THE SOCRATIC ENIGMA

The Library of Liberal Arts
OSKAR PIEST, FOUNDER

The Library of Liberal Arts

THE SOCRATIC ENIGMA

A Collection of Testimonies
Through Twenty-Four Centuries

Edited, with an Introduction, by

HERBERT SPIEGELBERG

Professor of Philosophy, Washington University

In collaboration with

BAYARD QUINCY MORGAN

Professor Emeritus of German, Stanford University

. . . .

The Library of Liberal Arts
published by
THE BOBBS-MERRILL COMPANY, INC.
A Subsidiary of Howard W. Sams & Co., Inc.
Publishers • Indianapolis • New York • Kansas City

To My Former Colleagues and Students
at Lawrence College

Preface

The best way to account for the present volume is to tell
about its origin. There was nothing deliberate about it. It
grew out of a concrete occasion. But it has grown into something which, I would like to hope, will meet more than the
needs of an occasion. That occasion was the demonstration to
American college freshmen of the significance of a person and
an event as seemingly remote as Socrates and his trial. The
framework was the Freshman Studies course inaugurated at
Lawrence College in 1945 by President Nathan M. Pusey, now
of Harvard University. In tackling this assignment I soon discovered that I had grown tired of the fatuous generalities
about his immortal fame, at best relieved by a contemptuous
reference to Nietzsche's sacrilegious villainy in attacking it. I
had for some time been suspicious of the traditional view,
shared even by students of classics, that Socrates had been re-
habilitated and canonized by a repenting posterity—a myth
which conceals the fact that Socrates has been steadily opposed
by anti-Socratism.

What I therefore wanted to do was to introduce some concrete evidence, in the shape of authentic testimonies from
some of the outstanding names in the history of Western civilization, of the actual impact of Socrates on posterity—evidence
which would not minimize the opposition to the gadfly of
Athens, whose Apology, taken seriously and read imagina-
tively, is anything but a safe bookshelf classic. Actually, this
plan first took the shape of a rather unconventional experiment, a dramatic presentation which attempted to re-enact the
trial of Socrates.

The conception of this book, however, developed after the first dramatic production. In collecting opinions for and against Socrates, I had become aware of the fact that there was an abundance of material which apparently had never been assembled and utilized. What is more, these opinions began to form a coherent story. Socrates turned out to be the persistent theme of a continuing argument in which nearly all the major figures in the history of ideas since Socrates' days had taken part. The pattern which thus began to unfold assumed increasingly the appearance of one of the most revealing chapters of intellectual history. Socrates has always been more or less an enigma to all the ages. We do not realize sufficiently that even the historic Socrates—assuming that we can ever hope to reconstruct a consistent core for the diverging stories and myths with which our patchy tradition supplies us —was a highly complex personality. It is high time to explode the legend of his universal or near-universal acceptance and acceptability. The pedestal is in any case a very un-Socratic and ineffective pulpit.

But to discover how Socrates is reflected in the mirror of posterity was not the only reason that this exploration seemed worth while. Socrates himself, no matter how imperfectly known to and variously interpreted by subsequent generations, holds up a mirror to the twenty-five centuries since his death— a mirror which reflects their concerns, their virtues, and their foibles with remarkable clarity. Socrates is still a midwife of ideas. He is also one of the watersheds from which the intellectual streams have flowed in different directions, fertilizing but at times even devastating the valleys.

It is this mutual mirroring, this continued meeting between the relentless life-examiner of Athens and the ages since, which I wanted to make accessible in the most direct and concentrated form possible, by presenting the documented reactions of the leading figures in the post-Socratic world. To let them speak for themselves, with as little commentary as possible, seemed to be the best way to tell the story. I submit that this undertaking can provide the most meaningful proof of the greatness of great men, of great ideas, and even of "great books."

Completeness is clearly an impossible and even a questionable goal for such a compilation. Representativeness rather than comprehensiveness is all I have attempted to achieve.

From the outset I omitted all statements which lacked any element of appraisal. Thus the merely factual accounts of Socrates' life and teaching by authors such as Diogenes Laërtius, Valerius Maximus, Clement of Alexandria, Hippolytus, Isidore of Seville, and Walter Burleigh (Burlaeus) were not included, much as a collection of such accounts might be desirable, not only in the interest of a better understanding of the Socratic tradition, but also to allow a better evaluation of the appraisals contained in our collection. For we must bear in mind that not all these appraisals are strictly comparable. They presuppose and refer to different pictures of the Socratic facts. Even today the "Socratic problem"—that is, the determination of the teachings which may be safely ascribed to Socrates—is as controversial, if not as insoluble, as ever. Another aspect of this problem is that quite a few of our witnesses do not distinguish between Socrates and Plato. In some cases it is quite apparent that in speaking about Socrates the appraiser really means the Plato of the *Republic* or even of the *Timaeus;* conversely, in referring to Plato he may really be thinking of Socrates. I saw no way of resolving this difficulty completely. I have therefore abided by the principle of including all those appraisals which use the name of Socrates, leaving it to the reader to decide how far the witness in question was aware of any difference between the two philosophers; I realize that in this way I may have neglected some appraisals which, while using Plato's name, actually refer to Socrates at the same time. It seems doubtful to me, however, that the total picture would be altered by their inclusion.

I am also aware of the fact that the separation of mere report from appraisal presents peculiar difficulties, known to all those who have struggled with the problem of eliminating value judgments. Even the driest chronicle, by the very selection of its items, expresses some measure of evaluation. On the other hand, the most meaningful appraisals are precisely those which also include factual material. The principle I have tried to follow is to include those statements about Socrates which, in addition to their informational (and sometimes misinformational) material, also show a pronounced interest in the significance of the phenomenon of Socrates beyond the mere facts of the case.

Another difficulty arose from the necessity of selecting among the appraisals thus selected. Of course there has been an abundance of foolish praise and a certain amount of stupid vilification, mostly unoriginal. No intrinsic interest attaches to such pronouncements. But at times the importance of the appraiser makes up for the unimportance of his verdict; if only as negative evidence, this seemed to justify some otherwise rather dubious inclusions, lest absence from our roster be taken as a sign of complete lack of interest in Socrates—a conclusion which in view of my admittedly incomplete search would never be quite safe. I also used the principle thus stated in the other direction by including some more penetrating comments by lesser authorities. Finally, there are a number of opinions which I decided to omit because their eccentricity was not redeemed by the importance of their authors.

Obviously, the result of my search falls short of an ideal goal. I had to stop, if only because of the limited facilities of a college library, where my explorations began, at a considerable distance from the larger depositories of learning. All the more do I wish to acknowledge the ready assistance of the librarians of Lawrence College, who bore up patiently and cooperatively under my accelerating requests for interlibrary loans.

Among the many friends and colleagues who have helped me in tracking down some of the testimonies I want to single out Craig R. Thompson, now Librarian and Professor of the

Department of English at Haverford College; Harry Bergholz, now Librarian at the University of North Carolina, who acted as my resourceful research agent at the University of Michigan; Walter Porges, now at the Los Angeles City College, then at the College of the University of Chicago, who helped me in a similar manner in the Chicago libraries; and John Hicks, now at Southern Florida University, who also assisted me greatly in the preparation of the manuscript. In addition, I am indebted to a large number of unnamed friends, without whose advice and references I could never have foraged as far beyond the field of philosophy as I had to in an enterprise which clearly calls for teamwork. My wife, Eldora Haskell Spiegelberg, assisted me valiantly in some of the translations, particularly those from the Russian.

In spite of this abundance of help, these labors might have been in vain but for the collaboration of Bayard Quincy Morgan of Stanford University. At a crucial stage in the revision of the text, which had already been set up in galleys by that time, he helped me in solving the problem of the new translations from the German. A number of the tougher ones were completely redone by him. In other cases his responsibility merely extends to the idiomatic reformulation. But his help in steering the production of the book as a whole has gone far beyond anything I can describe and acknowledge here. It is also on his experienced advice that certain poetic passages are rendered in prose in order to preserve as much as possible of the literal meaning. However, to avoid losing the poetic values altogether the original text is quoted as well.[1]

I also wish to express my grateful recognition of the guiding interest of my publisher, Oskar Piest, whose first response and advice have had considerable influence on the growth and the final shape of this book.

—HERBERT SPIEGELBERG

[1] Where no translator is given, the translation is to be credited to Professor Morgan alone, or to our joint cooperation.

Acknowledgments

For permission to reprint excerpts in this volume, acknowledgment is made to the following authors and publishers:

Edward Arnold & Co., for an excerpt from W. Macneile Dixon, *The Human Situation*.

Augsburg Publishing House, for an excerpt from David F. Swenson, *Something About Kierkegaard*.

The John Day Company, Inc., for an excerpt from Jawaharlal Nehru, *Glimpses of World History*.

Éditions Bernard Grasset, for an excerpt from Julien Benda, *La trahison des clercs*.

Harcourt, Brace & World, Inc., for excerpts from T. S. Eliot, *For Lancelot Andrewes. Essays on Style and Order*, and Vilfredo Pareto, *The Mind and Society*.

Harper & Row, Publishers, for an excerpt from Brand Blanshard, *Philosophy in American Education*.

Harvard University Press, for excerpts from *Holmes-Pollock Letters* and Charles Sanders Peirce, *Collected Papers*.

Holt, Rinehart & Winston, Inc., for excerpts from Henri Bergson, *The Two Sources of Morality*; Morris R. Cohen, *The Faith of a Liberal*; John Dewey, *The Influence of Darwin on Philosophy*, *Reconstruction in Philosophy*, and *Human Nature and Conduct*; John Dewey and James Tufts, *Ethics*; and Joseph Ratner, *The Philosophy of John Dewey*.

Houghton Mifflin Company, for excerpts from Irving Babbitt, *The New Laokoon*, *On Being Creative*, and *Rousseau and Romanticism*; and Paul Elmer More, *Shelburne Essays*.

Alfred A. Knopf, Inc., for excerpts from *The Journals of André Gide* and Oswald Spengler, *The Decline of the West*.

The Library of Living Philosophers, Inc., for an excerpt from Moritz Schlick, "The Future of Philosophy," in *College of the Pacific Publications in Philosophy,* Volume I (1932).

Little, Brown & Co., for excerpts from Epictetus, *Discourses,* translated by Thomas W. Higginson.

Longmans, Green & Co., Inc., for excerpts from William James, *Pragmatism* and *Some Problems of Philosophy.*

The Macmillan Company, for excerpts from Henry Festing Jones, *Samuel Butler;* Walter Lippmann, *A Preface to Morals;* Albert Schweitzer, *Civilization and Ethics;* Benedetto Croce, *Philosophy of the Practical;* and Alfred North Whitehead, *Adventures of Ideas* and *The Aims of Education.*

W. W. Norton & Company, Inc., for excerpts from Benedetto Croce, *History as the Story of Liberty;* José Ortega y Gasset, *The Modern Theme;* Harry A. Overstreet, *The Enduring Quest* and *The Mature Mind;* and Bertrand Russell, *Power. A New Social Analysis.*

Oxford University Press, Inc., for excerpts from Richard Howard Crossman, *Plato Today;* Søren Kierkegaard, *The Journals,* translated by Alexander Dru, *Christian Discourses* and *The Point of View,* translated by Walter Lowrie; Arnold Toynbee, *A Study of History;* and Max Weber, *Essays in Sociology,* translated by H. H. Gerth and C. W. Mills.

The Philosophical Library, for excerpts from John Dewey, *Problems of Man.*

Princeton University Press, for excerpts from Søren Kierkegaard, *Fear and Trembling, Sickness Unto Death,* and *Stages on Life's Way,* translated by Walter Lowrie, and *Concluding Unscientific Postscript* and *Philosophical Fragments,* translated by David Swenson.

Routledge and Kegan Paul Ltd., for excerpts from Karl R. Popper, *The Open Society and Its Enemies.*

Charles Scribner's Sons, for excerpts from *Ante-Nicene Fathers* and *Nicene and Post-Nicene Fathers;* Madison Grant, *The*

Passing of the Great Race; and from the following works by George Santayana: *Dialogues in Limbo; Dominations and Powers; The Idea of Christ in the Gospels; The Life of Reason. Reason in Common Sense;* Preface to the Second Edition, *The Life of Reason. Reason in Common Sense; The Life of Reason. Reason in Science; The Realm of Matter; The Realm of Truth; The Realm of the Spirit; Scepticism and Animal Faith;* and *Obiter Scripta,* edited by Justus Buchler and Benjamin Schwartz. Copyright 1936, 1940, 1946, 1951 Charles Scribner's Sons. Copyright 1937, 1938 George Santayana. Copyright 1948 Daniel M. Cory.

George Bernard Shaw, who in 1949 graciously gave his handwritten permission ("very willingly on my part") for the use of excerpts from *Prefaces, The Intelligent Woman's Guide to Socialism and Capitalism,* and *Everybody's Political What's What.*

Sheed & Ward, for an excerpt from Jacques Maritain, *An Introduction to Philosophy.*

Simon and Schuster, Inc., for an excerpt from Bertrand Russell, *A History of Western Philosophy.* Copyright 1945 by Bertrand Russell.

The University of Chicago Press, for an excerpt from John Dewey, *Essays in Experimental Logic.*

CONTENTS
. . . .

The Socratic Enigma

Introduction

"To write a history of Socrates' influence would be a gigantic task."[1] This verdict applies even to the limited task of tracing his prestige among the more prominent post-Socratics. At this stage it is chiefly the incompleteness of the materials here assembled which makes a more ambitious historical interpretation impossible. Nevertheless, some guideposts to the highlights and major trends in the history of Socratism and anti-Socratism may be helpful in the use of this volume.

The story begins with some of Plato's more explicit appraisals of Socrates, intended to show how Socrates' greatest and most congenial student—who, incidentally, never called him his teacher or master but only his older friend and companion—was well aware of many of his more puzzling and exasperating sides and never put him on as high a pedestal as the merely defending and adoring Xenophon had done. Aristotle, the detached pupil's pupil, at least in his extant writings, gives no signs of affection for the master of his own repudiated master, Plato. While he gives Socrates credit for his contributions to logic, he sees in him anything but a turning point in Greek philosophy and openly criticizes his ethics.

There is very little direct information about the minor Socratic schools like the Cynics and Cyrenaics. But it is apparent that the founder of hedonism, Aristippus, admired him. It is probably quite significant that among his Epicurean successors we find, after Epicurus'[2] own polite, telling silence, a later head of the garden school, Zeno of Sidon, attacking Soc-

1 Werner Jaeger, *Paideia: The Ideals of Greek Culture,* tr. Gilbert Highet (New York, 1943), II, 373, note 1.
2 Diogenes Laërtius, *Lives of the Philosophers* X.8.

3

rates openly as the crude buffoon of the Athenian streets. The
early Skeptics, judging from Timon's lampoon and Arcesilaus'
stricture, objected to his inconsistent skepticism. About the attitude of the older Stoics we have apparently as little firsthand
information as about that of their Cynic predecessors.[3] But
there is at least the story that the founder, Zeno of Citium,
upon reading the second book of Xenophon's *Memorabilia*,
was looking for followers of Socrates.[4]

It was apparently in Hellenized Rome that Socrates found a
much stronger following. True, the old diehards like Cato the
Elder opposed him, as they opposed everything Greek. But
Cicero, after initial resistance to the disparager of oratory,
naturalized him in Rome. To the later Stoics he became actually the model human being and even, through an apocryphal
tradition, the model world citizen. It seems to be a sign of the
subsequent times, interested primarily in religio-metaphysical
speculation, that Socrates with his sober critical reason is much
less prominent even among Platonists; thus, to an Apuleius,
he is chiefly an exhibit for the possibility of divination. Only
the apostate emperor Julian, in his belated attempt to revive
paganism, plays him off as a hero even against more famous
secular competitors. Socrates' last role in antiquity is that of
a comforter to the doomed Boethius in prison.

When Christianity in the persons of the Apologists takes up
permanent contact with ancient philosophy, we at once find
a very revealing division. There is the Socratism of such men
as St. Justin Martyr, from the very start his chief advocate
among Christians, and Origen, both of whom, in their belief
in the reasonableness of Christianity, see in Socrates a pacemaker, a fellow martyr, and even a Christian before Christ.
Simultaneously, however, there is the anti-Socratism of Tertullian, Lactantius, and Chrysostom, who cannot admit the rele-
vance and adequacy of reason in matters of faith, and who

[3] "Reference to Socrates is rare in the fragments of the Old Stoa." (Adolf
Dyroff, *Die Ethik der alten Stoa* [Berlin, 1897], p. 320.)
[4] Diogenes Laërtius, *Lives of the Philosophers* VII.1.3.

find the most amazing faults in Socrates, even though they like to call on him as a witness against pagan polytheism, as they believe they can. How embarrassing his spotless moral record must have been to them may be gathered from St. Jerome's opinion (see p. 46). Only the Platonist St. Augustine approached Socrates in a more objective manner and took exception merely to his hostility to metaphysics, as had Minucius Felix before him.

In order to understand the appraisals of Socrates during the Middle Ages we must project ourselves into an age which had practically nothing to go on but third- and fourth-hand information as to the Socratic facts. Plato's *Timaeus,* his only dialogue continuously known during the whole period, showed Socrates only in the introductory portions, where he briefly summarizes his political program, familiar to us from the long-submerged *Republic,* and then becomes a simple listener to the lecture of the Pythagorean Timaeus; not even Chalcidius' commentary, otherwise a major source of historical information for the Middle Ages, adds anything to this picture of Socrates, since it ignores the introductory section of the dialogue. Plato's *Apology,* the *Crito,* and the *Symposium* were inaccessible to the Western world until Leonardo Bruni (1369–1440), the pupil of the Byzantine refugee scholar Manuel Chrysoloras, supplied a Latin translation; only excerpts from Socrates' final speech in the *Apology* (40a-41), quoted without indication of the source and context in Cicero's *Tusculan Disputations,* were always available. During the twelfth century, at least the *Meno* and the *Phaedo* were recovered by the translations of Henricus Aristippus. Nothing of Xenophon's Socrates was known until Cardinal Bessarion (1403–1472) translated the *Memorabilia.* Thus in the Middle Ages most of the Socratic lore came from incidental information, found in Cicero and Seneca,[5] and anecdotes like those in Valerius Maxi-

5 Seneca's enthusiastic praise of Socrates might account for the strange tradition of Socrates as the head of the Stoics, as revealed by Albertus Magnus and documented also in a pictorial representation of Aristotle,

mus' *De factis dictisque memorabilibus* from the first century after Christ.

But even allowing for the poverty of the medieval picture of Socrates, we can discover significant differences in his prestige. Thus the cool, not to say indifferent, attitude of Aristotelians like Albertus Magnus and Thomas Aquinas stands in marked contrast to the much more sympathetic approach of a medieval Platonist like John of Salisbury or of the Augustine-inspired Scholastics like the Franciscans Bonaventura, Duns Scotus, and even Roger Bacon. For the later period of Scholasticism, as well as for the medieval mystics, the available sources are silent.

There were some interesting developments during the early Renaissance period. Whereas in Dante's list the philosophical hierarchy is headed by Aristotle, followed by Socrates and Plato, Petrarch's order of procession puts Plato in front of both Aristotle and Socrates, who appear to be on the same level. Among the Renaissance philosophers, Marsilio Ficino, head of the new Florentine Academy, rediscovered the hero of the *Apology* and drew a dangerously close parallel between his fate and Jesus' Passion. But it was Erasmus' near-canonization of the pagan sage which caused the real scandal. In Luther's war against the pagan humanists, Socrates becomes a symbolic target; for although the reformer more or less reluctantly admits some of his virtues, he still feels it his theological duty to condemn him in the name of the indispensable revelation which Socrates obviously could not share. While Melanchthon backs up Luther on this point, Zwingli, the most humanistic of the reformers, has the temerity to receive Socrates among the saved along with Heracles (perhaps a misreading for the name of the philosopher Heraclitus, christianized by St. Justin together with Socrates). Calvin, who admires Socrates for his civic virtues, apparently did not enter into this

Plato, Socrates, and Seneca reproduced in Raymond Klibansky's *The Continuity of the Platonic Tradition* (London, 1939), Table 4, where Socrates is called *Stoycus irreprehensibilis vitiorum aliorum.*

dispute. But the issue remained controversial among theologians for centuries, with Wesley finding him wanting in the virtue of hope, while the Quaker Barclay does not hesitate to give him full status in the invisible church.[6] Among Catholic thinkers it is particularly Bishop Bossuet who takes exception to the cult of Socrates, as was done before him by Guez de Balzac in his *Socrate Chrétien* (1632). Even today there would seem to be little chance to advance him beyond the limbo.[7] It is all the more remarkable that the most prominent neo-orthodox Protestant theologian, Karl Barth, thinks of Socrates as "immanent in Christ."

Among the philosophers we encounter in Montaigne the first modern thinker to whom Socrates' plainness and humor speak; in fact, the personality of Socrates seems to grow on him over and above the appeal of his being the model skeptic, as he is also to Charron. Otherwise the more systematic philosophers, rationalists though most of them are, do not take much interest in Socrates. Only Campanella and Francis Bacon recognize in him a possible ally in the struggle for freedom of thought and research. But in other regards Bacon as well as Hobbes, Descartes, Spinoza, and Leibniz remain surprisingly aloof from the father of self-critical philosophy; the inconsistency of his rationalism and his lack of system recommended him but little to the great metaphysical system-builders. Yet it seems worth noticing that the rationalist initiator of the new international law, Hugo Grotius, hails him

[6] For an interesting theological controversy released by a pro-Socratic remark in Jean François Marmontel's (1723–1799) novel *Bélisaire* (Chap. 15), which had been condemned by the Sorbonne, see L. Capéran, *Le problème du salut des infidèles* (new edn., 1934), I, 407 ff.; see also Craig R. Thompson's commentary on Desiderius Erasmus Roterodamus, *Inquisitio de Fide* (New Haven, 1950), pp. 101-21.

[7] See, for instance, the article on Socrates in the *Catholic Encyclopedia* (New York, 1912), in which Professor William Turner, of the Catholic University of America, points out that "he did not rise above the moral level of his contemporaries in every respect, and Christian apologists have no difficulty in refuting the contention that he was the equal of the Christian saints."

as an outstanding conscientious objector, whose nonconform-
ism would even have application to the case of an unjust war.

It is the eighteenth century which shows Socratism at its
peak. To Shaftesbury's enthusiasm Socrates seems a nearly
divine hero, yet human in the most natural manner. He also
becomes, as it were, the patron saint of the Deists, beginning
with John Locke and Anthony Collins and ending by inspiring such strange projects as John Toland's *Socratic Society*.[8]
Voltaire sees him as the greatest sage (with the possible exception of the Sage of Ferney), although he cannot always refrain
from ridiculing the less enlightened oddities of Socrates' personality. Diderot, the moving spirit of the *Encyclopédie*, worships Socrates with an almost touching sentimentalism; so did
Condorcet who, himself on the way to martyrdom, claimed
him as one of the pacemakers of science, apparently on the
basis of Aristophanes' portrait of him in the *Clouds*. However,
even during this period anti-Socratism remains alive. Thus to
Montesquieu Socrates is simply an objectionable absolutist à
la Plato. But the chief blast comes from the forerunner of romanticism, Rousseau, who dared to challenge Voltaire's admiration and who, besides belittling Socrates' martyrdom as
measured by Christian standards, included among his charges
not only his rationalism in morals, but also his lack of patriotism. It is less surprising that materialists like Holbach
objected to his ethics as vague and too submissive.

British thought since the eighteenth century shows some
rather interesting divisions. The ready acceptance of Socrates
by Chaucer, Spenser, Milton, Dryden, Addison, Steele, Swift,
and Johnson is raised to the superlative degree by Shelley's
and Keats's glorifications and by Byron's less consistent tributes. But there is also on the other side Jeremy Bentham,
boisterously debunking the empty prater, in such marked and
revealing contrast to John Stuart Mill's unstinted admiration,
so characteristic of the changed temper among the English

8 *Pantheisticon* (1720); excerpts in Paul Hazard, *La Crise de la conscience européenne, 1680–1715* (Paris, 1935), II, 44.

utilitarians. Then there is Landor's openly avowed antipathy. Carlyle is more subdued and speaks chiefly through his silence; indications are that he weakened temporarily under the influence of Emerson, but never to the extent of making Socrates the object of full-fledged hero worship. There is the interesting case of Coleridge, whose *Philosophical Lectures,* not published until 1949, credit Socrates with some of his own cherished imagination and with the religious genius which helped to prepare for the acceptance of the Christian revelation. Yet Coleridge cannot forgive him for his sophistic technique and for his utilitarian leanings, which put him far below Plato. Except for Thomas Moore's pledge to Socrates in his fight against intolerance, the most impressive tribute to Socrates comes from Matthew Arnold, who sees in him the man above politics and the hidden oracle in everybody's breast, although he too has reservations against his all too easygoing "Hellenism." Ruskin testifies for Socrates chiefly as his comforter in adversity. Samuel Butler's flippant rejection of the Socratic "humbug," though suppressed before publication, is hardly insignificant. It is all the more significant that Butler's twentieth-century admirer, George Bernard Shaw, stands by Socrates as the superior intellect, martyred by the middle classes, but too naïve for a full grasp of the issue, and missing his chance for a last dramatic stand for the right of free criticism. English philosophers since Hume's day have been somewhat noncommittal. The pragmatist "humanism" of F. C. S. Schiller ranks Socrates far below the Sophist Protagoras. Bertrand Russell ends by charging him with nearly unpardonable sins against the scientific spirit.

It seems rather remarkable that America, with its pronounced democratic heritage, should have been so strongly on the side of the merciless critic of ancient democracy; exceptions are Henry Adams, John Fiske, and Justice Oliver Wendell Holmes, whose brief and incidental strictures have no political implications; the same applies to the reservations of a churchman like Bishop Phillips Brooks. There is Benjamin Franklin's maxim of imitation of Socrates alongside the imitation of Christ. Thomas Paine invokes him only in passing in defense of his *Age of Reason*. More significant perhaps is Jefferson's tribute, considering his violent and sweeping rejection of Plato. But it was Emerson and his New England Transcendentalists to whom Socrates meant most and who have some of the most sensitive and refreshing praise for Socrates. Nor did Socrates mean less to Melville and Walt Whitman, or, on a more humorous plane, to Don Marquis. In American philosophy it is chiefly the pragmatists from Charles Sanders Peirce through William James to John Dewey who claim him as one of their ancestors and allies. Santayana's growing detachment from Socrates may be indicative of his estrangement from America. There are also the American "humanists," both of the classic-religious strain (Irving Babbitt and Paul Elmer More) and of the scientific-naturalist variety (*Humanist Manifesto* group), the former more passionately, the latter more reservedly, claiming the advocate of merely "human wisdom" for their ranks.

Chief landmarks in the French orbit after Rousseau are Lamartine's romantic hymn on Socrates, especially his poetic sequence on the philosopher's death, which to be sure was toned down considerably in favor of Christianity later on; the strictures of Auguste Comte against the man who, while deserving a prominent place on his calendar of positivist heroes, had touched off the orgy of metaphysics prior to the advent of genuine positive science; the scholarly arguments of Alfred Fouillée and Émile Boutroux for Socrates as the founder of an "independent" secular ethics; Bergson's interpretation of Socrates' ethics as fundamentally irrationalistic, mystic, and dynamic; and Léon Brunschvicg's claim that Socrates was the decisive force in starting the consciousness of mankind on its way to moral emancipation. Thus Socrates' hold seems to be equally strong on rationalists and irrationalists, though for different reasons. The same holds true for freethinkers like André Gide or Julien Benda and for neo-scho-

lastics like Jacques Maritain and Étienne Gilson. It also finds
striking expression in the fact that Gabriel Marcel, the chief
Catholic exponent of Christian existentialism, has now replaced that label with "neo-Socratism" or "Christian Socratism" as an expression of the attitude of interrogation, of communication by dialogue, and, in general, of anti-dogmatism,
for which he stands.[9] Even more recently the outstanding exponent of phenomenological existentialism, Maurice Merleau-
Ponty, paid a remarkable tribute to Socrates in his inaugural
lecture at the Collège de France in 1953.

The German writers, represented here only by examples
during and since the eighteenth century, pay their respects to
Socrates in terms typical of their authors and their develop-
mental stages, perhaps best illustrated in the case of Goethe.
Among the philosophers of German Idealism, Kant seems to
have considered Socrates' personality that of a freak, although
he looked upon his own *Critique of Pure Reason* as fundamentally a Socratic enterprise. Fichte and Schelling were the
first to see in Socrates a turning point in the history of the
human spirit. But it was Hegel who defined the place of Socrates' new principle in the drama of world history and of the
history of philosophy in particular, and who also saw the
tragic necessity of his fate. Schleiermacher's reflections on the
Socratic enigma were the first to show the full benefit of scholarly learning. To Schopenhauer, Socrates was basically the
illiterate philosopher—with, to be sure, some rather influential
ideas.

However, Socrates exerts his most momentous influence in
the nineteenth century on two figures destined to become
central to later developments, though seemingly outside the
main current of the intellectual events of the time: Kierkegaard, the Christian Socrates, and Nietzsche, Socrates' leading
modern antagonist. In the deeply moving case of Kierkegaard,
Socrates grows from the mere brilliant ironist of his master's

9 See Marcel's Preface to his English translation of the *Metaphysical
Journal* (Chicago, 1952), p. xiii.

thesis into the existentialist Socrates, whose Christian rein-
carnation Kierkegaard nearly felt himself to be. The notorious
case of Nietzsche is both far more complex and more tragic
than is commonly realized. For him, Socrates is a catalytic agent,
as it were, and a major pole of alternating attraction and re-
pulsion, a result very possibly of his frustrated love for Socrates. The case of Socrates is in that sense for Nietzsche another "Wagner case." As Nietzsche, after 1875, substitutes the
intellectual of the "gay science" for Wagner, the great artist,
so Socrates, whom he had first rejected as the destroyer of the
great art of tragedy, becomes the superman, since Wagner, first
hailed as the creator of new Dionysian tragedy, had returned
into the Christian fold. Yet by 1885 both Socrates and Wagner
are eclipsed by Cesare Borgia, the aristocratic will-to-power
edition of the immoralist superman, leaving Socrates, the
moralistic plebeian, in even worse disgrace, if possible. Oswald
Spengler, the twentieth-century disciple of Nietzsche, sees Socrates, in the curious company of Buddha and Rousseau, as
nothing but a symptom of decadence. To some extent this
interpretation is reflected even in the more appreciative view
of Count Hermann Keyserling, an admirer of Eastern wisdom.

Socrates finds at least some new response among the re-
newers of a more scientifically minded and intuitive German
philosophy. It is expressed in Franz Brentano's tribute to
Socrates' moral and social height and independence, in Edmund Husserl's recognition of Socrates, the initiator of a
philosophical reform in the name of an intuitive reason as
congenial to the new phenomenological approach, and even
in Max Scheler's and Martin Heidegger's less conspicuous
testimonies.

For an account of Italian Socratism since the Renaissance
a good deal more material is needed than the isolated testi-
monials of Vico, Leopardi, and Croce. The same is true of
the Spanish world, where Ortega's irrationalist revolt against
the discoverer of reason is possibly an expression of the Nietz-
sche-Bergson inspiration.

The Russians, whose first philosophy was religiously in-spired and is represented by Soloviev and more recently by Shestov, are remarkably hostile to Socrates. Though Tolstoy's passing pro-Socratic remark is hardly based on a more than saluting acquaintance, it explains Shestov's attack on both of them simultaneously.

As to Oriental developments, the Indian voice of Gandhi for Socrates, as the first nonviolent resister, as well as that of Nehru and, on a more philosophical level, of Radhakrishnan and Wadia, indicate some of the more remarkable conversions. Modern China, hardly represented by Lin Yutang, has not yet added a more explicit testimony beyond the obvious com-parisons with Confucius.[10]

This seems to be the proper place to record Socrates' strange fates at the hands of the political movements of our own time. To be sure, there was apparently little interest in Socrates among the early socialists and the original Marxists, for whom, as for Karl Marx—at that time still a Hegelian in his doctoral dissertation on Epicurus—the contrast between Plato and Democritus was all-important. It is not until we reach Georges Sorel, the French syndicalist, that Socrates becomes a major precipitating agent of political thought. Sorel's first book pre-sents a violent case against Socrates, based chiefly on the evi-dence of Aristophanes' *Clouds*. Written during his early na-tionalist phase, it holds Socrates up as the archphilosopher, responsible for all the major sins condemned by full-fledged fascism: antimilitarism, undermining of discipline, disbelief in myths, even indifference toward labor. In fact, his fellow prophet of fascism, the sociologist Vilfredo Pareto, saw Soc-

---

[10] Professor Y. L. Chin, as quoted in Fun Yu-Lan, *A Short History of Chinese Philosophy* (New York, 1949), p. 10: "Chinese philosophers were all of them different grades of Socrates." Also Professor Fung Yu-Lan's own characterization of Confucius, who "in this respect [consciousness of super-moral values] was like Socrates. Socrates thought that he had been appointed by a divine order to awaken the Greeks, and Confucius had a similar consciousness of divine mission" (*ibid.*, p. 46).

rates as the underminer of the indispensable nonlogical basis
of every society. Apparently even Mussolini, who was not a
favorite of either Sorel or Pareto, and his more philosophical
spokesmen were not aware of the Socrates problem, judging
from the fairly neutral article on Socrates in the Fascist *En-
ciclopedia Italiana* and from the fact of Mussolini's odd use
of Socrates as an authority on tough dealing with one's opponents.

But Socrates certainly had worse luck among the German
Nazis. In the eyes of the Nazi "philosopher" Alfred Rosenberg,
Socrates' major crime was his "inferior" race, combined with
his race-destroying, internationalizing doctrines. It is a matter of
conjecture who started the Nazi racists on this new tack, since
neither Nietzsche (except in passing) nor the detested pessimist
Spengler, anti-Socratic though they were, had suggested it.
Gobineau, the first racist, gives Socrates an exceptionally high
rating precisely because of his opposition to Greek city col-
lectivism. Houston Stewart Chamberlain, the Germanized second prophet of racism, rejects him, but rather for his philistine
attack upon the world of Homeric mythology than for racial
defects. The only writer before Rosenberg who publicly im-
pugned Socrates' racial stock was the American anthropologist
Madison Grant, who diagnosed him as a younger brother of
the Neanderthal man; Grant's work was, as a matter of fact,
widely read in translation in Germany during the nineteen-
twenties. The touching sonnet on Socrates written in prison
by Albrecht Haushofer, the doomed participant in the abor-
tive conspiracy against Hitler in 1944, reads like a symbolic
return to the spirit of Socratism.

The fascist and Nazi attacks upon Socrates have done little
to recommend him to the communists. There is, to be sure,
apart from Karl Marx's early and only incidental bow to
Socrates, the interesting case of Lenin, Sorel's designated
though scarcely appreciative heir. His private notes, suggested
by his study of Hegel's lectures on the history of philosophy
shortly before his historic return to Russia in 1917, show him
by no means hostile to Socrates and to the movement which he

initiated; after all, Socrates, the inventor of the dialectical half of dialectical materialism, need not be held responsible for the antimaterialistic idealism which Plato added to it. Yet it appears from later evidence that Socrates' stock in Soviet Russia, never too high anyway since Soloviev's attack upon him, dropped considerably after Lenin's death—witness especially the Great Soviet Encyclopedia. Socrates' critique of the natural science of his time, and even more his aristocratic sympathies, put him under additional suspicion. An official prospectus for a new text, to be written by a committee of thirty, states as its theme: "Idealistic philosophy (Socrates, Plato) was the reactionary ideology of the ancient Greek aristocracy."[11] To be thus convicted by the Nietzsches and the Rosenbergs of being plebeian and by the communists of being an aristocrat is indeed a rather desperate plight.

Has Socrates fared any better among liberal democrats? It would certainly be hard to convert him into a champion of democracy as such, which he criticized explicitly. Nevertheless, it can be maintained that the intellectual liberals and conscientious gadflies of democracy are usually champions of Socrates. This may explain the Socratism of such socially conscious democratic intellectuals as John Stuart Mill, John Dewey, Alfred North Whitehead, or Morris R. Cohen, for whom democracy is anything but the defense of the *status quo* in the interests of a restive majority. Nor are Churchill's and Nehru's tributes to Socrates any more historical accidents than those of a prominent Oxford laborite like R. H. Crossman, who plays him off against Plato's supposed proto-fascism.

A complete survey of the voices for and against Socrates would clearly require a sampling of evaluations by the major scholars who have discussed his significance for the history of mankind and his lasting contributions to specific fields of human endeavor. Reasons of space forced the omission of most of this testimony. However, in the Biographical Index (p.

11 *A Soviet History of Philosophy*, tr. William Edgerton (Washington, 1950), p. 9.

314 ff.), the reader will find references to the most significant appraisals. In addition, the following paragraphs will provide at least a preview of the evidence.

Ever since George Grote gave his appraisal, the historians of world and Greek history have been trying to be fair both to Socrates and to his judges. None of them, with the exception of Peter Wilhelm Forchhammer, have sided completely with Socrates' accusers. Some, but hardly the more penetrating ones, still decry his "judicial murder." Since most Western historians are individualists, the final verdict of men like Leopold von Ranke, Lord Acton, and Jacob Burckhardt is more favorable to Socrates' side of the argument. Perhaps the most impressive statement from the scholarly viewpoint is that of Eduard Meyer. Only the Russian historians seem to dissent —for obvious reasons.

In evaluating the appraisals by the historians of philosophy, more than in the case of nonphilosophers, proper allowance must be made for the perpetual "Socratic problem"—that is, the difficulty, if not the impossibility, of assigning to Socrates rather than to Plato any definite body of doctrines. This has led to any number of hypotheses, from the extreme affirmative side of A. E. Taylor, John Burnet, and Léon Robin, who credit Socrates with everything Plato puts into his mouth, to the negative side, which leaves him at best as much as Aristotle grants him. In spite of this basic difference in the picture of Socrates, most historians agree about his focal place in the history of Greek philosophy. After Hegel's largely speculative construction of this history, Eduard Zeller may be said to have set the tone for a genuinely scholarly appraisal. On this basis historians like Windelband and Gomperz are outspoken in taking Socrates' side. Robin credits him with a philosophical revolution. Heinrich Maier celebrates him as the bringer of a new gospel. Gilbert Murray sees in him the champion of truth at any price.

It is more difficult to collect representative estimates of Socrates' contributions to particular fields of philosophic and human endeavor. But the following evaluations deserve at least passing mention.

In the field of logic only the detailed and still classic *History of Logic* by Carl Prantl assigns to Socrates a significant place. Yet even some of the recent semanticists give him considerable credit for his effort to improve our linguistic habits, as do logical positivists like Moritz Schlick, and the philosophers of ordinary language like John L. Austin.[12]

Socrates' significance for ethics is stated clearly and soberly enough in Henry Sidgwick's still unsurpassed little *Outline of the History of Ethics*. That he is of importance even for the beginnings of esthetics is pointed out with good reasons by Professor Helmut Kuhn.

Scientists, remembering Socrates' disparaging comments on contemporary natural philosophy in the *Apology* and the *Phaedo,* usually do not think too highly of him, in spite of Galileo's and Condorcet's remarkable pleas. It is all the more interesting to note that such authorities in the field of the history of science as George Sarton and Sir William Dampier see him as exerting a much more constructive influence, if only indirectly, in the field of scientific methodology. Yet it must be admitted that Brett's standard history of psychology, for instance, sees in him chiefly a retarding influence in his field, in spite of—perhaps even because of—Socrates' concern about the "soul."

Socrates apparently ranks much higher among political scientists like Dunning, and among sociologists like Max Weber [13] and Karl Mannheim, who stresses his importance for the sociology of knowledge. Educationists have, of course, always supported the Socratic method, not always with much concern for the original article; but among the historians of education it is actually the classicist Werner Jaeger who makes

12 *La Philosophie analytique,* "Les Editions de Minuit" (Paris, 1962), p. 34.

13 See also P. Janet, *Histoire de la science politique dans ses rapports avec la morale* (Paris, 1887), I, 91, 102.

the highest claims for Socrates. His significance for the history of religion, specifically of the Christian religion, is attested most impressively by George Foot Moore's *History of Religion*.

What do all these currents and crosscurrents add up to? Hasn't Socrates been simply all things to all people, whether they liked him or not? Clearly not, for there is a definite grouping among his friends and his enemies. But it is not quite easy to state what holds either group together beyond the fact of their likes and dislikes.

Couldn't it be said simply that Socrates and Socratism have been the symbols of rationalism in the fight against irrationalism? That would be an oversimplification, and would seem to overlook the fact that, on the one hand, the most rationalistic philosophers have been singularly cool and reserved toward Socrates, and that among the admirers of Socrates there is no stronger antirationalist than Kierkegaard; after all, Socrates himself had his nonrationalist sides, which have appealed even to mystics as well. It might be a safer formulation to say that Socrates has always been the standard-bearer of individualism against collectivistic morality. But even so it must not be forgotten that an extreme individualist like Nietzsche took sides against him; it was certainly not self-assertive, antisocial individualism for which Socrates stood, but at best the individualism of a socially responsible personal conscience.

Any attempt to find a common denominator for Socratism seems rather questionable and apt to omit its best and most essential elements. But one might at least maintain as the minimum core of Socratism its unconditional insistence on the self-critical and responsible position of the individual in his courageous attempt to think for himself (if not to reason logically), without interference from authorities, guided only by his own free insight.

To discover a common denominator for the enemies of Socrates appears to be even harder. Not all of them resent the same thing, and many of them may be merely rationalizing their instinctive dislikes. What they object to, with more or less good reason, are such different and sometimes contradictory things as ethical intellectualism (Aristotle); general rationalism (Rousseau, Santayana, Ortega y Gasset, Pareto, Soloviev); sophistry (Bentham, Macaulay, Landor); hostility to great art and to the tragic spirit (Nietzsche); oversimplifying optimism (Dixon) or pessimism (Soloviev and, at one time, Nietzsche); insubordination (Sorel) and antipatriotism (Rousseau); racial inferiority (Rosenberg); plebeian tastes (Epicureans, Santayana, Nietzsche) and aristocratic leanings (Forchhammer, Winspear, and the Russian communists); antiscientific spirit (Comte, Santayana)—all this in addition to the ancient and sometimes revived charges of irreligion (Meletus) and subversiveness (Anytus) and the anonymous charges of the wider Athenian public.

No matter how ill-informed, unfair, and sometimes absurd these charges are, they all reveal a more than superficial revolt against the spirit of Socratism. But do they have a common root beyond the chance alliance of being *against* something or somebody? There is certainly a common ground in the general impatience with this contrary nonconformist, exasperating in his mixture of intellectual superiority toward his fellow men and humility toward the superhuman, with the clever debater and ironical question-master who evades definite and final answers, the professional ignoramus who is no skeptic, the antiauthoritarian who is neither a radical nor a reactionary, the believer in individual reason who still is not a rationalist, the believer in individual inspiration who still is not an irrationalist—in short, the man who is rather nothing than everything to all people. Is the root of this impatience the fact that Socrates is the first individual who dared to dissociate himself from the common mold, to stand aside, and to rise above his own time; the first emancipated spirit, and as such the great emancipator of critical thought?

Socrates was clearly a symbol for issues far bigger than his own person, and in this lies his major significance for posterity.

Is it possible to describe Socrates' impact on posterity more concisely? Has he been an influence for good or for evil? It is obviously not the compiler's business to make up the reader's mind on such questions. But it might seem unfair—unfair to Socrates and unfair to the reader—if the collector of the following array of testimonies should hide completely behind his cast without so much as indicating what seems to him the principal lesson of the story of Socrates' fame and infamy.

It is in this spirit that I would maintain that Socrates' memory—even more than the real Socrates, who remains unknown and unknowable—has been one of the most powerful liberators and defenders of man, the individual.

The memory of the man who dared to challenge calmly the totalitarian claims of a local political community has emancipated the thinking individual from the narrow bonds of merely national allegiance and prepared the ground for a cosmopolitan solidarity among all fellow thinkers.

The memory of the man who, though an undeniable pagan, was yet beyond the moralistic reproach of any but the most bigoted orthodoxy has been a constant embarrassment for and defense against religious fanaticism, with its claim of *no salvation outside the church,* and one of the strongest weapons in breaking its stranglehold on independent thought.

The memory of the man who lived the life of reason without dogmatic arrogance and skeptical despair offers one of the great inspiring patterns for a rational being whose last and best hope remains critical reason.

The memory of the man who was a hero of nonviolence, whose seeming defeat was the foundation of his continued though never final victories, has been in itself a gospel for a struggling and frustrated humanity.

1. *Antiquity*

PLATO (428–348 B.C.)

MENO: If I may venture to make a jest upon you [Socrates], 1
you seem to me both in your appearance and in your power
over others to be very like the flat torpedo fish, who torpifies
those who come near him and touch him, as you have now
torpified me, I think. For my soul and my tongue are really
torpid, and I do not know how to answer you. . . . I think that
you are very wise in not voyaging and going away from home,
for if you did in other places as you do in Athens, you would
be cast into prison as a magician. —*Meno*, tr. B. Jowett,
"Library of Liberal Arts," No. 12 (New York, 1957), pp. 35-36.

PHAEDO: Nothing is more pleasant to me than to recall Soc- 2
rates to my mind, whether by speaking of him myself or by
listening to others.

. . . .

I myself was strangely moved on that day. I did not feel that
I was being present at the death of a dear friend; I did not
pity him, for he seemed to me happy, . . . both in his bearing
and in his words, so fearlessly and nobly did he die. I could
not help thinking that the gods would watch over him still
on his journey to the other world, and that when he arrived
there it would be well with him, if it was ever well with any
man. Therefore I had scarcely any feeling of pity, as you
would expect at such a mournful time. —*Phaedo*, tr. F. J.
Church, "Library of Liberal Arts," No. 30 (New York, 1954),
p. 2.

. . . It seemed as if we were going to lose a father and to be 3
orphans for the rest of our life. —*Ibid.*, p. 71.

4   Such was the end . . . of our friend, a man, I think, who was
the wisest and justest, and the best man I have ever known.
——*Ibid.*, p. 74.

5   ALCIBIADES: I shall praise Socrates in a figure which will
appear to him to be a caricature, and yet I speak, not to make
fun of him, but only for the truth's sake. I say, that he is
exactly like the busts of Silenus, which are set up in the
statuaries' shops, holding pipes and flutes in their mouths;
and they are made to open in the middle, and have images of
gods inside them. I say also that he is like Marsyas the satyr.
. . . Aye, and there is a resemblance in other points too. For example, you [Socrates] are a bully, as I can prove by witnesses,
if you will not confess. And are you not a flute-player? That
you are, and a performer far more wonderful than Marsyas. He
indeed with instruments used to charm the souls of men by
the power of his breath. . . . [His melodies] alone possess the
soul and reveal the wants of those who have need of gods and
mysteries, because they are divine. But you produce the same
effect with your words only, and do not require the flute: that
is the difference between you and him. When we hear any
other speaker, even a very good one, he produces absolutely no
effect upon us, or not much, whereas the mere fragments of
you and your words, even at second-hand, and however imperfectly repeated, amaze and possess the souls of every man,
woman, and child who comes within hearing of them. And if
I were not afraid that you would think me hopelessly drunk,
I would have sworn as well as spoken to the influence which
they have always had and still have over me. For my heart
leaps within me more than that of any Corybantian reveller,
and my eyes rain tears when I hear them. And I observe that
many others are affected in the same manner. I have heard
Pericles and other great orators, and I thought that they
spoke well, but I never had any similar feeling; my soul was
not stirred by them, nor was I angry at the thought of my
own slavish state. But this Marsyas has often brought me to
such a pass, that I have felt as if I could hardly endure the

life which I am leading . . . ; and I am conscious that if I did not shut my ears against him, and fly as from the voice of the siren, my fate would be like that of others—he would transfix me, and I should grow old sitting at his feet. For he makes me confess that I ought not to live as I do, neglecting the wants of my own soul, and busying myself with the concerns of the Athenians; therefore I hold my ears and tear myself away from him. And he is the only person who ever made me ashamed, which you might think not to be in my nature, and there is no one else who does the same. For I know that I cannot answer him or say that I ought not to do as he bids, but when I leave his presence the love of popularity gets the better of me. And therefore I run away and fly from him, and when I see him, I am ashamed of what I have confessed to him. Many a time have I wished that he were dead, and yet I know that I should be much more sorry than glad, if he were to die: so that I am at my wit's end.

And this is what I and many others have suffered from the flute-playing of this satyr. Yet hear me once more while I show you how exact the image is, and how marvelous his power. For let me tell you; none of you know him; but I will reveal him to you; having begun, I must go on. See you how fond he is of the fair? He is always with them and is always being smitten by them, and then again he knows nothing and is ignorant of all things—such is the appearance which he puts on. Is he not like a Silenus in this? To be sure he is: his outer mask is the carved head of the Silenus; but . . . when he is opened, what temperance there is residing within! Know you that beauty and wealth and honour, at which the many wonder, are of no account with him, and are utterly despised by him: he regards not at all the persons who are gifted with them; mankind are nothing to him; all his life is spent in mocking and flouting at them. But when I opened him, and looked within at his serious purpose, I saw in him divine and golden images of such fascinating beauty that I was ready to do in a moment whatever Socrates commanded: they may have escaped the observation of others, but I saw them. . . .

I have felt the serpent's sting; and he who has suffered, as they say, is willing to tell his fellow-sufferers only, as they alone will be likely to understand him, and will not be extreme in judging of the sayings or doings which have been wrung from his agony. For I have been bitten by a more than viper's tooth; I have known in my soul, or in my heart, or in some other part, that worst of pangs, more violent in ingenuous youth than any serpent's tooth, the pang of philosophy, which will make a man say or do anything. . . . Many are the marvels which I might narrate in praise of Socrates; most of his ways might perhaps be paralleled in another man, but his absolute unlikeness to any human being that is or ever has been is perfectly astonishing. You may imagine Brasidas and others to have been like Achilles; or you may imagine Nestor and Antenor to have been like Pericles; and the same may be said of other famous men, but of this strange being you will never be able to find any likeness, however remote, either among men who now are or who ever have been—other than that which I have already suggested of Silenus and the satyrs; and they represent in a figure not only himself, but his words. For, although I forgot to mention this to you before, his words are like the images of Silenus which open; they are ridiculous when you first hear them; he clothes himself in language that is like the skin of the wanton satyr—for his talk is of pack-asses and smiths and cobblers and curriers, and he is always repeating the same things in the same words, so that any ignorant or inexperienced person might feel disposed to laugh at him; but he who opens the bust and sees what is within will find that they are the only words which have a meaning in them, and also the most divine, abounding in fair images of virtue, and of the widest comprehension, or rather extending to the whole duty of a good and honorable man. ——*Symposium,* in *The Dialogues of Plato,* tr. B. Jowett (New York, 1892), I, 586-9, 592-3.

6   Among their other deeds they [the Thirty Tyrants] named Socrates, an older friend of mine whom I should not hesitate

to call the wisest and justest man of that time, as one of a
group sent to arrest a certain citizen who was to be put to
death illegally, planning thereby to make Socrates willy-nilly
a party to their actions. . . . Those who returned from exile
acted with great restraint. By some chance, however, certain
powerful persons brought into court this same friend Socrates,
preferring against him a most shameless accusation, and one
which he, of all men, least deserved. For the prosecutors
charged him with impiety, and the jury condemned and put
to death the very man who, at the time when his accusers were
themselves in misfortune and exile, had refused to have a part
in the unjust arrest of one of their friends. —*Epistles*, tr.
Glenn R. Morrow, "Library of Liberal Arts," No. 122 (New
York, 1962), Epistle VII, pp. 216-17.

XENOPHON (430–*c.* 357 B.C.)

Socrates was evidently a friend of the common people, and 1
of a liberal disposition; for though he received numbers of
persons desirous to hear him discourse, as well citizens as
foreigners, he never required payment for his communications
from any one, but imparted to every one in abundance from
his stores, of which some, receiving fragments from him for
nothing, sold them at a great price to others, and were not,
like him, friends to the common people, for they declined to
converse with such as had not money to give them. But Socrates, in the eyes of other men, conferred glory on the city,
far more than Lichas, who was celebrated in this respect, on
that of the Lacedaemonians; for Lichas indeed entertained
the strangers that visited Lacedaemon at the *gymnopaediae,*
but Socrates, through the whole course of his life, freely imparted whatever he had to bestow, and thus benefited in the
highest degree all those who were willing to receive from him,
making those who associated with him better before he let
them go. To me, therefore, Socrates being a man of such a
character, appeared to be worthy of honour rather than of

death. ——*The Anabasis and the Memorabilia,* tr. J. S. Watson (London, 1880), pp. 367 ff.

2   To me, being such as I have described him, so pious that he did nothing without the sanction of the gods; so just, that he wronged no man even in the most trifling affair, but was of service, in the most important matters, to those who enjoyed his society; so temperate, that he never preferred pleasure to virtue; so wise, that he never erred in distinguishing better from worse, needing no counsel from others, but being sufficient in himself to discriminate between them; so able to explain and settle such questions by argument; and so capable of discerning the character of others, of confuting those who were in error, and of exhorting them to virtue and honour; he seemed to be such as the best and happiest of men would be. ——*Ibid.,* p. 507.

ARISTIPPUS OF CYRENE (*c.* 435–386 B.C.)

I myself would like to die as Socrates died. ——Diogenes Laërtius, *Lives of the Philosophers* II.70.

ARISTOTLE (384–322 B.C.)

1   Socrates was occupying himself with ethical questions; neglecting the world of nature as a whole, he sought what was universal in these ethical matters, and for the first time he focused thinking on definitions. ——*Metaphysics* I.987b 1-3. See also *De partibus animalium* 642a 28-29.

2   Socrates was concerned with the virtues of character, and in regard to them he was the first to search for general definitions. . . . It was with good reason that he should seek for the general essence. For he was seeking to syllogize, and the essence is the starting point of syllogisms. For there was then

no one with the dialectical power which enables people even
without knowledge of the essence to observe the extreme terms
[of a syllogism] and to inquire whether the same science deals
with such terms. For two things may be justly credited to
Socrates—inductive arguments and universal definitions, both
of which are concerned with the starting point of scientific
knowledge. But Socrates did not make the universals or definitions exist apart. His successors, however, gave them separate
existence, and this was the kind of thing they named Ideas.
——*Ibid.*, XIII.1078b 18-32.

After [Pythagoras] came Socrates, who spoke better and   3
further about this subject, but even he was not successful. For
he used to make the virtues sciences, and this is impossible.
For the sciences all involve reason, and reason is to be found
in the intellectual part of the soul. So that all the virtues, according to him, are to be found in the rational part of the
soul. The result is that in making the virtues sciences he is
doing away with the irrational part of the soul, and is thereby
doing away also both with passion and moral character, so
that he has not been successful in this respect in his treatment
of the virtues. ——*Magna Moralia* I.1182a 15-24.

Socrates in one respect was on the right track, while in an-   4
other he went astray; in thinking all the virtues were forms
of practical knowledge he was wrong, but in saying they implied practical wisdom he was right. ——*Nicomachean Ethics*
VI.1144b 17-21.

TIMON OF PHLIUS (*c.* 320–230 B.C.)

The sculptor Socrates turned away from the Sophists, he
who idly talked about the law, enchanted all Greece, and
fashioned arguments, making a mock of speech with an irony
that was not even Attic. ——Diogenes Laërtius, *Lives of the
Philosophers* II.70.

ARCESILAUS (*c.* 315–*c.* 241 B.C.)

Not even the residuum of knowledge that Socrates had left himself—the truth that nothing can be known—can be known. —Cicero, *Academica* I.12.45.

ZENO OF SIDON (150? B.C.)

Zeno called Socrates, the father of philosophy, an Attic buffoon (*scurra*), using a Latin word. —Cicero, *De natura deorum* I.34.93.

CATO THE ELDER (234–149 B.C.)

1   There is nothing else to admire in Socrates but that he was always kind and gentle in his dealings with his shrewish wife and stupid sons. —Plutarch, *Lives, Cato* XX.2.

2   Socrates is a mighty babbler, who tries to make himself the tyrant of his country, to dissolve its customs, and to entice its citizens into forming opinions contrary to law and order. —*Ibid.*, XXIII.1.

MARCUS TULLIUS CICERO (106–43 B.C.)

1   What Socrates used to say, namely, that all men were sufficiently eloquent in the field they knew, has some probability, but no truth. —*De oratore* (55 B.C.) I.14.63.

2   I believe that Socrates stood far above all others in this type of irony and feigned modesty by his humor and humaneness [*humanitas*]. —*Ibid.*, II.67.270.

3   But while there were some, and even many, who either were successful in public affairs because of their twofold wisdom

of action and speech, which cannot be separated, such as Themistocles, Pericles, and Theramenes, or who themselves were less active in these affairs, yet were teachers of this wisdom, such as Gorgias, Thrasymachus, and Isocrates, some there were who, with ample theoretical knowledge and intelligence, abhorred public business and affairs deliberately, and scouted and despised the practice of oratory. Foremost among these was Socrates, the man who, according to the testimony of all the learned and the judgment of all Greece, was easily first by virtue of prudence, acumen, charm, and subtlety as well as by eloquence, variety, and imagination. He denied to those who treated, considered, and taught the subject which we are now investigating the name commonly and exclusively used for all the knowledge and the practice of the best things, namely philosophy, and separated by his disputations the intrinsically coherent science of wise thinking from that of ornate speaking. . . . From here started that severance, as it were, of tongue and heart, utterly absurd, useless, and reprehensible, with the result that some taught wisdom, others speech. ——*Ibid.*, III.16.60-1.

I always consider Socrates to have shown greater wisdom 4 [than Panaetius] in refusing to take any interest in such matters [celestial phenomena] and maintaining that the problems of natural phenomena were either too difficult for the human understanding to fathom or else were of no importance whatever to human life. ——*De republica* (51 B.C.) I.10.15.

Socrates was right when he cursed, as he often did, the man 5 who first separated utility from justice; for this separation, he complained, is the source of all mischief.[1] ——*Leges* (after 52 B.C.) I.12.33.

I ask you not to consider me as the kind of philosopher who 6 will put before you a certain school system, a thing which I

1 This tradition goes back to the Stoic Cleanthes.

have never very much approved of even in genuine philosophers. For when did Socrates, who can rightly be called the
father of philosophy, ever do such a thing? ——*De finibus
bonorum et malorum* (45 B.C.) II.1.1.

7   Socrates sought out no advocate when on trial for his life,
and was not humble to his judges, but showed a noble obstinacy, derived from greatness of soul, not from pride, and
on the last day of his life he discussed at length this very subject [the immortality of the soul]; and a few days before,
though he could easily have been removed from prison, he
refused, and then, with the fatal cup almost actually in his
hands, he spoke in language which made him seem not as one
thrust out to die but as one ascending to the heavens. ——
Tusculanae Disputationes (45 B.C.) I.29.71. See also III.15.31.

8   Verily I should prefer above measure such a soul to the
possessions of all those who passed sentence upon him; also
he possesses the knowledge of what is known, as he says, to no
one except the gods, which of the two [life or death] is better
. . . but to the last he holds firmly to his principle of asserting
nothing. ——*Ibid.*, I.42.99.

9   All philosophers who disagree with Plato and Socrates and
the true and refined philosophy which, starting with Socrates,
has found its home till now among the Peripatetics, should be
called plebeians. ——*Ibid.*, I.33.55. See also IV.3.6.

10   Socrates was the first who called philosophy down from the
heavens, established her in the cities of men, introduced her
even into private houses, and compelled her to ask questions
about life and morality and things good and evil. ——*Ibid.*,
V.4.10. See also *Academica* I.4.15.

11   Two of my shops have collapsed and the others show cracks.
Hence not only the inhabitants but even the mice have
moved. Other people call this a calamity, but I do not even

call it a nuisance. O Socrates and you followers of Socrates, I
can never thank you enough. Immortal Gods, how little this
means to me! ——*Letters to Atticus* (17 April, 44 B.C., Puteoli)
XIV.9.9.

It is a fine thing to keep an unruffled temper, an unchang- 12
ing mien, and the same cast of countenance in every condition
of life; this, history tells us, was characteristic of Socrates.
——*De officiis* (44 B.C.) I.26.90.

No one ought to make the mistake of supposing that be- 13
cause Socrates . . . did or said anything contrary to the manners and established customs of his city, *he* has the right to
do the same; it was only on account of his great and divine
virtue that this famous man acquired that special privilege.
——*Ibid.,* I.41.148.

LUCIUS ANNAEUS SENECA (*c.* 4 B.C.–A.D. 65)

Plato, Aristotle, and the whole host of sages who were to 1
branch off in different directions derived more benefit from
the character of Socrates than from his words. ——*Epistulae
morales* VI.6.

Shall I receive in my mind with less than the highest honors 2
Marcus Cato the Elder and the Younger, the wise Laelius and
Socrates, together with Plato, Zeno, and Cleanthes? I worship
them most truly and always rise to honor such noble names.
——*Ibid.,* LXIV.10.

If you desire a model, take Socrates, an old man who had 3
suffered all and was buffeted by every hardship, and still was
unconquered both by poverty, rendered more difficult by his
domestic troubles, and by toil, among which there was also
that of military service. How sorely he was tried at home,
whether we think of his wife, a woman of ferocious manners

and shrewish language, or of his intractable children, so much
more like their mother than their father. And if you come to
think of it, he always lived under wartime conditions, under
the rule of tyrants, or under a "free" rule, which was even
more cruel than wars and tyrants. The war lasted for twenty-
seven years; after the end of the armed conflict the state
became the prey of the Thirty Tyrants, most of whom were
his personal enemies. At last came the crowning blow: his
condemnation under the gravest of indictments. He was
charged with violating religion and corrupting the youth,
whom, they maintained, he had incited against the gods, the city
fathers, and the whole state. Then followed prison and the
poison drink. But all these events changed Socrates' spirit so
little that they did not even change his expression. What
wonderful and singular distinction! To his very end no one
ever saw Socrates unusually cheerful or unusually depressed.
He remained even-tempered in all the unevenness of his fortunes. —*Ibid.,* CIV.27-28.

4   Fortune selects the bravest men with whom to vie. Some
men she bypasses in disgust. Those that are most steadfast
and virtuous she attacks, men against whom she may release
all her strength. . . . Socrates she tries by poison, Cato by
death. Only ill fortune uncovers the great exemplar. —*De
providentia* 3.4.

5   [During the rule of the Thirty Tyrants] Socrates was in the
midst of the Athenians and comforted the dejected city fathers.
He encouraged those who were despairing of the state; repri-
manded the rich, now fearing for their wealth in belated repentance of their perilous avarice; and showed those willing
to imitate him a magnificent example as he went about, a
free man among thirty masters. Yet this was the man whom
Athens herself killed in prison, and Freedom herself did not
support the freedom of the man who had challenged a host of
tyrants. —*De tranquillitate animi* 5.2-3.

PLUTARCH (*c.* 46–125)

Socrates surely was a philosopher, although he did not prepare benches or mount a chair or observe a fixed hour for con-
ferences or walks with his students, but joked with them, at
times went with some into the army or spent time in the
market place, and was finally arrested and drank poison. He
was the first to show that life at all times and in all parts, in
all that we suffer and do, always admits philosophy. ——
Moralia ("Should old men go into politics?") 796d.

EPICTETUS (*c.* 60–110)

If what philosophers say of the kinship between God and 1
men be true, what has any one to do but, like Socrates, when
he is asked what countryman he is, never to say that he is a
citizen of Athens, or of Corinth, but of the universe? ——*Discourses,* tr. Thomas W. Higginson (Boston, 1918), I, 35. See
also Cicero, *Tusculanae Disputationes* V.37.108.

. . . it was the principal and most peculiar characteristic of 2
Socrates, never to be provoked in a dispute, nor to throw out
any reviling or injurious expression; but to bear patiently
with those who reviled him, and thus put an end to the controversy. ——*Ibid.,* II, 15.

Go to Socrates, and see him placed beside his beloved, yet 3
not seduced by youth and beauty. Consider what a victory he
was conscious of obtaining; what an Olympic triumph! How
near does he rank to Hercules! So that, by Heaven! one might
justly salute him, Hail! wondrous victor! instead of those sorry
boxers and wrestlers, and the gladiators who resemble them.
By placing such an example before you, you will conquer any
alluring semblance, and not be drawn away by it. ——*Ibid.,*
I, 181.

4   Pray did not Socrates love his own children? But it was as
became one who was free, and mindful that his first duty was
to gain the love of the gods. Hence he violated no part of the
character of a good man, either in his defense or in fixing a
penalty on himself. Nor yet before, when he was a senator or
a soldier. ——*Ibid.*, II, 99 f.

5   Take Socrates, and consider him, who had a wife and children, but held them not as his own; had a country, friends,
relations, but held them only so long as it was proper, and in
the manner that was proper; submitting all these to the law
and to the obedience due to it. Hence, when it was proper to
fight, he was the first to go out, and exposed himself to danger
without the least reserve. But when he was sent by the thirty
tyrants to apprehend Leon, because he esteemed it a base
action, he did not even deliberate about it; though he knew
that, perhaps, he might die for it. But what did that signify to
him? For it was something else that he wanted to preserve, not
his mere flesh; but his fidelity, his honor, free from attack or
subjection. And afterwards, when he was to make a defense
for his life, does he behave like one having children, or a wife?
No, but like a single man. And how does he behave, when required to drink the poison? When he might escape, and Crito
would have him escape from prison for the sake of his children, what says he? Does he esteem it a fortunate opportunity?
How should he? But he considers what is becoming, and
neither sees nor regards anything else. "For I am not desirous," he says, "to preserve this pitiful body; but that part
which is improved and preserved by justice, and impaired and
destroyed by injustice." Socrates is not to be basely preserved.
He who refused to vote for what the Athenians commanded;
he who contemned the thirty tyrants; he who held such discourses on virtue and moral beauty—such a man is not to be
preserved by a base action, but is preserved by dying, instead
of running away. . . . "What then will become of your children?" "If I had gone away into Thessaly, you would have
taken care of them; and will there be no one to take care of

them when I am departed to Hades?" You see how he ridicules and plays with death. . . . Now the remembrance of the death of Socrates is not less, but even more useful to the world than that of the things which he did and said when alive.   —*Ibid.*, p. 145.

. . . Death is nothing terrible, else it would have appeared   6
so to Socrates.   —*Enchiridion*, tr. Thomas W. Higginson, "Library of Liberal Arts," No. 8 (New York, 1948), p. 19.

When you are going to confer with anyone, and especially   7
with one who seems your superior, represent to yourself how Socrates or Zeno would behave in such a case, and you will not be at a loss to meet properly whatever may occur.   —*Ibid.*, p. 32.

. . . Socrates became perfect, improving himself by every-   8
thing, following reason alone. And though you are not yet a Socrates, you ought, however, to live as one seeking to be a Socrates.   —*Ibid.*, pp. 38-39.

MARCUS AURELIUS (121–180)

How do we know that Telauges [the son of Pythagoras] was not superior in character to Socrates? For it is not enough that Socrates died a more glorious death and disputed more effectively with the Sophists; that he held out with more endurance through whole nights in the frost, and when ordered to arrest the Salaminian Leon deemed it nobler to disobey; and that he "carried his head high as he walked," which is easy to establish. What has to be examined is this: what kind of a soul had Socrates? Was it enough for him to be just in his dealings with men and religious in his attitude toward the gods? Was he indignant about wickedness? Did he kowtow to the ignorance of anyone? Did he regard as alien to himself anything allotted to him from the Whole, or bear it as an intolerable

load? Did he allow his intelligence to be moved by the affections of the flesh?   ——*Meditations* VII.66.

DEMONAX (SECOND CENTURY)

All philosophers are admirable. But I personally worship
Socrates, I marvel at Diogenes, and I love Aristippus.   ——
Quoted in Lucian, *Demonax* 62.

LUCIAN (SECOND CENTURY)

1   MENIPPUS: Was then this fellow [Socrates] merely a Sophist?
Did he not, as a matter of fact, show contempt for the fact of
death?

CERBERUS: No, he did not. But when he saw eventually that
it was necessary and inevitable, he started putting on a bold
front, as though he were really ready to suffer willingly what
he had to undergo anyhow, in order that the spectators would
admire his behavior.   ——*Dialogues of the Dead* 21.

2   SIMON: There is nobody who can give the name of a philosopher who was killed in battle. Either they did not go into
military service at all, or, if they did, they all ran away. Antisthenes, Diogenes, Crates, Zeno, Plato, Aeschines, Aristotle,
and all that crowd never even saw a battle line. The only one
who dared to set out for the battle of Delium, their wise Socrates, fled all the way home from Parnes to the school of
Taureas.[2] He considered it far more urbane to sit down and
make love to boys and put sophistries to the first comer than
to fight a real Spartan.

TYCHIADES: My noble friend, I have already learned this
from others who by no means wished to ridicule and to
slander them; so I certainly do not think that you are telling
lies about them out of bias for your art [rhetoric].   ——*The
Parasite* 43.

  [2] See, however, Plato, *Laches* 181b.

PLOTINUS (204–*c.* 270)

"Celebrating the natal days of Plato and Socrates, Plotinus invited his friends to a philosophic banquet, at which each one was required to deliver an oration suited to the occasion."
——Porphyrius, *De vita Plotini* II.96.

JULIAN THE APOSTATE (331?–363)

And what are we to say about Socrates? Socrates, who disclaimed theory and loved the practical life, was a ruler neither of his wife nor his child. Now, was it not in his power to rule these two or three citizens? Was he after all not practical, since he was not the ruler of anybody? But in my eyes the achievements of Alexander are outdone by the son of Sophroniscus. I ascribe to him the wisdom of Plato, the generalship of Xenophon, the fortitude of Antisthenes, the Eretric and Megaric philosophies together with Cebes and Simmias and countless others. And I do not even mention the colonies that he planted, the Lyceum, the Stoa, and the Academies. Whoever found salvation in the victories of Alexander? What city had better citizens because of him? Who developed into a better private person [on his account]? For you might find many who [thanks to him] became richer, but no one who became wiser or more healthy-minded than before, some indeed more irresponsible and haughty. Whereas it is thanks to Socrates that all who find salvation in philosophy are being saved even now. And that is not only my opinion, but Aristotle seems to have thought and said so before me. ——*Letter to Themistius* 264b-d.

1

[Among Ulysses, Alexander the son of Philip of Macedon, Achilles the son of Thetis, and many other glorious personalities of illustrious birth] Socrates alone, I believe, with very few of his disciples, truly happy and blessed men, succeeded in

2

laying down the last of the garments of which the soul divests itself, the love of [worldly] honor. ——*Oration* II. 69c.

BOETHIUS (*c.* 480–*c.* 525)

Socrates had the victory of an unjust death. Subsequently such rabble as the Epicureans, Stoics, and others all tried hard to appropriate him, each group for its own school. ——*De Consolatione philosophiae* 1.3.

2. *Early Christianity*

JUSTIN MARTYR (*c.* 105–*c.* 165)

Lest some should, without reason, and for the perversion of   1
what we teach, maintain that we say that Christ was born
one hundred and fifty years ago under Cyrenius, and subsequently, in the time of Pontius Pilate, taught what we say He
taught; and should cry out against us as though all men who
were born before Him were irresponsible—let us anticipate
and solve the difficulty. We have been taught that Christ is
the first-born of God, and we have declared above that He is
the Word of whom every race of men were partakers; and
those who lived reasonably are Christians, even though they
have been thought atheists; as, among the Greeks, Socrates and
Heraclitus, and men like them. ——*The First Apology* 46, in
The Ante-Nicene Fathers (Grand Rapids, 1950), I, 178.

[Those before Christ] when they attempted to consider and   2
prove things by reason, were brought before the tribunals as
impious persons and busybodies. And Socrates, who was more
zealous in this direction than all of them, was accused of the
very same crimes as ourselves. For they said that he was introducing new divinities, and did not consider those to be gods
whom the state recognized. But he cast out from the state both
Homer and the rest of the poets, and taught men to reject the
wicked demons and those who did the things which the poets
related; and he exhorted them to become acquainted with
the God who was to them unknown by means of the investigation of reason, saying "that it is neither easy to find the
Father and Maker of all, nor, having found Him, is it safe to
declare Him to all." (*Republic* 10.595.) But these things our

Christ did through His own power. For no one trusted in Socrates so as to die for this doctrine, but in Christ, who was partially known even by Socrates (for He was and is the Word who is in every man, and who foretold the things that were to come to pass both through the Prophets and in His own person when He was made of like passions, and taught these things), not only philosophers and scholars believed, but also artisans and people entirely uneducated, despising both glory, and fear, and death; since he is a power of the ineffable Father, and not the mere instrument of human reason. ——*The Second Apology* 10, in *The Ante-Nicene Fathers* (Grand Rapids, 1950), I, 191-92.

TERTULLIAN (*c.* 155–*c.* 222)

1   [In my treatment of the soul] I shall evidently have mostly to contend with the philosophers. In the very prison of Socrates they skirmished with the state of the soul. I have my doubts at once whether the time was an opportune one for their (great) master—(to say nothing of the place), although *that* perhaps does not much matter. For what could the soul of Socrates then contemplate with clearness and serenity? The sacred ship had returned (from Delos), the hemlock draft to which he had been condemned had been drunk, death was now present before him: (his mind) was, as one may suppose, naturally excited at every emotion; or if nature had lost her influence, it must have been deprived of all power of thought. Or let it have been as placid and tranquil as you please, inflexible, in spite of the claims of natural duty, at the tears of her who was so soon to be his widow, and at the sight of his thenceforward orphan children, yet his soul must have been moved even by its very efforts to suppress emotion, and his constancy itself must have been shaken, as he struggled against the disturbance of the excitement around him. Besides, what other thoughts could any man entertain who had been unjustly condemned to die, but such as should solace him for the

injury done to him? Especially would this be the case with
that glorious creature, the philosopher, to whom injurious
treatment would not suggest a craving for consolation, but
rather the feeling of resentment and indignation. Accordingly,
after his sentence, when his wife came to him with her effemi-
nate cry, "O Socrates, you are unjustly condemned!" he seemed
already to find joy in answering, "Would you then wish me
justly condemned?" It is therefore not to be wondered at if,
even in his prison, from a desire to break the foul hands of
Anytus and Meletus, he, in the face of death itself, asserts the
immortality of the soul by a strong assumption such as was
wanted to frustrate the wrong (they had inflicted upon him).
So that all the wisdom of Socrates, at that moment, proceeded
from the affectation of an assumed composure, rather than the
firm conviction of ascertained truth. For by whom has truth
ever been discovered without God? By whom has God ever
been found without Christ? By whom has Christ ever been explored without the Holy Spirit? By whom has the Holy Spirit
ever been attained without the mysterious gift of faith? Socrates, as none can doubt, was actuated by a different spirit. For
they say a demon clave to him from his boyhood—the very
worst teacher certainly, notwithstanding the high place assigned to it by poets and philosophers—even next to (nay
along with) the gods themselves. The teachings of the power
of Christ had not yet been given—(that power) which alone
can confute this most pernicious influence of evil that has
nothing good in it, but is rather the author of all error, and
the seducer from all truth. Now if Socrates was pronounced
the wisest of men by the oracle of the Pythian demon, which,
you may be sure, neatly managed the business for his friend,
of how much greater dignity and constancy is the assertion of
the Christian wisdom, before the very breath of which the
whole host of demons is scattered! The wisdom of the school
of heaven frankly and without reserve denies the gods of the
world, and shows no such inconsistency as to order a "cock to
be sacrificed to Aesculapius"; no new gods and demons does
it introduce, but it expels the old ones; it does not corrupt

youth, but instructs them in all goodness and moderation; and so it bears the unjust condemnation, not of one city only, but of all the world, in the cause of that truth which incurs indeed the greater hatred in proportion to its fulness; so that it tastes death not out of a (poisoned) cup almost in the way of jollity, but it exhausts it in every kind of bitter cruelty, on gibbets and in holocausts. Meanwhile, in the still gloomier prison of the world amongst your Cebeses and Phaedos, in every investigation concerning (man's) soul, it directs its inquiry according to the rules of God. ——*A Treatise on the Soul*, II, in *The Ante-Nicene Fathers* (Grand Rapids, 1950), III, 181-82.

2   This name of philosopher has no power to put demons to rout. Why are they not able to do that too, since philosophers consider demons inferior to gods? Socrates used to say, "If the demon grant permission." Yet he too, though in denying the existence of your [the pagan's] divinities he had a glimpse of the truth, at his dying ordered a cock to be sacrificed to Aesculapius, I believe in honor of his father; for Apollo had pronounced Socrates the wisest of men. Thoughtless Apollo! testifying to the wisdom of the man who denied the very existence of his race. . . . If we challenge you to comparison in the virtue of chastity, I turn to a part of the sentence passed by the Athenians against Socrates, who was pronounced a corrupter of youth. ——*Apology* 46, in *The Ante-Nicene Fathers* (Grand Rapids, 1950), III, 51. See also *Ad Nationes*, chap. 4, *ibid.*, p. 112.

3   In contempt of your gods, Socrates swears by an oak, a dog, and a goat. Now, although he was condemned to die for that very reason, the Athenians afterwards repented of that condemnation and even put to death his accusers. By this conduct of theirs the testimony of Socrates is replaced at its full value, and I am enabled to meet you with the retort that in this case you have approbation bestowed on that which is

nowadays reprobated in us. ——*Ad Nationes,* chap. 10, in *The Ante-Nicene Fathers* (Grand Rapids, 1950), III, 120.

ORIGEN (185–*c.* 253)

Socrates knew that he would die after drinking the hem- 1
lock, and it was in his power, if he had allowed himself to be persuaded by Crito, by escaping from prison, to avoid these calamities; but nevertheless he decided, as it appeared to him consistent with right reason, that it was better for him to die as became a philosopher, than to retain his life in a manner unbecoming one. ——*Contra Celsum* IX.17, in *The Ante-Nicene Fathers* (Grand Rapids, 1950), IV, 438-39.

Those who [like Plato] have written . . . regarding the 2
"chief good" will go down to the Piraeus and offer prayer to Artemis,[1] as if she were God, and will look (with approval) upon the solemn assembly held by ignorant men; and after giving utterance to philosophical remarks of such profundity regarding the soul, and describing its passage (to a happier world) after a virtuous life, they pass from those great topics which God has revealed to them, and adopt mean and trifling thoughts, and offer a cock to Aesculapius! ——*Ibid.,* VI.4, in *The Ante-Nicene Fathers,* IV, 574.

Jesus did indeed meet with a most sad death; but the same 3
might be said of Socrates. . . . If the death of Jesus was a miser-able one, was not that of the others so too? ——*Ibid.,* VI.56, in *The Ante-Nicene Fathers,* IV, 633-34.

[1] See *Republic* 327a.

ST. ATHANASIUS (*c.* 298–373)

Strange to say, even Plato, the sage admired among the Greeks, with all his vaunted understanding about God, goes down with Socrates to Piraeus [2] to worship Artemis, a figment of man's art.   —*Against the Heathen,* chap. 10, in *The Nicene and Post-Nicene Fathers* (2nd series; New York, 1925), IV, 9.

ARNOBIUS (*c.* 300)

. . . Socrates, condemned by the decision of his fellow citizens, suffered capital punishment: have his discussions on morals, on virtues, and on duties been rendered vain, because he was unjustly hurried from life?   —*Against the Heathen,* I, 40, in *The Ante-Nicene Fathers* (Grand Rapids, 1950), VI, 424.

LACTANTIUS (*c.* 300)

1   Let us now see what there was so great in Socrates himself, that a wise man [Plato] deservedly [3] gave thanks that he was born in his times. I do not deny that he was a little more sagacious than the others who thought that the nature of things could be comprehended by the mind . . . no one descends from heaven to pass sentence on the opinions of individuals; wherefore no one can doubt that those who seek after these things are foolish, senseless, and insane. Socrates therefore had something of human wisdom, who, when he understood that these things could not possibly be ascertained,

---

[2] Apparently an allusion to Plato's *Republic* 327a. See also ORIGEN, p. 43, no. 2.

[3] This word is clearly meant to be ironic.

removed himself from questions of this kind; but I fear that he so acted in this alone. For many of his actions are not only undeserving of praise, but also most deserving of censure, in which things he most resembled those of his own class. Out of these I will select one which may be judged of by all. Socrates used this well-known proverb: "That which is above us is nothing to us." . . . He undoubtedly meant that which he said, that we are not to devote ourselves to religion. . . . If he wished to overthrow those public superstitions, I do not disapprove of this; yea, I shall rather praise it, if he shall have found anything better *to take their* [i.e., the pagans'] *place*. But the same man swore by a dog and a goose. Oh buffoon (as Zeno the Epicurean says), senseless, abandoned, desperate man, if he wished to scoff at religion: madman, if he did this seriously, so as to esteem a most base animal as God! . . . I should consider him most mad if he had died under the influence of disease. But since he did this [i.e., asked his friends to sacrifice for him a cock which he had vowed to Aesculapius] in his sound mind, he who thinks that he was wise is himself of unsound mind. Behold one in whose times the wise man [Plato] congratulates himself as having been born! —*Divine Institutes,* chap. 20, in *The Ante-Nicene Fathers* (Grand Rapids, 1950), VII, 91.

. . . Socrates held the first place in philosophy, who was 2 pronounced most wise even by the oracle, because he confessed that he knew one thing only—namely, that he knew nothing. And on the authority of this oracle it was right that the natural philosophers should restrain themselves, lest they should either inquire into those things which they could not know, or should think that they knew things which they did not know. Let us, however, see whether Socrates was most wise, as the Pythian god proclaimed. He often made use of the proverb that that which is above us has also no reference to us. He has now passed beyond the limits of his opinions. For he who said that he knew one thing only found another thing to speak of, as though he knew it; but that in vain. For God, who is plainly above us, is to be sought for; and religion is to be undertaken, which alone separates us from the brutes, which indeed Socrates not only rejected, but even derided, in swearing by a goose and a dog, as if in truth he could not have sworn by Aesculapius, to whom he had vowed a cock. Behold the sacrifice of a wise man! And because he was unable to offer this in his own person, since he was at the point of death, he entreated his friends to perform the vow after his death, lest forsooth he should be detained as a debtor in the lower regions. He assuredly both pronounced that he knew nothing, and made good his statement. ——*The Epitome of the Divine Institutes,* chap. 37, in *The Ante-Nicene Fathers* (Grand Rapids, 1950), VII, 236.

EUSEBIUS (*c.* 260–*c.* 340)

Socrates . . . elated by his skill in argumentation, indulging his power of making the worse appear the better reason, and playing continually with the subtleties of controversy, fell a victim to the slander of his own countrymen and fellow citizens. ——*The Oration of Constantine, which he addressed to the Assembly of Saints,* chap. 9, in *The Nicene and Post-Nicene Fathers* (2nd series; New York, 1925), I, 566.

ST. JEROME (*c.* 340–420)

I would refer to our shame to the frugality of Pythagoras, Socrates, Antisthenes and the rest, if this were not a long story and were without proper purpose here. But certainly this is the place for the story of Antisthenes, who, after he had gloriously taught rhetoric and had heard Socrates in a disputation about poverty, is reported to have said to his students: "Leave me and look for a [real] teacher; for I have already found one." ——*Adversus Jovinianum* II.14; *Porphyrii philosophi opuscula selecta,* ed. Augustus Nauck (Leipzig, 1886).

JOHN CHRYSOSTOM (347?–407)

That the honor to be had from the many is not to be despised, this Socrates himself shows, for all that he may philosophize without end on this point: for in everything he did, he had an eye to fame. And if you were conversant with his discourses, I might go at great length into this subject, and show what a deal of insincerity (*eironeia*) there was in them— if at least we may believe what his disciple says of him—and how that all his writings have their ground-work in vainglory. ——*Homily on The Acts of the Apostles,* 36, in *The Nicene and Post-Nicene Fathers* (1st series; New York, 1886– 90), XI, 226.

1

[Plato's] master is in a stupid awe of these idols, for he it is that bids them sacrifice the cock to Aesculapius, [in whose temple] are the images of these beasts, and creeping things. ——*Homily on Epistle to the Romans,* 3:23, in *The Nicene and Post-Nicene Fathers* (1st series; New York, 1886–90), XI, 353.

2

But among [the philosophers] also, it will be said, many have been found contemners of death. Tell me who? Was it he who drank the hemlock? But if thou wilt, I can bring forward ten thousand such from within the Church. For had it been lawful when prosecution befell them to drink hemlock and depart, all had become more famous than he. And besides, he drank when he was not at liberty to drink or not to drink; but willing or against his will he must have undergone it: no effect surely of fortitude, but of necessity, and nothing more. . . . This then you see is no great wonder, that he whom I was mentioning drank hemlock; it being no longer in his power not to drink, and also when he had arrived at a very great age. For when he despised life he stated himself to be seventy years old; if this can be called despising. For I for my

3

part could not affirm it: nor, what is more, can anyone else.
——*Homily on First Corinthians*, 4:7, in *The Nicene and Post-Nicene Fathers* (1st series; New York, 1886–90), XII, 19.

4   . . . It is said that Plato, although well aware that all about the gods was a sort of imposture, condescended to all the feasts and all the rest of it, as being unable to contend with custom: and as having in fact learnt this from his master. For he, too, being suspected of some such innovation, was so far from succeeding in what he desired that he even lost his life: and this, too, after making his defence.   ——*Ibid.*, 4:15, p. 40.

5   Why, I at this moment [i.e., in considering Socrates' patience with Xanthippe] am greatly mourning, when heathens prove better lovers of wisdom than we.   ——*Ibid.*, 26:8, p. 156.

ST. AUGUSTINE (354–430)

1   . . . The charm and subtlety which Socrates possessed in moral matters.   ——*Contra Academicos* III.37.

2   In my estimate it cannot be determined with certainty whether Socrates directed the entire effort of philosophy to the correction and regulation of conduct because he was wearied of obscure and uncertain matters and thus wished to direct his mind to the discovery of something manifest and certain, which was necessary in order to obtain a blessed life . . . or whether (as some yet more favorable to him suppose) he did it because he did not wish that minds defiled with earthly desires should attempt to raise themselves upward to matters divine. For he saw that they were seeking the causes of things—which causes he believed to be ultimately reducible to nothing else but the will of the true and supreme God, wherefore he thought they could only be comprehended by a purified mind; and therefore that all diligence ought to be given to the purification of life by good morals, in order that

the mind, delivered from the depressing weight of lusts, might raise itself upward by its native vigor to eternal things and might, with purified understanding, contemplate that nature which is incorporeal and unchangeable light, where live the causes of all created natures. It is evident, however, that he hunted out and pursued, with a wonderful pleasantness of style and argument, and with a most pointed and insinuating urbanity, the foolishness of ignorant men, who thought that they knew this or that—sometimes confessing his own ignorance and sometimes dissimulating his knowledge, even in those very moral questions to which he seems to have applied the whole vigor of his mind. And hence there arose hostility against him, which ended in his being slanderously impeached and condemned to death. . . . Illustrious therefore both in his life and his death, Socrates left very many disciples. . . . Because in his disputations, where he raises all manner of questions, he makes assertions and then demolishes them, it was not fully evident what he held to be the chief good. Thus everyone took from these disputations what pleased him best, and everyone placed the final good in whatever it appeared to him to consist. ——*De civitate Dei* VIII.3.

SOCRATES SCHOLASTICUS (*c.* 380–*c.* 450)

Even Socrates, the most celebrated of [the Greek] philosophers, despised these absurdities [of Greek literature], and was condemned on account of it, as if he had attempted to violate the sanctity of their deities. ——*Ecclesiastical History* III.16, in *The Nicene and Post-Nicene Fathers* (2nd series; New York, 1925), II, 87. See also Vol. IV, p. xxiii.

3. *The Middle Ages*

PETER ABÉLARD (1079–1142)

1   Who exhort us more to show contempt of the world, by their writings as well as by their deeds, than do the philosophers? They write down the elements of true immortality and are guided by their own writings and distinguish carefully the vices as well as the virtues, and have persisted steadfastly in correcting the depraved until death, as did Socrates, who was killed for the sake of truth by those whose vices he constantly discussed. . . . You admire the life of Job, his patience and his other virtues. What about them? Socrates, Diogenes, and many others also [showed them]. That Socrates and many others left everything behind like the Apostles is testified by Hieronymus (*Ad Jovinianum*). ——*Theologia "Summi Boni,"* ed. H. Ostlender (Münster, 1939), p. 25.

2   Remember, Socrates was tied to a wife, and through a nasty accident he wiped out this blot [his marriage] upon philosophy so that others after him might be more cautious; a story which not even Jerome omits in his first book against Jovinianus (I, 278), where he writes about Socrates: "At one time when Xanthippe had put her foot down about his endless bringing in of dinner guests of higher rank and he was met by a bucket of slops, he simply said, after wiping his head, 'I knew such thunder would bring rain.' " ——Héloïse' First Letter to Abélard in *Historia calamitatum*.

ALBERTUS MAGNUS (*c.* 1193–1280)

Plato took over the view that man is the cause of good and not of evil things from his teacher Socrates, who was the head of the Stoics [1] and stated that all the virtues within man were conferred upon the soul by divine gift. . . . But this view is ridiculous, according to the Peripatetics, because it proceeds from a wrong hypothesis.   —*In Ethicam Aristotelis,* in *Opera,* ed. P. Jammy and A. Borgnet (Paris, 1890–99), IV, 203a.

ST. JOHANNES BONAVENTURA (1221–1274)

All true philosophers worshiped one God. Which is also **1** the reason why Socrates, because he forbade men to sacrifice to Apollo, was killed, since he worshiped one God. It is true that Plato advised him to flee. "Far be it from me," said Socrates, "to deny the truth which I have asserted." And for that reason Plato was not present at his death, ashamed of having advised him to escape.   —*In Hexaemeron,* Sermon V, in *Opera omnia,* ed. A. C. Peltier (Paris, 1867), IX, 57.

Socrates, that philosopher who was famous for such great **2** wisdom, said, according to Valerius Maximus, that in his opinion we should not request anything from the gods save that they give us good things. Socrates used many arguments to confirm this, according to Valerius, who at the end of the chapter concludes that the following was a wise verdict about that criminal sentence passed against him by the Athenians: "When Socrates had accepted with brave spirit and steadfast expression the poison drink from the hand of the executioner, with his lips already at the cup, he told his wife Xanthippe, who clamored amid tears and lamentations that he was being killed without guilt, "How then? Would you have considered it better for me to die guilty?" Valerius adds, "What immense wisdom, which could not forget itself even at the end of life." It is for this reason that Socrates received with brave spirit and cheerful expression the poison drink from the hand of the executioner and drank it at once.   —*First Sermon on St. Agatha, Virgin and Martyr,* in *Opera omnia,* XIII, 530b.

1 This bit of misinformation recurs repeatedly.

3   Socrates, during the ninety-nine years [*sic*] of his life, was so
intent upon teaching that he disputed even at his death. Wisdom, for which human concern is so strong, is therefore a great
good.   —*Fifth Sermon on Several Martyr Saints,* in *Opera
omnia,* XIII, 60b.

ST. THOMAS AQUINAS (*c.* 1225–1274)

1   The opinion of Socrates, who (according to Aristotle) said
that virtue is a kind of prudence, is based on a false supposi-
tion, although there is some truth to it.   —*Summa theologica*
Ia IIae, q. 58 art. 2.

2   Socrates, in his opinion that knowledge can never be overcome by passion, that virtue is a kind of knowledge, and that
every sin is a kind of ignorance, was somewhat right, because
the will, since its object is a good or an apparent good, is
never moved to an evil unless that which is not good appear
to reason to be good in some respect.   —*Ibid.,* q. 77 art. 2.

3   To a certain extent Socrates, as reported by Valerius Maximus, is right in believing that we should ask the immortal
gods for nothing but that they should grant us good things
because they at any rate know what is good for each one.
—*Ibid.* IIa IIae, q. 83 art. 5.

4   It was proper for Christ not to write down his teaching . . .
which is also the reason why, among the pagans, Pythagoras
and Socrates, who were most excellent teachers, did not want
to write anything.   —*Ibid.* IIIa, q. 42 art. 4.

JEAN DE MEUN (*c.* 1250–1305)

1   REASON: . . . Make
                No count of Fortune and her wheel
                (Not worth a prune is she), but steel

Thy heart like Socrates, who ne'er
In all his life was swayed by her.
She smiled, his heart grew nowise gay;
She frowned, he laughed her frowns away.
Whatso of good or ill he met,
Was each 'gainst each in balance set,
Nor deigned he say that this was good
Or that was fraught with drearihood,
No evil chances could destroy
His peace, nor good luck move to joy.
Of all who lived was he the man
Judged by Apollo Pythian
For wisest, as Solinus saith;
For ne'er could Fortune's changeful breath
Alter his visage—still 'twas seen,
In joy unmoved—in woe serene.
And even when, because, quoth he,
"There is but one great Deity,"
They brought to him the poison cup,
Calmly he drank the potion up,
Charging his gaolers they should ne'er
By more than one God use to swear.

—*Roman de la Rose*, tr. F. S. Ellis (London, 1900), I, 209.

REASON: In thine heart   2
Bethink thou well of Socrates
(Too wise a foolish world to please);
My love I gave him, and to me
He gave his love all utterly.

—*Ibid.*, I, 221.

DANTE ALIGHIERI (1265–1321)

When I raised my eyelids a little higher, I saw the master
of those who know sitting in the midst of the philosophic

family. All look at him, all do him honor; there I saw Socrates
and Plato, who stand nearest to him and before the rest.[2]

 ——*Divina Commedia,* Inferno, Canto IV, 130-34.

JOHANNES DUNS SCOTUS (*c.* 1265–1308)

Men as good and as wise as Pythagoras, Socrates, Plato, and
Aristotle and other outstanding followers of wisdom received
from God special revelations in which they obtained many insights about God. ——Quoted in Latin in Charles R. S.
Harris, *Duns Scotus* (Oxford, 1927), I, 125.

[2] Poi ch' innalzai un poco più le ciglia,
    Vidi 'l maestro di color che sanno,
    Seder tra filosofica famiglia.
  Tutti lo miran, tutti onor li fanno,
    Quivi vid' io Socrate e Platone,
    Che 'nnanzi a li altri più presso li stanno.

4. *The Renaissance*

PETRARCH (1304–1374)

But now a different troop my notice drew: 1
The sage Palladian tribe, a nobler train,
Whose toils deserve a more exalted strain.
Plato majestic in the front appear'd,
Where wisdom's sacred hand her ensign rear'd.
Celestial blazonry! by heaven bestow'd,
Which, waving high, before the vanguard glow'd:
Then came the Stagyrite, whose mental ray
Pierced through all nature like the shafts of day;
And he that, by the unambitious name,
Lover of wisdom, chose to bound his fame.
Then Socrates and Xenophon were seen . . .

> ——*The Triumph of Fame,* Pt. III, tr. Hugh Boyd
> in *The Sonnets, Triumphs, and Other
> Poems of Petrarch* (London, 1883), p. 391.

Socrates says: "This one thing I know, that I know noth-   2
ing" . . . a most humble confession. ——*De sua ignorantia,* in
E. Cassirer (ed.), *The Renaissance Philosophy of Man* (Chicago, 1948), pp. 126.

GEOFFREY CHAUCER (*c.* 1344–1400)

O Socrates, thou stedfast champioun,
She [Fortune] never mightè be thy tormentour;
Thou never dreddest hir oppressioun,
Ne in hir cherè founde thou no savour.

55

Thou knewe wel the deceit of hir colour
And that hir mostè worshipe is to lye.
——"Fortune," lines 17-24, in *Works,* ed. A. W.
Pollard *et al.* (London, 1899), p. 629; See
also *Book of the Duchess,* lines 717–19.

NICOLAUS CUSANUS (1401–1464)

Knowledge of the precise numerical relations in physical
objects and the proper coordination of the known to the unknown exceeds human reason; that is why it seemed to Socrates that he knew nothing except that he knew nothing.
——*De docta ignorantia* I.1.

MARSILIO FICINO (1433–1499)

1   Marsilio Ficino to Paolo Ferrobanti, the distinguished theologian, greetings.

If I were not afraid, excellent Paul, that there are quite a
few who, either because of intellectual dishonesty or pettiness
of judgment, took my words in a sense different from the one
in which I use them, I would demonstrate in detail that Socrates, if not, to use a rather bold figure, like John the Baptist,
yet by way of adumbration, if I may say so, foreshadowed
Christ, the author of our salvation. I would do so principally
for the purpose of confounding that detractor Lucian who,
after detracting everybody, finally did not even spare good
Christians, when he dared to ridicule the martyrs of our faith
because they, being somewhat simple-minded, had voluntarily
given up all the things which are considered good by the people; and further because, being rather pitiable, they had exposed themselves even to tortures and slaughter. But the man
who should be held up to Lucian when he ridicules the simple-
minded is Socrates, the wisest of all, thus pronounced by the
testimony of the great philosophers as well as by the oracle of
Apollo. Now this man, not from some crude simple-minded-

ness, but from his singular mental excellence and, as witness
Plato and Xenophon, divinity and innate or oracular inspiration, throughout his life preferred the eternal values to the
corruptible ones, sustained physical inconveniences and particularly lack of food and clothing and all other misfortunes
besides, fearing only the perpetual evil and harm of the
soul, intent alone on his duty of piety and charity. He is the
one who neglects his own advantages and is stopped by no
danger, he who like a physician of souls is engaged in purging
the minds of men everywhere within the borders of the country, while he detests pride above everything but approves of
mildness, charity, and religiousness, professes alone the study
of true love and charity and excludes the pretentious pursuit
of the sciences. Everywhere he relies on divine testimonies,
holds on to them in firm faith, is content with pious and just
customs and, what is marvelous, does so without hope for human reward for such a strenuous duty, even undergoing for its
sake danger and death. In fact, he asserted that he had been
sent by God for that one very purpose and stated that he
would rather obey God than men. But let us listen to Socrates
himself, who will shortly exclaim before his unjust judges:
"That I am one who is obviously given to the city by God,
you can see from the following: It certainly does not seem to
be human that I have neglected all my interests and have persisted in this neglect of my affairs and in my poverty for so
many years, always concerned for your good whenever I meet
someone, advising him to care for virtue, like a father or an
elder brother. If I received some reward for my service, there
would have been a human reason for that." [1] Therefore, while
he takes the sinners to task, even while being kicked, he
salutes the one who kicks him, and, smitten on the cheek,
turns the other cheek. Finally he earned such hatred by telling the truth that he was accused of impiety by the very people to whom he had openly preached the duty of piety. And
what am I to say about the fact that, while he could have

[1] *Apology* 31a.

easily defended himself in court, he neither did so nor apolo-
gized, but accused his judges; and, when he could have left
prison, did not want to and most willingly suffered an unjust
death as the man who was to bequeath to posterity examples
of supreme steadfastness and patience? I leave out at present
the price of thirty minae offered by Socrates, the prophecies
of Socrates, the divine retaliation which immediately followed
his death,[2] the washing instituted by Socrates in the evening
shortly before his death, and Socrates' exhortation to piety in
the hour of the meal. What am I to say about the fact that,
in the same hour, he refers to the chalice, to the benediction,
and, in the very hour of his death, to the cock? I omit besides
many deeds as well as sayings of Socrates which were written
down, not by himself, but principally by his four disciples, by
which the Christian faith is greatly confirmed against Lucian.
For there are many things, and those to be sure of supreme
importance, which are handed down about the divine spirit
breathed into him, about the detachment of his mind from his
body and, as it were, transfiguration. But this letter could
neither easily encompass such things nor could many people
accept them in good faith without thinking that I was presenting Socrates here as a competitor [of Christianity] while I
make him a defender [of it]. ——*Opera omnia* (Basel, 1562),
p. 868.

2   Socrates, Plato, and Varro, although secretly because of the
masses, rightly ridiculed the superstitions of the pagans. Jesus
finally destroyed them, that men might not be destroyed [by
them]. ——*Ibid.*, p. 25.

3   Plato wrote that the whole concern of his mind was directed toward the investigation of divine things. Socrates believed that this investigation can achieve the desired end by

  [2] The widespread tradition concerning Athenian repentance and concerning the banishment or execution of Socrates' accusers, to which this
phrase apparently refers, can be traced back as far as Diodorus Siculus,
Plutarch, and Diogenes Laërtius.

means of the purgation of the mind. Therefore, by neglecting at times his customary caution in questioning, he resorted to physical (*mortalis*) philosophy in order that the mind, by its benefit, after dissipating the material clouds of the body, be made more serene and grasp the light of the divine sun and the other lights always and everywhere simultaneously. Which is what Socrates himself, to start with, and then Plato, by imitation of Socrates, seem to have achieved. ——*Ibid.,* p. 267.

GIOVANNI PICO DELLA MIRANDOLA (1463–1494)

Who would not like to be inspired by that Socratic enthusi- 1
asm (*Socratici furores*) which Plato describes in the *Phaedo,* so that, with the rudder (*remigium*) of wings and feet, he could flee quickly from this world, steeped as it is in evil, and be transferred by the fastest possible course to the heavenly Jerusalem? Oh, let us be driven, Fathers, by that Socratic en-thusiasm, which thus takes us beyond our minds in such a way that it puts our minds and ourselves into God. . . . When the dying Socrates was in hope to wed his own divine mind to the divinity of the larger universe, he stated, from where he was already beyond all risk of illness, that he owed to Aescu-lapius, i.e., to the physician of souls, a rooster. ——*Oratio de dignitate hominis,* in E. Cassirer (ed.), *The Renaissance Phi-losophy of Man* (Chicago, 1948), pp. 233-34.

It is his [Epictetus'] opinion that a person who finds himself 2
suffering from however tormented an imagination acts best if he considers what either Socrates or Zeno would do if they had fallen into this type of adversity. But I believe that one ought to observe this as well under favorable gusts of fortune as under unfavorable countergusts, not in imitation of Soc-rates and Zeno, but of the most saintly Christians, who not only taught that the slippery force of appetite and the swell-ing furor of anger ought to be kept by the fences of other men's reason, but, having very often experienced the harm of

these forces, actually restrained them by their own efforts.
——*Liber de imaginatione,* ed. Harry Caplan (New Haven,
1930), p. 94.

DESIDERIUS ERASMUS OF ROTTERDAM (1466–1536)

1   You will find in Socrates' life what is in harmony with
Christ's life. ——*Enchiridion* (1502), in *Opera* (Leiden, 1703–
06), V, 92b.

2   FOLLY: How inept these philosophers are for the work of
everyday life is demonstrated by the unique Socrates, who was
judged the wisest of men by the not equally wise oracle of
Apollo. When he tried to make a motion in public for I know
not what, he had to sit down amid universal laughter. Still
Socrates was not completely foolish in declining the title
"wise" and leaving all to God; he also espoused the opinion
that a wise man should refrain from getting mixed up with
the public business of the community. To be sure, he ought
rather to have exhorted those who want to take their place in
the ranks of mankind to abstain from wisdom itself. Besides,
what wisdom made him, once he had been indicted, drink
the hemlock? For while he philosophized about clouds and
ideas, and measured the feet of a flea and marveled at the
sound of a gnat, he had no idea of the most common affairs
of life. ——*The Praise of Folly* (1509), chap. 24 (New York,
n.d.); also in *Stultitiae Laus,* ed. I. B. Kan (The Hague, 1898),
pp. 38-39.

3   Hardly anything has been brought out in the Gospels that
had not been brought out many centuries before in the volumes of the Old Testament and some also in the books of the
philosophers. That souls survive the bodies and receive rewards and penalties for the merits of their past life is taught
by Plato's Socrates among others. . . . Don't these things agree

with the teaching of the Gospels? ——*Epistula de Philosophia Evangelica* (1516), in *Opera*, VI, *4 verso.

What else is Christ's philosophy, which he himself calls re- 4
birth (*renascentia*), but the restoration of a well-constituted nature? In fact, although none has ever transmitted this in more absolute and efficacious form than Christ, a great many things can be found in the books of the pagans that agree with his doctrine. . . . According to Plato, Socrates teaches in many forms that injustice should not be paid by injustice; he also says that, since the soul is immortal, those ought not to be deplored who with the confidence of a life well lived migrate toward a happier life; also that the soul should be diverted by all possible means from being affected by the body, and that it be led to those things that truly are, while they do not seem to be. ——*Paraclesis* (1516), in *Opera*, VI, *4.

EUSEBIUS: First authority always belongs to the Scriptures. 5
Yet sometimes I hit upon some statements, made by the an-cients or written by pagans and even by poets, which are so chaste, so saintly, so divinely inspired that I cannot help be-lieving some good genius had been moving their hearts when they wrote this. And perhaps Christ's spirit spreads farther than we interpret it, and many are in the fellowship of the saints who are not included in our catalogue of them.

NEPHALIUS: No less appealing (*elegans*) is what Socrates says in Plato's account, namely, that the human soul has been put into this body, as it were, on guard, whence it is becoming not to leave without the order of the commander, nor to stay there any longer than seems good to the one who has put us there.[3]

CHRYSOGLOTTUS: How blessed are those who in such a spirit expect death. But in Cato's speech, however famous it is, some-one could still charge his trust as proceeding from arrogance, which must be completely absent in a Christian man. How-

3 *Phaedo* 62b.

ever, I seem to have never read anything in the ancient writers that would befit such a person better than what Socrates said to Crito, shortly before he accepted the hemlock drink. "Whether God will approve of our works," he said, "I do not know; certainly we have tried assiduously to please him. Yet I have good hope that he will accept our efforts in good part." [4] This man was so diffident regarding his own works that only his eager willingness to do God's will led him to hope that God in His goodness would feel assured of his having endeavored to lead a good life.

NEPHALIUS: Truly an admirable spirit in a man who did not know Christ and the Scriptures. In fact, when I read such things about men of this kind, I can hardly refrain from saying: "Saint Socrates, pray for us." ——*Convivium Religiosum* (1522), in *Opera,* I, 683.

6   Zeno's self-control, Xenocrates' integrity, Socrates' patience are praised; but since they occurred independently of Christ, they did not contribute to true felicity. ——*De Amabili Ecclesiae Concordia* (1533), in *Opera,* V, 485d-e.

JEAN BODIN (1530–1596)

TARALBA: This seems to me completely alien to any reason, merely to assert that Christ suffered death for the salvation of the human race in order that he might obtain not only forgiveness for its enormous misdeeds but also [for himself] the highest glory by his justice and integrity, yet that the just Aristides, Solon, Lycurgus, Socrates, Chilon, Phocion, and Plato, who, according to the verdict of all mortals, have achieved immortal glory because of their virtues, should be tortured and crucified with most cruel penalties, as if they were the worst criminals and evildoers. ——*Heptaplomeres* VI, ed. Ludwig Noack (1857), p. 320.

[4] *Phaedo* 69d. Actually, these words are addressed to Simmias and Cebes; nor is this a literal translation of the passage.

HUGO GROTIUS (1583–1645)

If those under the rule of another are ordered to do military service, as frequently happens, they should refuse to do so altogether if it is clear to them that the cause of the war is unjust. For that God must be obeyed, rather than men, has been said not only by the Apostles (Acts 5:22), but also by Socrates (*Apology* XVII). ——*De iure belli ac pacis* (1625), Bk. II, chap. 26, sec. 3.

5. *The Reformation*

MARTIN LUTHER (1483–1546)

1   In some places you might see the philosophers argue not ineptly about God and the providence by which God rules everything. To some, such ideas appear put with so much piety that they barely fail to make prophets of Socrates, Xenophon, and Plato. But since they argue these things in such a manner as to ignore the fact that God sent his son Christ for the salvation of sinners, these very fine disputations represent supreme ignorance of God and mere blasphemies in the light of this passage [Genesis 6:5], which proclaims plainly that all imagination, all study of the human heart is only evil. —*Vorlesungen über I. Moses* (1533–43), in *Werke* (Weimar, 1833), XI, 292.

2   It is rather easy to slip, after one has abandoned the Word. For that splendor of the political virtues captivates the minds of men marvelously. Thus Erasmus makes Socrates into an almost perfect Christian.   —*Ibid.*, XI, 350.

3   Erasmus praises in grand style the vitrues of the pagans, of a Socrates, a Cicero, an Atticus, and others, and makes a comparison. He says: "You will hardly find among Christians men who would perform what Pomponius, Atticus, or others have done. Rather do you find among Christians many who are manifestly evil and disgraceful, to whom these pagans were far superior." The proper answer to this is: Philosophically and according to the material of the action (*materia*), that is, according to the general kind of life (*genus vitae*), they are the same, but not according to the specific and differentiating

nature (*in specie et differentia*). For even if Cicero or Socrates had sweated blood, that would not make it pleasing to God. —*Ibid.*, XLIII, 614. (The quotation from Erasmus could not be located.)

The poets leave their [the pagans'] gods alone, don't do anything, except for Socrates, who did a little; and since he also talked against their gods, he was "truncated." —*Neue Tischreden*, 7076, in *ibid.*, XLVIII, 684.   4

These philosophers, although they did not make a display or a boast of their righteousness before the people, but adhered to it because of true affection for virtue and wisdom, as did the best and most sincere—very few apart from Socrates— could yet not abstain from self-satisfaction and inner boasting in their hearts as being wise, just, and good men. —*Epistula ad Romanos*, in *ibid.*, LVI, 157.   5

The highest wisdom is that none can know wisdom. Thus Socrates said, "This I know, that I know nothing"—if he knew that correctly. —*Zu Prediger Salomonis* V, 28, 29, in *Werke* (Walch edn.; Halle, 1740–53), V, 1518.   6

Socrates said rightly: "It is better to suffer injustice than to do it." For he who suffers does not sin. —*Auslegung I. Moses* 37, 31, sec. 313, in *ibid.*, II, 1147.   7

The heathen Socrates knew this [that there should be no specific requests in prayers] when he said one ought to ask God to give what is good for us, for He knew best. —*Auslegung I. Moses*, in *ibid.*, XX, 871.   8

Goat Emser, if only you . . . had sworn by your horns and your beard, as Socrates swore by the dog, that would have been most terrifying to me and a truly philosophical oath. —Answer to the Superchristian, Superspiritual, and Superlearned Book of Goat Emser of Leipzig, in *Works* (Philadelphia, 1930), III, 310.   9

HULDREICH ZWINGLI (1484–1531)

Here [in the heavenly company] you will see Hercules, Theseus, Socrates, Aristides, Antigonus, Numa, Camillus, the Catos, the Scipios. . . . What more cheerful and pleasant, and, besides, what more honorable spectacle could one imagine? ——*Christianae Fidei Brevis et Clara Expositio* (1531), in *Zwinglis Sämtliche Werke* (Zurich, 1878 ff.), IV, 42-43.

PHILIPP MELANCHTHON (1497–1560)

Granted that there was a certain steadfastness in Socrates . . . since it resided in an impure soul, in fact because it arose from self-love, such phantom virtues ought not to be considered true virtues but vices. ——*Loci communes rerum theologicarum* (1521), in *Corpus Reformatorum* (Halle, 1834 ff.), XXI, 100-01.

JOHN CALVIN (1509–1564)

1   Socrates died like Christ; yet by killing him men achieved no valid refutation of his doctrine. ——*Epistula Pauli ad Timotheum*, Bk. I, VI, in *Corpus Reformatorum*, LII, 530.

2   The foolish softness of those to whom it seems intolerable that there be unjust affliction is confounded by that noble answer of Socrates when his wife lamented in his prison that he had been condemned unjustly, and he said, "Would you then prefer my dying guilty?" ——*De Psalmo LXIX*, in *Corpus Reformatorum*, XXXI, 639. See also p. 446.

6. *Modern Thought*

BRITISH

EDMUND SPENSER (*c.* 1552–1599)

.... and *Cicuta* bad
With which th'vniust Atheniens made to dy
Wise *Socrates,* who thereof quaffing glad
Poured out his life, and last Philosophy
To the faire *Critias* [*sic*] his dearest Belamy.
——*Faerie Queene,* Bk. II, Canto VII, stanza
52, in *Works* (Oxford, 1909), I, 254.

FRANCIS BACON (1561–1626)

In fame of learning the flight will be slow without some 1
feathers of ostentation. They that write books on the worth-
lessness of fame, put their names on the title page. Socrates,
Aristotle, Galen were men full of ostentation. ——"Of Vainglory," in *Works,* ed. J. Spedding *et al.* (London, 1857–74),
XII, 262.

(Elenches [refutations] are excellently handled) . . . even in 2
Socrates himself; who professing to affirm nothing, but to in-
firm that which was affirmed by another, hath exactly expressed all the forms of objection, fallace, and redargution.
——*Of the Advancement of Learning* (1623), in *Works,* VI, 274.

Socrates, a true and unfeigned inquisitor of truth. ——*Ibid.,* 3
p. 186.

4   Men ought not to fall . . . into Socrates his ironical doubting of all things.   ——*Ibid.*, p. 133.

5   As for the accusation of Socrates, the time must be remem-
bered when it was prosecuted; which was under the thirty
tyrants, the most base, bloody, and envious persons that have
governed; which revolution of state was no sooner over, but
Socrates, whom they had made a person criminal, was made
a person heroical, and his memory accumulate with honours
divine and human; and those discourses of his, which were
then termed corrupting of manners, were after acknowledged
for sovereign medicines of the mind and manners, and so have
been received ever since, till this day. Let this therefore serve
for answer to politicians, which in their humorous severity, or
in their feigned gravity, have presumed to throw imputations
upon learning; which redargution nevertheless (save that we
know not whether our labours may extend to other ages) were
not needful for the present, in regard of the awe and reverence
towards learning, which the example and countenance of two
so learned princes, queen Elizabeth and your majesty [James
I], being as Castor and Pollux, . . . stars of excellent light and
most benign influence, hath wrought in all men of place and
authority in our nation.   ——*Ibid.*, pp. 105-06. See also p. 321.

6   [Anytus' accusations] have rather a countenance of gravity
than any ground of justice. . . .   ——*Ibid.*, p. 98.

THOMAS HOBBES (1588–1679)

1   But in after times, Socrates is said to have been the first who
truly loved this civil science [*De Cive*]; although hitherto not
thoroughly understood, yet glimmering forth as through a
cloud in the government of the commonweal: and that he set
so great a value on this, that utterly abandoning and despising
all other parts of philosophy, he wholly embraced this, as

judging it only worthy the labour of his mind. ——*De Cive* (1642), in *Works,* ed. W. Molesworth (London, 1839 ff.), II, x.

Though Socrates be acknowledged for continent, yet the *continent* have the passion they *contain,* as *much* and more than they that *satiate* the appetite; which maketh me suspect this *platonic* love for merely sensual. . . . ——*Human Nature* (1650), in *Works,* IV, 50.

2

JOHN MILTON (1608–1674)

Poor *Socrates* (who next more memorable?)
By what he taught and suffer'd for so doing,
For truths sake suffering death unjust, lives now
Equal in fame to proudest Conquerours.
    ——The Saviour speaking in *Paradise Regained,*
        Bk. III. lines 95-98, in *The Works of John
        Milton* (New York, 1931), II, 2, 445.

1

To sage Philosophy next lend thine ear,
From Heaven descended to the low-rooft house
Of *Socrates,* see there his Tenement,
Whom well inspir'd the oracle pronounc'd

Wisest of men; from whose mouth issu'd forth
Mellifluous streams that water'd all the schools. . . .
The first and wisest of them all profess'd
To know this only, that he nothing knew;
    ——Satan speaking in *Paradise Regained,* Bk.
        IV, ll. 272-7, 293-4, in *Works,* II, 2, 469.

2

JOHN DRYDEN (1631–1700)

. . . Those who follow'd *Reasons* Dictates right,
Liv'd up, and lifted high their *Natural Light;*
With *Socrates* may see their Maker's Face,

1

While Thousand *Rubrick-martyrs* want a place.
Nor does it baulk my Charity to find
Th' *Egyptian* bishop [1] of another mind. . . .
——*Religio Laici* (1682), ll. 208-13,
in *Poems* (Oxford, 1929), p. 102.

2   What *Socrates* said of him [i.e., God], what *Plato* writ, and
the rest of the heathen philosophers of several nations, is all
no more than the Twilight of Revelation, after the Sun of it
was set in the Race of Noah. ——Preface to *Religio Laici*
(1682), in *Poems*, p. 95.

JOHN LOCKE (1632–1704)

There was no part of mankind, who had quicker parts, or
improved them more; that had a greater light of reason, or
followed it further in all sorts of speculations, than the
Athenians; and yet we find but one Socrates amongst them,
that opposed and laughed at their polytheism, and wrong
opinions of the Deity; and we see how they rewarded him for
it. Whatsoever Plato, and the soberest of the philosophers,
thought of the nature and being of the one God, they were
faïn, in their outward professions and worship, to go with the
herd, and to keep to their religion established by law. ——*The
Reasonableness of Christianity* (1695), in *The Works of John
Locke* (London, 1824), VI, 136.

ROBERT BARCLAY (1648–1690)

It appears that they [the heathen philosophers] knew Christ;
and by his working *in* them, were brought from unrighteous-
ness to righteousness, and to love that power by which they felt
themselves redeemed; so that, as saith the apostle, *They show
the work of the law written in their hearts, and did the things*

[1] I.e., Athanasius.

contained in the law; and, therefore, as *all doers of the law are,
were no doubt justified,* and saved thus by the power of Christ
in them. And as this was the judgment of the apostle, so was it
of the primitive Christians. Hence *Justin Martyr* stuck not to
call *Socrates a Christian.* ——*An Apology for the True Christian Divinity,* in . . . *Principles and Doctrines of the . . . Quakers* (New York, 1826), pp. 192-93.

JONATHAN SWIFT (1667–1745) [2]

> In points of Honour to be try'd   1
> All Passions must be laid aside:
> Ask no Advice, but think alone,
> Suppose the Question not your own:
> How shall I act? is not the Case,
> But how would *Brutus* in my place?
> In such a cause would *Cato* bleed?
> And how would *Socrates* proceed?
> ——"To Stella, Visiting Me in My Sickness" (1720),
>   ll. 35-42, in *The Poems of Jonathan Swift,*
>   ed. Harold Williams (Oxford, 1937), II, 724.

Junius [Brutus], Socrates, Epaminondas, Cato the Younger,   2
Sir Thomas More and himself [Brutus the Younger] . . . a
Sextumvirate to which all the Ages of the World cannot add a
Seventh. ——*A Voyage to Laputa,* chap. 7, in *The Prose
Works of Jonathan Swift,* ed. Herbert Davis (Oxford, 1941),
XI, 180.

. . . When I [Gulliver] used to explain to him [my master]   3
our several Systems of *Natural Philosophy,* he would laugh
that a Creature pretending to *Reason,* should value itself upon
the Knowledge of other Peoples Conjectures, and in Things,
where that Knowledge, if it were certain, could be of no use.
Wherein he agreed entirely with the Sentiments of *Socrates,*

2 See also footnote under ANTHONY COLLINS, below, p. 77.

as *Plato* delivers them; which I mention as the highest Honour I can do that Prince of Philosophers. ——*A Voyage to the Houyhnhnms,* chap. 8, in *Prose Works,* XI, 251-52.

4   It is true there hath been all along in the world a notion of rewards and punishments in another life; but it seems to have rather served as an entertainment to poets, or as a terror to children, than a settled principle, by which men pretended to govern any of their actions. The last celebrated words of Socrates, a little before his death, do not seem to reckon or build much upon any such opinion. ——"On the Excellency of Christianity" (1765), in *Irish Tracts and Sermons* (Oxford, 1948), p. 245.

5   The two virtues most celebrated by ancient moralists were fortitude and temperance, as relating to the government of man in his private capacity, to which their schemes were generally addressed and confined; and the two instances, wherein those virtues arrived at the greatest height, were Socrates and Cato. But neither those, nor any other virtues possessed by these two, were at all owing to any lessons or doctrines of a sect. For Socrates himself was of none at all.   ——*Ibid.,* p. 249.

6   Of those who have made great figures in some particular action or circumstance of their lives.
     Alexander the Great, after his victory at the straits at Mount Taurus.
     Socrates, the whole last day of his life, and particularly from the time he took the poison until the moment he expired.
     [*Cicero and nineteen other names follow on this list.*]
     ——"Of Mean and Great Figures, Made by Several Persons" (1772), in *The Works of Jonathan Swift* (London, 1843), II, 310.

ANTHONY ASHLEY COOPER, THIRD EARL OF
SHAFTESBURY (1671–1713)

The philosophical Hero of these [the Platonic] Poems, whose   1
Name they carry'd both in their Body and Front, and whose
Genius and Manner they were made to represent, was in himself *a perfect Character;* yet, in some respects, so veil'd, and in
a Cloud, that to the unattentive Surveyor he seem'd often to
be very different from what he really was: and this chiefly by
reason of a certain exquisite and refin'd Raillery which belong'd to his Manner, and by virtue of which he cou'd treat
the highest Subjects, and those of the commonest Capacity
both together, and render 'em explanatory of each other.
——"Advice to an Author" (1710), Pt. I, sec. 3, in *Characteristics of Men, Manners, Opinions, Times* (5th edn.; Birming-
ham, 1773), I, 194.

. . . The greatest of philosophers, the very founder of phi-   2
losophy itself.   ——"Miscellaneous Reflections" (1711), Pt. V,
sec. 1, in *Characteristics,* III, 244.

. . . The philosophical Patriarch . . . containing within him-   3
self the several Genius's of Philosophy, gave rise to all those
several manners in which that Science was delivered.   ——"Advice to an Author," Pt. II, sec. 2, in *Characteristics,* I, 254.

The divinest Man who had ever appear'd in the Heathen   4
World was in the height of witty Times, and by the wittiest of
all Poets, most abominably ridicul'd in a whole Comedy writ
and acted on purpose. But so far was this from sinking his
Reputation, or suppressing his Philosophy, that they each in-
creas'd the more for it; and he apparently grew to be more the
Envy of other Teachers. He was not only contented to be
ridicul'd; but, that he might help the Poet as much as possible, he presented himself openly in the Theater; that his

real Figure (which was no advantageous one) might be compar'd with that . . . on the stage. Such was his *good Humour!* Nor could there be in the World a greater Testimony of the invincible Goodness of the Man or a greater Demonstration that there was no Imposture either in his Character or Opinions. ——"A Letter on Enthusiasm" (1708), Pt. I, sec. 3, in *Characteristics,* I, 31.

JOSEPH ADDISON (1672–1719)

1   If we would imitate the behaviour of a single spectator [of a play], let us reflect upon that of Socrates, in a particular which gives me as great an idea of that extraordinary man, as any circumstance of his life; or, what is more, of his death. This venerable person often frequented the theatre, which brought a great many thither out of a desire to see him. On which occasion it is recorded of him, that he sometimes stood, to make himself the more conspicuous, and to satisfy the curiosity of the beholders. He was one day present at the first representation of a tragedy of Euripides, who was his intimate friend, and whom he is said to have assisted in several of his plays. In the midst of the tragedy, which had met with very great success, there chanc'd to be a line that seemed to encourage vice and immorality. This was no sooner spoken, but Socrates rose from his seat, and without any regard to his affection for his friend, or to the success of his play, showed himself displeased at what was said, and walked out of the assembly. ——*The Tatler,* No. 122 (January 18, 1710), in *Works* (Philadelphia, 1888), IV, 130.

2   Socrates introduced a catechical method of arguing. He would ask his adversary question upon question, till he had convinced him out of his own mouth that his opinions were wrong. This way of debating drives an enemy up into a corner, seizes all the passes through which he can make an escape,

and forces him to surrender at discretion. Aristotle changed
this method of attack, and invented a great variety of little
weapons called syllogisms. As in the Socratic way of dispute
you agree to every thing which your opponent advances; in
the Aristotelic you are still denying and contradicting some
part or other of what he says. Socrates conquers you by strata-
gem; Aristotle by force; the one takes the town by sap, the
other sword in hand. ——*The Spectator*, No. 239 (December
4, 1711), in *Works*, V, 560.

This divine philosopher was so well fortified in his own in- 3
nocence, that he neglected all the impotence of evil tongues
which were engaged in his destruction. This was properly the
support of a good conscience, that contradicted the reports
which had been raised against him, and cleared him to himself. ——*The Guardian*, No. 135 (August 15, 1713), in *Works*,
IV, 427.

RICHARD STEELE (1672–1729)

When the iniquity of the times brought Socrates to his 1
execution, how great and wonderful is it to behold him, un-
supported by any thing but the testimony of his own conscience and conjectures of hereafter, receive the poison with
an air of mirth and good humour, and, as if going on an agreeable journey, bespeak some deity to make it fortunate!
——*The Spectator*, No. 133 (August 2, 1711), in *Selections* (Oxford, 1885), p. 83.

The divine Socrates is here [in Cicero's *Tusculan Disputa- 2
tions*, Bk. I] represented in a figure worthy his great wisdom
and philosophy, worthy the greatest mere man that ever
breathed. ——*Ibid.*, No. 146 (August 17, 1711).

Socrates, who is by all accounts the undoubted head of the 3
sect of the hen-pecked, owned and acknowledged that he owed

a great part of his virtue to the exercise which his useful wife constantly gave it. There are several good instructions that may be drawn from his wise answers to people of less fortitude than himself on her subject. A friend, with indignation, asked how so good a man could live with so violent a creature? He observed to him, that they who learn to keep a good seat on horseback, mount the least manageable they can get; and, when they have mastered them, they are sure never to be discomposed on the backs of steeds less restive. At several times, to different persons, on the same subject he has said, "My dear friend, you are beholden to Xanthippe, that I bear so well your flying out in a dispute." To another, "My hen clacks very much, but she brings me chickens. They that live in a trading street are not disturbed at the passage of carts." I would have, if possible, a wise man be contented with his lot, even with a shrew; for, though he cannot make her better, he may, you see, make himself better by her means. ——*Ibid.,* No. 479 (September 9, 1712), p. 106.

ANTHONY COLLINS (1676–1729)

At the end of his Discourse of Free-Thinking, *Collins answers the objection "that freethinkers are irrational, infamous and wicked people," and adds that "they have in fact been the most understanding and virtuous people in all ages," for which he introduces as evidence a list of nineteen names, headed by Socrates, Plato, Aristotle, and Epicurus, and ending with "My Lord Bacon, Hobbes, and Tillotson."*

Socrates, the divinest Man that ever appear'd in the Heathen World and to whose Virtue and Wisdom all Ages since have done justice, was a very great *Free-Thinker.* He not only disbeliev'd the Gods of his Country, and the common Creeds about them, and *declar'd his Dislike,* when he heard Men attribute *Repentance, Anger,* and other *Passions* to the *Gods,* and talk of *Wars and Battles in Heaven,* and of the *Gods getting Women with Child,* and such-like fabulous and blas-phemous Storys: [3] but obtain'd a just Notion of the Nature and Attributes of God, exactly agreeable to that which we have receiv'd by Divine Revelation, and became a true Chris-tian (if it be allow'd that the Primitive Fathers understood what true Christianity was): [Here follow quotations from ST. JUSTIN MARTYR and ERASMUS. See pp. 39, 62.]

Socrates could not be suppos'd to have made Notions, or Speculations, or Mysteries, any parts of his Religion, when he *Demonstrated all men to be Fools who troubled themselves with Inquiries into* Heavenly *things* and ask'd such Inquirers *whether they had attain'd a perfect Knowledge of Human things, since they search'd into Heavenly things; or if they could think themselves wise in neglecting that which concern'd them, to employ themselves in that which was above their Capacity to understand.*

Lastly, As a further Evidence of his *Free-Thinking,* Socrates had the common Fate of *Free-Thinkers,* to be calumniated in his life time for an Atheist (though the God Apollo by his *Oracle* declar'd him the *wisest Man upon earth*) and at length suffer'd that Punishment for *Free-Thinking,* which Knavery and Folly, whenever they are arriv'd to a due pitch, and are

---

[3] Jonathan Swift, in his satirical rendering of Collins, after quoting the preceding sentences almost correctly, continues: "I pick out these par-ticulars, because they are the very same with what the priests have in their Bibles, where repentance and anger are attributed to God; where it is said, there was 'war in heaven'; and that 'the Virgin Mary was with child by the Holy Ghost,' whom the priests call God; all fabulous and blas-phemous stories. Now, I affirm Socrates to have been a true Christian. You will ask, perhaps, how that can be, since he lived three or four hundred years before Christ? I answer, with Justin Martyr, that Christ is nothing else but reason; and I hope you do not think Socrates lived before reason. Now, this true Christian Socrates never made notions, speculations, or mysteries, any part of his religion; but demonstrated all men to be fools who troubled themselves with inquiries into heavenly things. . . . For I argue thus, that if I never trouble myself to think whether there be a God or no, and forbid others to do it, I am a freethinker, but not an atheist." —Swift, *Works* (London, 1883), VIII, 183.

well confederated together, are ever ready to inflict on all
those who have the Honesty and Courage to endeavour to
imitate him. ——*A Discourse of Free-Thinking* (London,
1713), pp. 123-26.

EDWARD YOUNG (1683–1765)

Speaking of the "boasted friends of reason":
"As wise as Socrates," if such they were,
(Nor will they 'bate of that sublime renown,)
"As wise as Socrates," might justly stand
The definition of a modern fool.
A christian is the highest style of man. . . .
——"Christian Triumph," in *The Po-
etical Works* (Boston, 1804), I, 89.

GEORGE BERKELEY (1685–1753)

1   . . . Anything of that excellent philosopher, whose divine
sentiments are preserved to us by Plato and Xenophon, could
not fail of being agreeable to a man of sense and virtue. . . .
His whole employment was the turning men aside from vice,
impertinence, and trifling speculations to the study of solid
wisdom, temperance, justice, and piety, which is the true business of a philosopher. . . . But if you need any motive to peruse
a discourse of Socrates, I know none more apposite than the
authority of Squire Bickerstaff, a man I think of excellent
sense and whom you may have observed on all occasions to
express a very high esteem of that philosopher. For my own
part, so far as I can judge by what notions of his I have seen,
I cannot forbear thinking him the best and most admirable
man that the heathen world produced.   ——Letter to Sir John
Percival (written from Trinity College, December 27, 1709),
in *The Works of George Berkeley,* ed. A. A. Luce and T. E.
Jessop (Edinburgh, 1948–56), VIII, 28-29.

Certainly had the philosophy of Socrates and Pythagoras 2
prevailed in this age among those who think themselves too
wise to receive the dictates of the Gospel, we should not have
seen interest take so general and fast hold on the minds of
men, nor public spirit reputed to be *gennaian euetheian,* a
generous folly, among those who are reckoned to be the most
knowing as well as the most getting part of mankind. ——*Siris*
(1714), No. 331, in *Works,* V, 151.

ALEXANDER POPE (1688–1744)

Much-suff'ring heroes next their honours claim, 1
Those of less noisy, and less guilty fame,
Fair Virtue's silent train: supreme of these
Here ever shines the godlike *Socrates.*
 ——"The Temple of Fame" (1710), lines 168-
 71, in *The Works of Alexander Pope,* ed.
 W. Elwin (London, 1871), I, 212-13.

The oracle pronounced Socrates the wisest of all men living, 2
because he judiciously made choice of human nature for the
object of his thoughts; an inquiry into which as much exceeds
all other learning, as it is of more consequence to adjust the
true nature and measures of right and wrong, than to settle
the distance of the planets, and compute the times of their
circumvolutions. ——*The Spectator,* No. 408 (June 18, 1712),
written by "Z" (supposed to be Pope).

Who noble ends by noble means obtains, 3
Or, failing, smiles in exile or in chains,
Like good Aurelius let him reign, or bleed
Like Socrates, that man is great indeed.
 ——*Essay on Man* (1733), Epistle IV,
 lines 232-35, in *Works,* II, 445.

JAMES THOMSON (1700–1748)

1   . . . I throw aside
The long-lived Volume; and, deep-musing, hail
The sacred Shades, that, slowly rising, pass
Before my wondering eyes. First Socrates,
Who, firmly good in a corrupted State,
Against the rage of tyrants single stood,
Invincible; calm Reason's holy law,
That Voice of God within the attentive mind,
Obeying, fearless, or in life, or death:
Great moral teacher! Wisest of Mankind!
——*The Seasons*, "Winter" (1726), ll. 436-45, in *The Poetical Works of James Thomson* (Boston, 1848), II, 202.

2   O'er all shone out the great Athenian Sage,
And Father of Philosophy: the sun,
From whose white blaze emerged, each various sect
Took various tints, but with diminish'd beam.
Tutor of Athens! he, in every street,
Dealt priceless treasure: goodness his delight,
Wisdom his wealth, and glory his reward.
Deep through the human heart, with playful art,
His simple question stole; as into truth,
And serious deeds, he smiled the laughing race;
Taught moral happy life, whate'er can bless,
Or grace mankind; and what he taught he was.
——"Greece," ll. 222-33, in *Liberty* (1735),
Pt. II, in *Poetical Works*, I, 162.

JOHN WESLEY (1703–1791)

1   If reason could have produced a hope full of immortality in any child of man, it might have produced it in that great man

whom Justin Martyr scruples not to call "a Christian before Christ." For who that was not favoured with the written word of God, ever excelled, yea, or equalled, Socrates? In what other Heathen can we find so strong an understanding, joined with so consummate a virtue? But had he really this hope? Let him answer for himself. What is the conclusion of that noble apology which he made before his unrighteous judges? "And now, oh judges, ye are going hence to live; and I am going hence to die: which of these is best, the gods know; but, I suppose, no man does." *No man knows!* How far is this from the language of the little Benjamite? "I desire to depart, and to be with Christ; which is far better." [St. Paul, *Letter to the Philippians,* 1:23.] ——"The Case of Reason Impartially Considered" (Sermon LXX), in *The Works of the Reverend John Wesley* (London, 1826), VI, 357.

Our philosophical poet justly terms Socrates, "The wisest of   2
all moral men"; that is, of all that were not favoured with Divine Revelation. Yet what evidence had he of another world when he addressed those that had condemned him to death? "And now, O ye judges, ye are going to live, and I am going to die. Which of these is best, God knows; but I suppose no man does." Alas! What a confession is this! Is this all the evidence that poor dying Socrates had either of an invisible or an eternal world? ——"The Difference between Walking by Sight, and Walking by Faith" (Sermon CXIII), in *Works,* VII, 259.

SAMUEL JOHNSON (1709–1784)

I have Socrates on my side. It was his labour to turn phi-   1
losophy from the study of nature to speculations upon life: but the innovators whom I oppose are turning off attention from life to nature. They seem to think that we are placed here to watch the growth of plants, or the motions of the stars. Socrates was rather of opinion, that what we had to

learn was, how to do good, and avoid evil. ——"Milton," in
The Lives of the English Poets (Philadelphia, 1868), I, 124.

2   The great praise of Socrates is, that he drew the wits of
Greece, by his instruction and example, from the vain pursuit
of natural philosophy to moral inquiries, and turned their
thoughts from stars, and tides, and matter, and motion, upon
the various modes of virtue and relations of life. All his lectures were but commentaries upon this saying. ——*The
Rambler* No. 24 (June 9, 1750).

3   Were Socrates and Charles the Twelfth of Sweden both
present in any company, and Socrates to say, "Follow me, and
hear a lecture on philosophy"; and Charles, laying his hand
on his sword, to say, "Follow me, and dethrone the Czar"; a
man would be ashamed to follow Socrates. Sir, the impression
is universal; yet it is strange. ——*Boswell's Life of Johnson*,
ed. G. B. Hill (New York, 1925), III, 301.

DAVID HUME (1711–1776)

1   For except the banishment of Protagoras and the death of
Socrates, which last event proceeded partly from other motives, there are scarcely any instances to be met with, in ancient history, of this bigoted jealousy with which the present
age is so much infested. ——*An Inquiry Concerning Human
Understanding* (1748). "Library of Liberal Arts," No. 49 (New
York, 1957), p. 142.

2   Who admires not Socrates, his perpetual serenity and contentment amidst the greatest poverty and domestic vexations,
his resolute contempt of riches, and his magnanimous care of
preserving liberty, while he refused all assistance from his
friends and disciples, and avoided even the dependence of an
obligation? . . . Among the ancients, the heroes in philosophy

as well as those in war and patriotism have a grandeur and force of sentiment which astonishes our narrow souls, and is rashly rejected as extravagant and supernatural. —*An Inquiry Concerning the Principles of Morals* (1751). "Library of Liberal Arts," No. 62 (New York, 1957), pp. 79-80.

JEREMY BENTHAM (1748–1832)

While Xenophon was writing history and Euclid giving   1
instruction in geometry, Socrates and Plato were talking non-sense under pretense of teaching wisdom and morality. This morality of theirs consisted in words—this wisdom of theirs was the denial of matters known to every man's experience, and the assertion of other matters opposed to every man's experience. And exactly in the proportion in which their notions on this subject differed from those of the mass of mankind, exactly in that proportion were they below the level of mankind.[4]   —*Deontology, or The Science of Morals* (London, 1834), I, 39-40.

Fanny Wright told me Socrates was pure as an icicle. I an-   2
swered that it was my misfortune to read Greek, and to know better. What I read of Socrates was insipid. I could find in

4 John Stuart Mill, in his essay on Bentham (1838), referred to this passage in the following words: "In almost the only passage of the *Deontology* which, from its style, and from its having before appeared in print, may be known to be Bentham's, Socrates and Plato are spoken of in terms distressing to his greatest admirers; and the incapacity to appreciate such men is a fact perfectly in unison with the general habits of Bentham's mind" (*Mill on Bentham and Coleridge*, ed. F. R. Leavis [New York, 1950], pp. 58-59).

Later, the same passage was quoted by Matthew Arnold in *Sweetness and Light* with the following comment: "From the moment of reading that, I am delivered from the bondage of Bentham! The fanaticism of his adherents can touch me no longer. I feel the inadequacy of his mind and ideas for supplying the rule of human society, for perfection" (*Culture and Anarchy* [New York, 1924], p. 35).

him nothing that distinguished him from other peoples, except his manner of putting questions. This would have been good, had it been explained why; but the devil a bit of explanation was there. For didactic purposes, it is good for bringing forward the appropriate subject of speculation. ——Conversation reported in *The Works of Jeremy Bentham* (Edinburgh, 1843), X, 583.

SAMUEL TAYLOR COLERIDGE (1772–1834)

1   . . . As if the Almighty, either by direct interference as in the case of the Hebrews, or by particular providence, never left man wholly without an aid in the worst times (and if he refused it, left him wholly without excuse), at that time and in this age was Socrates born, whose whole life was one contest against the Sophists, but who yet marked the necessity of revelation by an intermixture of weakness, nay even of sophistry, in his own mode of contending against them. He did the best it was [possible] for unassisted man to do. He lived holily and died magnanimously. . . .

He was a man (if I may speak of him as a man and as far as we can learn of his biographer Xenophon or the more suspicious representations of Plato, who however is very faithful in his portraits) [one who] generally appears to have possessed a fine and active but yet not very powerful imagination—an imagination instrumental and illustrative rather than predominant and creative; but beyond all doubt what characterized him was—pardon the play on words—the UNCOMMON excellence of common sense. Naturally and by observation he excelled in this and cultivated it. There was in his character an exquisite balance, an equilibrium and harmony of all the various faculties, so that everywhere his mind acted by a sort of tact, as it were, rather than arithmetically or by examining the process. This without genius would have been the character of a wise, natural, unaffected man; but Socrates doubtless possessed genius in a high degree, a peculiar turn for contemplation, not for the purposes of physical truth, but in aid of prior truths or anticipations found in his own nature by meditation.

. . . .

This turn for meditative observation was connected in him, as we find it in others of our times, with a species of humour and keen perception of the extravagant, the irrational, the absurd; and with the freedom of a republican city it led him frequently into good-humoured conversations with his fellow-citizens [in a city] THEN ALL ALIVE with the Sophists and with their disciples. So hard is it for virtue to wrestle with vice or good sense with folly without receiving some stain on its outward garments, it cannot be denied, I fear, that from this practice he fell at times into the very errors he was opposing. At all events, by his example he gave currency to a mode of argument which may be as easily, perhaps more easily, adapted to delusion than [to] sound conviction. It has the misfortune at least, by entangling a man in a number of questions the answers to which he does not anticipate, of leaving a final conviction, as if the man were cheated INTO a conclusion though he could see no hole afterwards to escape from it. But with minds truly ingenuous nothing is more desirable than this method of leading the mind to a consciousness of its own ignorance by degrees, and of securing every step behind before there was any undue progress forward. These are the faults and excellence of the Socratic mode as they appear to me.

But this was not all. All these qualities would not of themselves have formed a Socrates. He had, and in that all of his contemporaries and all who followed joined, a deep, nay what our enlightened men of the present day would perhaps call a superstitious, and earnest piety, which disposed him to the reverence of the unknown, whatever it was, nay even to a reverence of the best signs of it (however he might disapprove of them) which secured his fellow creatures from being merely as the beasts that perish. He was in every sense of the word a religious man, and as the natural result of religion, combined a firm love of his fellow creatures [with his love of truth].

. . . .

The clamour of the Sophists against Socrates, and his death (or what it might be truly called, his martyrdom) I will not detail to you. You must be all acquainted with them from childhood. It is sufficient to state that in his philosophy he had the design, and he certainly produced the effect, of making the moral being of man the especial and single object of thought and of human institution. Disheartened by the gross incongruity of the opinions of the elder philosophers, seeing no good arising at that time, perhaps despairing far too easily of any good which might arise from their physical, astronomical and astrological speculations, he said, "Whether these things be true or not and whether anything or nothing is to come out of them, still men must be men before generally they can receive any advantage. Our great object at present is to render ourselves susceptible of any truths for good purposes which God may hereafter grant us. The proper knowledge of mankind is man." Consequently all his reasoning, and I may add all his sophistry, tends to this one point, to withdraw the human mind from all other subjects as of main or important interest till it had entered into that, the last, the most important. Before his death and his condition—the state of his own moral being (from the influences of Socrates, from the celebrity if I may say so of his death, from the hasty repentance of the Athenians afterwards) this undoubtedly produced on the pagan world a greater effect than any other single event can be supposed to do; it undoubtedly did draw the mind of Plato and others to more and more speculations concerning the heart of man; and then at last the whole came to be this, that with the better and profounder kind it excited an anticipation of some clearer knowledge which doubtless prepared greatly for the reception of Christianity; in the lower orders, who were incapable of understanding these abstract speculations, [it] still produced a sense of their necessity which made them receive Christianity with gratitude and with fervour.

This must be stated as a defect, likewise, as indeed is the case in the writings before the time of Socrates, and even in a number of the dialogues of Plato himself: there is a confusion arising from the word "happiness." . . .

Now Socrates was constantly vacillating. At one time things were to be revered and honoured for their utility, which at times meant the quantum of agreeable sensations; sometimes other things were evil and then it signified an intellectual harmony. At other times he has a still higher flight and he speaks with true piety of blessedness but again relapses and considers this but another mode of pleasure. ——*The Philosophical Lectures* (1818–19), ed. Kathleen Colburn (New York, 1949), pp. 136-41.

In this emergency Providence vouchsafed to raise up Socrates. . . . I endeavoured to shew and I believe proved, in my former lecture, that Socrates himself was not free from the errors which it was his object to oppose and (I must not say that without adding) to his imperishable glory did oppose, in so many and in such important points. For little, and with a poor spirit, does he estimate the merits of a great man by the mere quantum of direct truth which he happens to teach first, or detract from that merely by the quantum of error with which that truth was mingled through human imperfections and the state of the times in which he lived. No, these are but small and comparatively trifling portions of a great man's merits. It is to have awakened an idea, to have excited a spirit, to have opened a road and to have given the first impulse to it. He is working in hundreds in after ages who are working in his spirit, and to him they will all, in proportion as they possess his genius, give praise and honour. Not that this and that was done well, or this or that erroneously, but that it was done at all; that it was attempted, that the path was opened, that the light was given, that the impulse was provided—the power of doing this constitutes the power of a great man. I could not mention the name of Socrates with anything that resembles detraction without saving myself from infamy by this explanation. ——*Ibid.*, pp. 148-49.

3   When Socrates, though in the most tolerant (and almost timid) form conceivable, led even to the great truths which, being told, this diabolical system of polytheism must necessarily have fallen, he was poisoned. ——*Ibid.*, p. 182.

4   Throughout they [the Stoics] confounded God and Nature. For this was the grand error of Socrates himself and common to all his disciples as far as they were his exclusively. ——*Ibid.*, pp. 219-20.

5   Socrates attempted a compromise by excluding all earnest investigations except into human nature. . . . But by his own vacillating between the good and the useful, whether [crime] guilt was or was not more and other than an error in calculation, he gave rise to new schisms—the Stoic Bully and the Cyrenaic Sensualist. ——*Ibid.*, p. 398.

WALTER SAVAGE LANDOR (1775–1864)

1   DIOGENES: Truth is a point; the subtilest and finest, harder than adamant; never to be broken, worn away, or blunted. Its only bad quality is, that it is sure to hurt those who touch it; and likely to draw blood, perhaps the life-blood, of those who press earnestly upon it. Let us away from this narrow lane skirted with hemlock, and pursue our road again through the wind and dust, toward the *great* man and the *powerful*. Him I would call the powerful one, who controls the storms of his mind, and turns to good account the worst accidents of his fortune. The great man, I was going on to demonstrate, is somewhat more. He must be able to do this, and he must have an intellect which puts into motion the intellect of others.

PLATO: Socrates, then, was your great man.

DIOGENES: He was indeed; nor can all thou hast attributed to him ever make me think the contrary. I wish he could have kept a little more at home, and have thought it as well worth his while to converse with his own children as with others.

PLATO: He knew himself born for the benefit of the human race.

DIOGENES: Those who are born for the benefit of the human race, go but little into it; those who are born for its curse, are crowded.

PLATO: It was requisite to dispel the mists of ignorance and error.

DIOGENES: Has he done it? What doubt has he elucidated, or what fact has he established? Although I was but twelve years old and resident in another city when he died, I have taken some pains in my inquiries about him from persons of less vanity and less perverseness than his disciples. He did not leave behind him any true philosopher among them; any who followed his mode of argumentation, his subjects of disquisition, or his course of life; any who would subdue the malignant passions or coerce the loser; any who would abstain from calumny or from cavil; any who would devote his days to the glory of his country, or, what is easier and perhaps wiser, to his own well-founded contentment and well-merited repose. Xenophon, the best of them, offered up sacrifices, believed in oracles, consulted soothsayers, turned pale at a jay, and was dysenteric at a magpie. ——*Complete Works,* ed. T. E. Welby (London, 1927), I, 70-71.

DIOGENES: Art thou certain thou hast given to Socrates all   2
his irony and perspicacity, or even all his virtue?

PLATO: His virtue I think I have given him fully.

DIOGENES: Few can comprehend the whole of it, or see where it is separated from wisdom. Being a philosopher, he must have known that marriage would render him less contemplative and less happy, though he had chosen the most beautiful, the most quiet, the most obedient, and most affectionate woman in the world; yet he preferred what he considered his duty as a citizen to his peace of mind.

PLATO: He might hope to beget children in sagacity like himself.

DIOGENES: He can never have hoped it at all, or thought about it as became him. He must have observed that the sons of meditative men are usually dull and stupid; and he might foresee that those philosophers or magistrates whom their father had excelled would be, openly or covertly, their enemies. —*Ibid.*, p. 106.

3   I think it was of Socrates that Landor dared to say—so far can a humorous man indulge a whim—"He was a vulgar sophist and he [Landor] could not forgive vulgarity in any-body; if he saw it in a wise man, he regretted it the more." [5] —*The Journals of Ralph Waldo Emerson* (Boston, 1910), III, 117-18.

4   ASPASIA: I do not love . . . my friend Socrates so much as perhaps I should, who however, beside his cleverness, has many good qualities. He . . . is endowed with an extraordinary share of intellect; but [he has not] attained the fixed and measured scope of true philosophy . . . being in perpetual motion to display his surprising tricks of rhetorical ingenuity, which tend only to the confusion of truth and falsehood, and consequently to indifference in the choice of them. —*Complete Works*, ed. T. E. Welby (London, 1927), X, 173.

5   ASPASIA: Our epithalamiast, intending nothing satirical, tells Socrates (whom neither celibacy nor marriage have detained

[5] According to John Forster (*Walter Savage Landor: A Biography* [London, 1869], II, 268), Landor in a letter to Ralph W. Emerson from Florence (March 28, 1851) protested, "Socrates he had never undervalued. Incomparably the cleverest of all the sophists, he had turned them all into ridicule; and for this he honoured him, though as a philosopher he counted him inferior to Epicurus and Epictetus."

at home, and who never could resist an opportunity of wrangling, while a Sophist or a straw was before him) that he first brought Philosophy from heaven into private houses! I hope he will find her in his own as often as he wants her; but if he is resolved to bring her down into ours, such as we have seen her lately, the city will be all in a bustle with the double-bolting of doors. Let the archons look to it. ——*Ibid.*, p. 190.

THOMAS MOORE (1779–1852)

... That canting crew,
So smooth, so godly,—yet so devilish too;
Who, arm'd at once with prayer-books and with whips,
Blood on their hands, and Scripture on their lips,
Tyrants by creed, and torturers by text,
Make *this* life hell, in honor of the *next!*
Your Redesdales, Percevals,—great, glorious Heaven,
If I'm presumptuous, be my tongue forgiven,
When here I swear, by my soul's hope of rest,
I'd rather have been born, ere man was blest
With the pure dawn of Revelation's light,
Yes,—rather plunge me back in Pagan night,
And take my chance with Socrates for bliss,
Than be the Christian of a faith like this,
Which builds on heavenly cant its earthly sway,
And in a convert mourns to lose a prey ...
——"Intolerance, A Satire," in *The Poetical Works
of Thomas Moore* (New York, 1873), pp. 195-96.

LORD BYRON (1788–1824)

Well didst thou speak, Athena's wisest son!   1
    "All that we know is, nothing can be known."
——*Childe Harold's Pilgrimage* (1812), Canto II, vii, in *The
Complete Works of Lord Byron* (Boston, 1905), p. 20.

2   ARNOLD: What! that low, swarthy, short-nosed, round-
                          eyed satyr,
                     With the wide nostrils and Silenus' aspect,
                     The splay feet and low stature! I had better
                     Remain that which I am.
      STRANGER: And yet he was
                     The earth's perfection of all mental beauty,
                     And personification of all virtue.
                          ——*The Deformed Transformed,* Pt. I, Scene 1, lines
                          217-22, in *Poetical Works* (London, 1904), p. 598.

3   The hackneyed and lavish title of Blasphemer—which, with
     Radical, Liberal, Jacobin, Reformer, etc., are the changes
     which the hirelings are daily ringing in the ears of those who
     will listen—should be welcome to all who recollect on *whom*
     it was originally bestowed. Socrates and Jesus Christ were put
     to death publicly as *blasphemers,* and so have been and may
     be many who dare to oppose the most notorious abuses of the
     name of God and the mind of man. But persecution is not
     refutation, nor even triumph; the "wretched infidel," as he is
     called, is probably happier in his prison than the proudest of
     his assailants.   ——*Don Juan* (1812), Canto VI, in *Poetical
     Works,* p. 717.

4   Socrates said, our only knowledge was
              "To know that nothing could be known"; a pleasant
          Science enough, which levels to an ass
              Each man of wisdom, future, past, or present.
                               ——*Ibid.,* Canto VII, v, p. 730.

5   Alas! must noblest views, like an old song,
              Be for mere fancy's sport a theme creative,
          A jest, a riddle, Fame through thick and thin sought!
              And Socrates himself but Wisdom's Quixote?
                               ——*Ibid.,* Canto XIII, x, p. 794.

6   And persecuted sages teach the schools
              Their folly in forgetting there are fools.

Was it not so, great Locke? and greater Bacon?
Great Socrates?
> ——*Ibid.*, Canto XV, xvii-xviii, p. 818.

And Socrates, that model of all duty   7
Own'd to a penchant, though discreet, for beauty.
> ——*Ibid.*, Canto XV, lxxxv, p. 825.

Pythagoras, Locke, Socrates—but pages   8
   Might be fill'd up, as vainly as before,
With the sad usage of all sorts of sages,
   Who, in his life-time, each, was deem'd a Bore!
The loftiest minds outrun their tardy ages;
   This they must bear with and, perhaps, much more;
The wise man's sure when he no more can share it, he
   Will have a firm *Post Obit* on posterity.
> ——*Ibid.*, Canto XVII, ix, pp. 997-98.

PERCY BYSSHE SHELLEY (1792–1822)

If I were one whom the loud world held wise,   1
I should disdain to quote authorities
In commendation of this kind of love:—
Why there is first the God in heaven above,
Who wrote a book called Nature, 'tis to be
Reviewed, I hear, in the next *Quarterly;*
And Socrates, the Jesus Christ of Greece,
And Jesus Christ Himself, did never cease
To urge all living things to love each other,
And to forgive their mutual faults, and smother
The Devil of disunion in their souls.
> ——"Fragments connected with Epipsychidion," lines 27-
>   37, in *The Complete Works* (New York, 1904), p. 469.

When virtuous spirits through the gate of Death   2
Pass triumphing over the thorns of life,

> Sceptres and crowns, mitres and swords and snares,
> Trampling in scorn, like Him [Jesus], and Socrates.
> ——Prologue to "Hellas," lines 152-
> 55, in *Complete Works,* p. 447.

3   In a late number of the *Quarterly Review* I observe an attack on the character of Socrates, which appearing to proceed
from the pen of an accomplished scholar gave me the severer
pain. A portion of Cumberland's Observer is dedicated to the
same purpose of defaming that illustrious person by taking
advantage against him of a change which has been operated
in certain conventional notions of morals, which he is accused,
but as I feel myself prepared to prove, falsely accused of having violated. I conceive him to have been the author of some
of the most elevated truths of ethical philosophy; to have been
to the science of the conduct of men in their social relations,
what Bacon was to the science of the classifications of the material world, and metaphysics. I conceive him personally to
have presented a grand and simple model of much of what
we can conceive, and more than in any other instance we have
seen realized, of all that is eminent and excellent in man. I
conceive that many of those popular maxims which under the
name of Christianity have softened the manners of modern
Europe are channels from the fountain of his profound yet
overflowing mind. These sentiments are with me a kind of
religion; yet how wickedly absurd I should be if I should go
from study to study of all the Greek scholars in London and
Cambridge, and excite them to seize upon the author of the
article on the Grecian Philosophy, and carry him off to some
solitary dungeon, and instead of arguments give him bread
and water, and then publish a violent tirade against him and
his opinions. I have a strong inclination if my health will
permit me to take the more unChristian method of presenting
the same subject to the public—without any disrespect to
Aristophanes or his learned translator—in a very different
point of view.   ——*Complete Works,* ed. Robert Ingpen and
Walter E. Peck (London, 1926–29), X, 116. [The reference is

to an article in the *Quarterly Review* of April, 1819, under
the title "View of Grecian Philosophy.—*The Clouds,* etc."]

JOHN KEATS (1795–1821)

I have no doubt that thousands of people never heard of   1
have had hearts completely disinterested: I can remember but
two—Socrates and Jesus—their Histories evince it. ——Letter
123 (1819), in *The Poetical Works and Other Writings* (New
York, 1939), VII, 257.

The most interesting question that can come before us is,   2
How far by the persevering endeavors of a seldom appearing
Socrates Mankind may be made happy. ——*Ibid.,* p. 284.

THOMAS CARLYLE (1795–1881)

EMERSON: We [Carlyle and Emerson] talked of books. Plato   1
he does not read, and he disparaged Socrates. ——*English
Traits,* in *The Complete Works of Ralph Waldo Emerson*
(Boston, 1876), V, 16.

EMERSON: Strange is it to me that you should not sym-   2
pathize (yet so you said) with Socrates, so ironical, so true, and
who "tramped in the mire with wooden shoes whenever they
would force him into the clouds." I seem to see him offering
the hand to you across the ages which some time you will
grasp.[6] ——Letter of Emerson to Carlyle (November 20, 1834),
in *The Correspondence of Thomas Carlyle and Ralph Waldo
Emerson, 1834–72* (Boston, 1833), p. 32.

The difference between Socrates and Jesus Christ! The great   3
Conscious; the immeasurably great Unconscious. The one
cunningly manufactured; the other created, living, and life-

---

6 See also Carlyle's comment to Emerson, p. 134*n.*

giving. The epitome this of a grand and fundamental diversity
among men. Did *any* truly great man ever go through the
world without *offense;* all rounded in, so that the current
moral systems could find no fault in him? Most likely, never.
——"Journal," October 28, 1833, quoted in J. A. Froude,
Thomas Carlyle (New York, 1882), II, 300.

4   I have a screen at home, and on it I have put portraits, the
best I can anyhow get—often enough I have to be content with
very poor ones—of all the . . . brave-hearted creatures whose
deeds and words have made life a term of years to bear with
patience and faith, and I see what manner of men most of
these were—Socrates and Plato, Alexander, Pompey, Caesar,
aye, and Brutus, and many another man of the old time who
won or lost in the struggle to do what they deemed the justest
and wisest thing. ——Carlyle, according to a report by Hol-
man Hunt, the Pre-Raphaelite painter, about his visit to
Carlyle in 1853 (quoted in David Alec Wilson, *Carlyle at His
Zenith* [London, 1924], p. 488).

5   "Plato has not been of much use to me," Carlyle confessed;
"a high, refined man: '*Odi profanum vulgus.*' Socrates—I did
not get much benefit from *him.*"
       "His discourse before his death?"
       "Well, in such a case, I should have made no discourse;
should have wished to be left alone, to profound reflections."
       Froude came in during another discussion of Plato as Carlyle
was saying: "Plato's style is admirable, but he has nothing
particular to tell you."
       "One wonders how much is Socrates," Allingham said.
       "Socrates one suspects to be a myth mainly," Carlyle re-
plied. "I could get nothing out of Plato. What do you mean
then? The devil a word!"
       "You would have liked me to meet him?" Froude asked, re-
ferring to Socrates.
       "O yes; I dare say I should have found him highly inter-
esting in himself." ——Conversation of 1872, reported in

D. A. Wilson, *Carlyle in Old Age* (New York, 1934), pp. 263-64.

Socrates is terribly at ease in Zion. ——Dubious saying; see 6
MATTHEW ARNOLD, p. 104, no. 2.

THOMAS BABINGTON MACAULAY (1800–1859)

The character of Socrates does not rise upon me. The more 1
I read about him, the less I wonder that they poisoned him.
——Letter to Mr. Ellis (May 29, 1835), in G. Otto Trevelyan,
Lord Macaulay, Life and Letters (New York, 1878), I, 283.

I read the *Protagoras* at dinner. The childish quibbling of 2
Socrates provokes me. It is odd that such trumpery fallacies
should have imposed on such powerful minds. . . .
I imagine that, with all his skill in logomachy, Socrates was
a strange, fanciful, superstitious old fellow. . . . I do not
much wonder at the violence of the hatred which Socrates had
provoked. He had, evidently, a thorough love for making men
look small. There was a meek maliciousness about him which
gave wounds such as must have smarted long, and his command of temper was more provoking than noisy triumph and
insolence would have been. ——Diary for July, 1853, *ibid.*, II,
235 ff.

The philosophers adopted the form of dialogue, as the most 3
natural mode of communicating knowledge. Their reasonings
have the merits and the defects which belong to that species
of composition, and are characterized rather by quickness and
subtilty [*sic*] than by depth and precision. Truth is exhibited
in parts, and by glimpse. Innumerable clever hints are given;
but no sound and durable system is erected. The *argumentum
ad hominem,* a kind of argument most efficacious in debate,
but utterly useless for the investigation of general principles,
is among their favorite resources. Hence, though nothing can

be more admirable than the skill which Socrates displays in the conversation which Plato has reported or invented, his victories, for the most part, seem to us unprofitable. A trophy is set up; but no new province is added to the dominions of the human mind. ——"History" (1828), in *Critical, Historical and Miscellaneous Essays* (New York, 188–), I, 275-76.

4   . . . The English ladies of the sixteenth century . . . who, while the horns were sounding and the dogs in full cry, sat in the lonely oriel, with eyes riveted to that immortal page which tells how meekly and bravely the first great martyr of intellectual liberty took the cup from his weeping jailer.
——"Lord Bacon," in *ibid.*, II, 152.

JOHN HENRY NEWMAN (1801–1890)

The common sense of mankind has associated the search after truth with seclusion and quiet. The greatest thinkers have been too intent on their subject to admit of interruption; they have been men of idiosyncratic habits, and have, more or less, shunned the lecture room and the public school. . . . I do not say that there are not great examples the other way, perhaps Socrates, certainly Lord Bacon; still I think it must be allowed on the whole that, while teaching involves external engagements, the natural home for experiment and speculation is retirement. ——*The Idea of a University* (1873; New York, 1947), p. xxxi.

JOHN STUART MILL (1806–1873) [7]

Mankind can hardly be too often reminded that there was 1
once a man named Socrates, between whom and the legal
authorities and public opinion of his time there took place a
memorable collision. Born in an age and country abounding
in individual greatness, this man has been handed down to
us by those who best knew both him and the age as the most
virtuous man in it; while *we* know him as the head and proto-
type of all subsequent teachers of virtue, the source equally
of the lofty inspiration of Plato and the judicious utilitarianism of Aristotle, *"i maestri di color che sanno,"* [8] the two head-
springs of ethical as of all other philosophy. This acknowledged master of all the eminent thinkers who have since lived
—whose fame, still growing after more than two thousand
years, all but outweighs the whole remainder of the names
which make his native city illustrious—was put to death by
his countrymen, after a judicial conviction, for impiety and
immorality. Impiety, in denying the gods recognized by the
State; indeed, his accuser asserted (see the *Apologia*) that he
believed in no gods at all. Immorality, in being, by his doctrines and instructions, a "corruptor of youth." Of these
charges the tribunal, there is every ground for believing, hon-
estly found him guilty, and condemned the man who probably of all then born had deserved best of mankind to be put
to death as a criminal.

To pass from this to the only other instance of judicial
iniquity, the mention of which, after the condemnation of
Socrates, would not be an anticlimax: the event which took
place on Calvary rather more than eighteen hundred years ago.
——*On Liberty* (1859), "Library of Liberal Arts," No. 61 (New
York, 1956), pp. 29–30.

[7] For Mill's earlier statement on Bentham's Socrates (1838) see under
JEREMY BENTHAM, p. 83*n*.

[8] Mill changes Dante's singular to the plural to make a point which is
characteristic of his broad-mindedness.

2   Socrates was put to death, but the Socratic philosophy rose
like the sun in heaven and spread its illumination over the
whole intellectual firmament.   ——*Ibid.,* p. 39.

3   These last-mentioned contests [the school disputations of
the Middle Ages] had indeed the incurable defect that the
premises appealed to were taken from authority, not from reason; and, as a discipline to the mind, they were in every respect inferior to the powerful [Socratic] dialectics which
formed the intellects of the *"Socratici viri"*; but the modern
mind owes far more to both than it is generally willing to admit, and the present modes of education contain nothing
which in the smallest degree supplies the place either of the
one or of the other.   ——*Ibid.,* p. 54.

4   It is better . . . to be Socrates dissatisfied than a fool satisfied.   ——*Utilitarianism,* "Library of Liberal Arts," No. 1
(New York, 1957), p. 10.

5   It was reserved for Socrates, and for Plato, who, whether as
the interpreter or continuator of Socrates, can never be severed
from him, to exalt this negative arm of philosophy [i.e., that
which tests the truth of theories by the difficulties which they
are bound to meet] to a perfection never since surpassed, and
to provide it with its greatest, most interesting, and most indispensable field of exercise, the generalities relating to life
and conduct. These great men originated the thought, that,
like every other part of the practice of life, morals and politics
are an affair of science, to be understood only after severe study
and special training; an indispensable part of which consists
in acquiring the habit of considering, not merely what can
be said in favor of a doctrine, but what can be said against it;
of sifting opinions, and never accepting any until it has
emerged victorious over every logical, still more than over
every practical objection. These two principles—the necessity
of a scientific basis and method for ethics and politics, and of
rigorous negative dialectics as a part of that method—are the

greatest of the many lessons to be learned from Plato; and it is because the modern mind has in a great measure laid both these lessons, especially the latter of them, aside, that we regard the Platonic writings as among the most precious of the intellectual treasures bequeathed to us by antiquity. Mr. Grote is of the same opinion. . . . ——"Plato," *Edinburgh Review* (April, 1866), in *Dissertations and Discussions* (New York, 1893), IV, 236-37.

This cross-examination is the Socratic Elenchus which, **6** wielded by a master such as Socrates was, and as we can ourselves appreciate in Plato, no more appearance of knowledge without the reality was able to resist. Its pressure was certain, in an honest mind, to dissipate the false opinion of knowledge, and make the confuted respondent sensible of his own ignorance, while it at once helped and stimulated him to the mental effort by which alone that ignorance could be exchanged for knowledge. Dialectics, thus understood, is one branch of an art which is a main portion of the Art of Living —that of not believing except on sufficient evidence; its function being that of compelling a man to put his belief into precise terms and take a defensible position against all the objections that can be made to it. The other, or positive arm of Plato's dialectics, of which he and Socrates may be regarded as the originators, is the direct search for the common feature of things that are classed together, or, in other words, for the meaning of the class-name. ——*Ibid.*, p. 273.

Even at the very early age (before my eighth year) at which **7** I read with [my father] the *Memorabilia* of Xenophon, I imbibed from that work and from his comments a deep respect for the character of Socrates; who stood in my mind as a model of ideal excellence. . . . ——*Autobiography*, "Library of Liberal Arts," No. 91 (New York, 1957), p. 31.

The same inspiring effect which so many of the benefactors **8** of mankind have left on record that they had experienced from Plutarch's *Lives*, was produced on me by Plato's pictures of Socrates, and by some modern biographies. . . .   —*Ibid.,* p. 73.

9   . . . The idea that Socrates, or Howard, or Washington, or Antoninus, or Christ would have sympathized with us, or that we are attempting to do our part in the spirit in which they did theirs, has operated on the very best minds as a strong incentive to act up to their highest feelings and convictions. —"Utility of Religion" (1874), in *Nature and Utility of Religion,* "Library of Liberal Arts," No. 81 (New York, 1958), p. 71.

JOHN RUSKIN (1819–1900)

1   . . . The Reader . . . will not any more think it wrong in me to place invention so high among the powers of man. Nor any more think it strange that the last act of the life of Socrates [to make and cultivate music] should have been to purify himself from the sin of having negligently listened to the voice within him, which, through all his past life, had bid him "labour, and make harmony."   —*Modern Painters,* Pt. VIII (1860), in *The Works of Ruskin* (London, 1903–12), VII, 215-16.

2   It is no use for me to talk or hear talking as yet.[9] What can be said for good, I have for the most part well heard and thought of—no one much comforts me but Socrates. Is not this a glorious bit of antimaterialism, summing nearly all that can be said: [there follows a quotation from Xenophon, *Memorabilia* I, 4, 8].   —From a letter to Charles Eliot Norton (Holyhead, August 26, 1861), in *Works,* XXXVI, 380.

3   Well, we poor Gentiles, though we cannot share in the blessings of the Jews, can at least emulate them in hardness of

[9] During this period of his life, Ruskin suffered from acute depressions.

heart, and we also treat our best teachers in like manner, for I suppose the three greatest of the wise men and scribes, uninspired, who have been sent to teach us, were Socrates, and Dante, and Milton, of whom one was indeed killed, and another indeed persecuted from city to city, and another, in all the spiritual sense of the word, scourged in our synagogues, together with his master, the ashes of whose body we scattered to the winds. But of our treatment of them I do not speak. The mystery of the matter to me is *their* treatment of us, the little of trustworthy saying which they have left to us, about what we most desired . . . to know. Socrates, indeed, altogether refused to converse about the things above, saying that until he knew more of the things round about him, he held it no business of his to meddle with those above him. . . .   ——Manuscript variation of *Sesame and Lilies* (1871), in *Works,* XVIII, 156-57, note.

In heaven I mean to go and talk to Pythagoras and Socrates   4 and Valerius Publicola. ——From a letter to Miss Susan Beever (from Assisi, Sacristan's Cell, June 25, 1874), in *Works,* XXXVII, 117.

HERBERT SPENCER (1820–1903)

Let it be observed that the conception of ethics thus set   1 forth [regarding absolute and relative ethics], strange as many will think it, is one which really lies latent in the beliefs of the moralists at large. Though not definitely acknowledged it is vaguely implied in many of their propositions. From early times downwards we find in ethical speculations, references to the ideal man, his acts, his feelings, his judgments. When Socrates said that well-doing is the thing to be chiefly studied, and that he achieved it who devoted to the study searching and labour, he made the actions of the superior man his standard, since he gave no other. ——*The Principles of Ethics* (New York, 1898), I, 277-78.

2   Turning to ancient civilizations, we meet with various
denials of the right of free belief. . . . There is the death of
Socrates for attacking the current views concerning the gods.
—*Ibid.*, II, 138.

MATTHEW ARNOLD (1822–1888)

1   For my part I do not wish to see men of culture asking to
be entrusted with power; and, indeed, I have freely said, that
in my opinion the speech most proper, at present, for a man
of culture to make to a body of his fellow countrymen who get
him into a committee-room is Socrates' *Know thyself!* and this
is not a speech to be made by men wanting to be entrusted
with power. —*Culture and Anarchy* (1869) (New York,
1924), p. 2.

2   . . . Human life in the hands of Hellenism is invested with
a kind of aërial ease, clearness, and radiancy; they are full of
what we call sweetness and light. Difficulties are kept out of
view, and the beauty and rationalness of the ideal have all
our thoughts. "The best man is he who most tries to perfect
himself, and the happiest man is he who most feels that he *is*
perfecting himself"—this account of the matter by Socrates,
the true Socrates of the *Memorabilia,* has something so simple,
spontaneous, and unsophisticated about it, that it seems to fill
us with clearness and hope when we hear it. But there is a saying which I have heard attributed to Mr. Carlyle about Socrates—a very happy saying, whether it is really Mr. Carlyle's
or not—which excellently marks the essential point in which
Hebraism differs from Hellenism. "Socrates," this saying goes,
"is terribly *at ease in Zion.*" Hebraism—and here is the source
of its wonderful strength—has always been severely preoccupied with an awful sense of the impossibility of being at ease
in Zion; of the difficulties which oppose themselves to man's
pursuit of attainment of that perfection of which Socrates talks
so hopefully, and, from this point of view one might almost

say, so glibly. It is all very well to talk of getting rid of one's
ignorance, of seeing things in their reality, seeing them in their
beauty; but how is this to be done when there is something
which thwarts and spoils all our efforts?—This something is
sin. . . . Apparently it was the Hellenic conception of human
nature which was unsound, for the world could not live by it.
—*Ibid.*, pp. 116-18.

Pericles was perhaps the most perfect public speaker who   3
ever lived, for he was the man who most perfectly combined
thought and wisdom with feeling and eloquence. Yet Plato
brings in Alcibiades declaring, that men went away from the
oratory of Pericles, saying it was very fine, it was very good,
and afterwards thinking no more about it; but they went
away from hearing Socrates talk, he says, with the point of
what he had said sticking fast in their minds, and they could
not get rid of it. Socrates has drunk the hemlock and is dead;
but in his own breast does not every man carry about with
him a possible Socrates, in that power of a disinterested play
of consciousness upon his stock notions and habits, of which
this wise and admirable man gave all through his lifetime the
great example, and which was the great secret of his incomparable influence? And he who leads men to call forth and exercise in themselves this power, and who busily calls it forth
and exercises it in himself, is at the present moment, perhaps,
as Socrates was in his time, more in concert with the vital
working of men's minds, and more effectually significant, than
any House of Commons' orator, or practical operator in
politics. —*Ibid.*, pp. 204-05.

THOMAS HUXLEY (1825–1895)

They [i.e., the Greeks] fell short of the Jews in morality.
How curious is the tolerant attitude of Socrates, like a modern
man of the world talking to a young fellow who runs after
the girls. —*Life and Letters of Thomas Huxley* (New York,
1916), II, 452.

SAMUEL BUTLER (1835–1902)

There is a sentence in Chapter XIII of *Alps and Sanctuaries*
(1881), "Considerations on the Decline of Italian Art," which
in the manuscript originally ran thus: "As for the old masters,
the better plan would be never even to look at one of them,
and to consign Raffaele, along with Socrates, Virgil, Marcus
Aurelius Antoninus, Goethe, Beethoven, and another, to
limbo, as the Seven Humbugs of Christendom." Butler struck
out Socrates and Virgil and substituted Plato and Dante.
——Henry Festing Jones, *Samuel Butler* (London, 1920), I, 364.

WALTER PATER (1839–1894)

1   Strange! out of the practical cautions of Socrates for the
securing of clear and correct and sufficient conceptions about
one's actual experience, for the attainment of a sort of thoroughly educated common sense, came the mystic intellectualism of Plato—Platonism, with all its hazardous flights of soul.

A rich contributor to the philosophic consciousness of Plato,
Socrates was perhaps of larger influence still on the religious
soul in him. As Plato accepted from the masters of Elea the
theoretic principles of all natural religion—the principles of a
reasonable monotheism—so from Socrates he derived its indispensable morality. It was Socrates who first of pagans com-
prised in one clear consciousness the authentic rudiments of
such natural religion, and gave them clear utterance. Through
him, Parmenides had conveyed to Plato the notion of a "Perfect Being," to brace and satisfy the abstracting intellect; but
it was from Socrates himself Plato had learned those corre-
spondent practical pieties, which tranquillise and re-assure the
soul, together with the genial hopes which cheer the great
teacher on the day of his death.

Loyal to the ancient beliefs, the ancient usages, of the religion of many gods which he had found all around him,

Socrates pierces through it to one unmistakable person, of perfect intelligence, power and goodness, who takes note of him. In the course of his seventy years he has adjusted that thought of the invisible to the general facts and to many of the subtler complexities of man's experience in the world of sight. *Sitivit anima mea,* the Athenian philosopher might say, *in Deum, in Deum vivum,* as he was known at Sion. He has at least measured devoutly the place, this way and that, which a religion of infallible authority must fill; has already by implication concurred in it; and in fact has his reward at this depressing hour, as the action of the poison mounts slowly to the centre of his material existence. . . .

Comfort himself and his friends, however, as he may, it does tax all his resources of moral and physical courage to do what is at last required of him: and it was something quite new, unseen before in Greece, inspiring a new note in literature—this attitude of Socrates in the condemned cell, where, fulfilling his own prediction, multitudes, of a wisdom and piety, after all, so different from his, have ever since assisted so admiringly, this anticipation of the Christian way of dying for an opinion, when, as Plato says simply, he consumed the poison in the prison. . . . It was amid larger consolations, we must admit, that Christian heroes did that kind of thing. But bravery, you need hardly be reminded, was ever one of the specially characteristic virtues of the pagan world—loyalty even unto death. It had been loyalty, however, hitherto to one's country, one's home in the world, one's visible companions; not to a wholly invisible claimant, in this way, upon one, upon one's self.

Socrates, with all his singleness of purpose, had been . . . by natural constitution a twofold power, an embodied paradox. The infinitely significant Socrates of Plato, and the quite simple Socrates of Xenophon, may have been indeed the not incompatible oppositions of a nature from the influence of which, as a matter of fact, there emerged on one hand the Cynic, on the other the Cyrenaic School, embodying respectively those opposed austerities and amenities of character,

which, according to the temper of this or that disciple, had
seemed to predominate in their common master. And so the
courage which declined to act as almost any one else would
have acted in that matter of the legal appeal which might
have mitigated the penalty of death, bringing to its appropriate end a life whose main power had been an unrivalled
independence, was contrasted in Socrates, paradoxically, with
a genuine diffidence about his own convictions which explains
some peculiarities in his manner of teaching. The irony, the
humour, for which he was famous—the unfailing humour
which some have found in his very last words—were not merely
spontaneous personal traits, or tricks of manner; but an essential part of the dialectical apparatus, as affording a means
of escape from responsibility, convenient for one who has
scruples about the fitness of his own thoughts for the reception of another, doubts as to the power of words to convey
thoughts, such as he thinks cannot after all be properly conveyed to another, but only awakened, or brought to birth in
him, out of himself—who can tell with what distortions in
that secret place? ——"Plato and Socrates," in *Plato and
Platonism* (London, 1893), pp. 74-78.

2   The very thoroughness of the sort of self-knowledge [Socra-
tes] promoted had in it something sacramental, so to speak;
if it did not do [the young Athenians] good, must do them
considerable harm; could not leave them just as they were.
He had not been able in all cases to expand "the better self,"
as people say, in those he influenced. Some of them had
really become very insolent questioners of others, as also of
a wholly legitimate authority within themselves; and had
but passed from bad to worse. That fatal necessity had been
involved of coming to years of discretion. His claim to have
been no teacher at all, to be irresponsible in regard to those
who had in truth been his very willing disciples, was but
humorous or ironical; and as a consequence there was after
all a sort of historic justice in his death. ——*Ibid.*, p. 80.

Socrates in truth was a sophist; but more than a sophist. 3
Both alike handled freely matters that to the fathers had
seemed beyond question; encouraged what seemed impious
questioning in the sons; had set "the hearts of the sons against
the fathers"; and some instances there were in which the
teaching of Socrates had been more conspicuously ruinous
than theirs. "If you ask people at Athens," says Socrates in
the *Meno,* "how virtue is to be attained, they will laugh in
your face and say they don't so much as know what virtue
is." And who was responsible for that? Certainly that Dialogue, proposing to discover the essential nature of virtue, by
no means re-establishes one's old prepossessions about it in
the vein of Simonides, or Pindar, or one's elders. Sophist, and
philosopher; Protagoras, and Socrates; so far their effect was
the same—to the horror of fathers, to put the minds of the
sons in motion regarding matters it were surely best to take
as settled once and for ever. ——*Ibid.,* p. 90.

GEORGE BERNARD SHAW (1856–1950)

The happiness of credulity is a cheap and dangerous quality 1
of happiness, and by no means a necessity of life. Whether Socrates got as much happiness out of life as Wesley is an un-
answerable question; but a nation of Socrateses would be
much safer and happier than a nation of Wesleys; and its individuals would be higher in the evolutionary scale. At all
events it is in the Socratic man and not in the Wesleyan that
our hope lies now. ——Preface to *Androcles and the Lion*
(1916), in *Prefaces* (London, 1934), p. 576.

Even Socrates, for all his age and experience, did not defend 2
himself at his trial like a man who understood the long accumulated fury that had burst on him, and was clamoring for
his death. His accuser, if born 2300 years later, might have
been picked out of any first class carriage on a suburban rail-

way during the evening or morning rush from or to the City; for he had really nothing to say except that he and his like could not endure being shown up as idiots every time Socrates opened his mouth. Socrates, unconscious of this, was paralyzed by his sense that somehow he was missing the point of the attack. He petered out after he had established the fact that he was an old soldier and a man of honorable life, and that his accuser was a silly snob. He had no suspicion of the extent to which his mental superiority had roused fear and hatred against him in the hearts of men towards whom he was conscious of nothing but good will and good service. . . . Now Socrates was a man of argument, operating slowly and peacefully on men's minds. . . . That, no doubt, is why the contemporaries of Socrates endured him so long. . . . But both of them [Socrates and Joan] combined terrifying ability with a frankness, personal modesty, and benevolence which made the furious dislike to which they fell victims absolutely unreasonable, and therefore inapprehensible by themselves. ——Preface to *Saint Joan* (1924), in *Prefaces*, p. 583.

3   Grown-up geniuses are seldom liked until they are dead. Considering that we poisoned Socrates, crucified Christ, and burnt Joan of Arc amid popular applause, because, after a trial by responsible lawyers and Churchmen, we decided that they were too wicked to be allowed to live, we can hardly set up to be judges of goodness or to have any sincere liking for it. ——*The Intelligent Woman's Guide to Socialism and Capitalism* (New York, 1929), p. 54.

4   Even in ancient Greece, where our proletarians were represented by slaves, and only what we call the middle and upper classes voted, there was the same reaction [of disgust with democracy], which is hardly surprising in view of the fact that one of the famous feats of Athenian democracy was to execute Socrates for using his superior brains to expose its follies. ——*Ibid.*, p. 453.

There have been summits of civilization at which heretics 5
like Socrates, who was killed because he was wiser than his
neighbors, have not been tortured, but ordered to kill themselves in the most painless manner known to their judges. But
from that summit there was a speedy relapse into our present
savagery. ——Preface to *On the Rocks* (1933), in *Prefaces*, p.
356.

It is a historical misfortune that the most world-famous vic- 6
tims of persecution made no valid defence. Socrates and Jesus
are the most talked of in Christian countries. Socrates at his
trial was in full possession of his faculties, and was allowed
to say everything he had to say in his defence; but instead of
defending his right to criticize he infuriated his accusers by
launching at them a damning contrast between their infamous
corruption and mendacity and his own disinterestedness and
blameless record as citizen and soldier. ——*Ibid.*, p. 367.

These refined people worship Jesus and take comparatively 7
no account of Socrates and Mahomet, for no discoverable reason, except that Jesus was horribly tortured, and Socrates
humanely drugged, whilst Mahomet died unsensationally in
his bed. ——*Everybody's Political What's What* (London,
1944), p. 129.

ALFRED NORTH WHITEHEAD (1861–1947)

For some of the most fertile minds composition in writing, 1
or in a form reducible to writing, seems to be an impossibility.
In every faculty you will find that some of the more brilliant
teachers are not among those who publish. Their originality
requires for its expression direct intercourse with their pupils
in the form of lectures, or of personal discussion. Such men
exercise an immense influence; and yet, after the generation
of their pupils has passed away, they sleep among the innu-

merable unthanked benefactors of humanity. Fortunately, one of them is immortal—Socrates. —*The Aims of Education* (New York, 1929), pp. 148-49.

2   Plato's own writings constitute one prolonged apology for freedom of contemplation, and for freedom for the communication of contemplative experiences. In the persistent exercise of this right Socrates and Plato lived, and it was on its behalf that Socrates died. —*Adventures of Ideas* (New York, 1933), p. 64.

3   It is interesting to speculate on the analogies and differences between the deaths of Socrates and Paul. Both were martyrs. Socrates died because his speculative opinions were held to be subversive of the communal life. It is difficult to believe that the agents of Claudius, or Nero, or Galba, were much concerned with Paul's speculative opinions as to the ways of God to man. —*Ibid.*, p. 69.

F. C. S. SCHILLER (1864–1937)

1   The philosophical discovery of the Concept's function is, perhaps, to be credited to Socrates, but it is not probable that he used it as the basis for a complete *Weltanschauung*. The Socratic Concept was still used merely in its natural "pragmatic" way, as the ideal unity whereby the human mind classifies and controls the confusing and confused multitude of particulars, and orders its experience. It was thus essentially an instrument of human cognition; but it may be doubted whether Socrates had recognized its fundamental importance for logic. —*Studies in Humanism* (2nd edn.; London, 1912), p. 52.

2   PROTAGORAS: Were none of [the sages] truly great and wise?
     ANTIMORUS: One there was upon whose like the sun will not shine again for ten thousand years.

PROTAGORAS: And that, I suppose, was Socrates?

ANTIMORUS: What! The boon companion of all the dissolute young swells in Athens! I knew him well, as well as I wanted to. At times, and for a little while, he was not unamusing. It was as stupid as it was cruel to make him drink the hemlock. But he had angered the Athenians beyond endurance, and when fools get angry they are as likely to commit a crime as a blunder. No one, however, who knew him, and wished to speak the truth, would speak of him as I have spoken of the wisest of men from the foolishest of cities, Protagoras from Abdera. ——"Protagoras the Humanist," in *Studies*, pp. 304-05.

W. MACNEILE DIXON (1866–1945)

So perilous is the situation [of ethics] that in the attempt to find an indestructible basis for conduct even philosophers will flout every law of logic, and torture words out of every vestige of meaning. Listen to Socrates, the most admirable and most lovable of men. "No evil," he told his judges, "can befall a good man, neither in this life nor in that which is to come." What meaning can be attached to these words? His statement is certainly false if the word "evil" be used in the sense it has invariably borne throughout the whole of history, in all times and in every language under the sun. "No evil can befall a good man." How interesting a discovery! A good man, therefore, has never suffered in mind or body, never been bereaved of friends or children, never sickened at the sight of cruelty or injustice, at the miseries of the innocent. Epictetus talks in the same lofty strain. The good man is known by his complete indifference to all experiences of this kind. May we not say to Socrates and Epictetus, "My good friends, we cannot sufficiently admire your constancy, your noble sentiments, but we should have preferred you to use words in a human and intelligible sense. And have you considered the case of the simple souls, or of children? Have they never suffered? Have evils never befallen them? Have they never been bewildered by misery they could not understand, never wept in the desolation of their gentle hearts? No doubt, like you, they should have reflected that all was well with them, that they were not in any way afflicted, and like you should have remained serene in the consciousness of their virtue. We fear, my dear Socrates and Epictetus, that it was hardly possible for them, and that in your commendable zeal for good conduct you have outstripped your wonderful wisdom, for which you have been so justly celebrated." ——*The Human Situation,* Gifford Lectures (London, 1937), pp. 285-86.

BERTRAND RUSSELL (1872——)

1   Socrates was concerned mainly with ethics. . . . The views of the ancients on ethics are better worth studying than their views on (say) physical science; the subject has not yet proved amenable to exact reasoning, and we cannot boast that the moderns have as yet rendered their predecessors obsolete. ——*Philosophy* (New York, 1927), pp. 226-27.

2   Socrates acts as his daemon commands, not as the legally constituted authorities desire; he is prepared to suffer martyrdom rather than be untrue to the inner voice. All these men were rebels in their day, and all have come to be honored. Something of what was new in them has come to be taken as a matter of course. But it is not altogether easy to say what this something is.   ——*Power. A New Social Analysis* (New York, 1938), p. 243.

3   There is every reason to suppose that Socrates practised and developed the [dialectic] method. As we saw, when Socrates is condemned to death he reflects happily that in the next world he can go on asking questions for ever, and cannot be put to death, as he will be immortal. Certainly, if he practised dialectic in the way described in the *Apology,* the hostility to him

is easily explained: all the humbugs in Athens would combine against him.—The dialectic method is suitable for some questions, and unsuitable for others. . . . Some matters are obviously unsuitable for treatment in this way—empirical science, for example. . . . The matters that are suitable for treatment by the Socratic method are those as to which we have already enough knowledge to come to a right conclusion. ——*A History of Western Philosophy* (New York, 1945), pp. 92-93.

The Platonic Socrates was a pattern to subsequent philoso-   4
phers for many ages. What are we to think of him ethically? (I am concerned only with the man as Plato portrays him.) His merits are obvious. He is indifferent to worldly success, so devoid of fear that he remains calm and urbane and humourous to the last moment, caring more for what he believes to be truth than for anything else whatever. He has, however, some very grave defects. He is dishonest and sophistical in argument, and in his private thinking he uses intellect to prove conclusions that are to him agreeable, rather than in a disinterested search for knowledge. There is something smug and unctuous about him, which reminds one of a bad type of cleric. His courage in the face of death would have been more remarkable if he had not believed that he was going to enjoy eternal bliss in the company of the gods. Unlike some of his predecessors, he was not scientific in his thinking, but was determined to prove the universe agreeable to his ethical standards. This is treachery to truth, and the worst of philosophic sins. As a man, we may believe him admitted to the communion of saints; but as philosopher he needs a long residence in a scientific purgatory. ——*Ibid.,* p. 142.

WINSTON LEONARD SPENCER CHURCHILL (1874——)

Reporting on his private studies while an army officer in Bangalore, India, 1895-6:

Someone had used the phrase "the Socratic method." What   1 was that? It was apparently a way of giving your friend his head in an argument and prodding him into a pit by cunning questions. Who was Socrates, anyhow? A very argumentative Greek who had a nagging wife and was finally compelled to commit suicide because he was a nuisance! Still, he was beyond doubt a considerable person. He counted for a lot in the minds of learned people. I wanted "the Socrates story." Why had his fame lasted through all the ages? What were the stresses which had led a government to put him to death merely because of the things he said? Dire stresses they must have been: the life of the Athenian Executive or the life of this talkative professor! Such antagonisms do not spring from petty issues. Evidently Socrates had called something into being long ago which was very explosive. Intellectual dynamite! A moral bomb! But there was nothing about [it] in The Queen's Regulations. ——*A Roving Commission: My Early Life* (New York, 1930), p. 110.

2   He [i.e., Lord Balfour] would very soon have put Socrates in his place, if that old fellow had played one of his dialectical tricks on him. When I go to Heaven, I shall try to arrange a chat between these two on some topic, not too recondite for me to follow. ——*Great Contemporaries* (New York, 1937), p. 207.

THOMAS STEARNS ELIOT (1882——)

. . . The attitude of Socrates and that of Erasmus toward the religion of their place and time were very different from what I take to be the attitude of Professor Babbitt. How far Socrates believed, and whether his legendary request of the sacrifice of a cock was merely gentlemanly behaviour or even irony, we cannot tell; but the equivalent would be Professor Babbitt receiving extreme unction, and that I cannot at present conceive. But both Socrates and Erasmus were content to

remain critics, and to leave the religious fabric untouched.
——*For Lancelot Andrewes. Essays on Style and Order* (New
York, 1929), p. 147.

ARNOLD TOYNBEE (1889——)

If the Roman administrator was an altruistic agent of the   1
Hellenic dominant minority's practical ability, the Greek
philosopher was a still nobler exponent of its intellectual
power; and the golden chain of creative Greek philosophers,
which ends with Plotinus in the generation that lived to see
the Roman public service collapse, had begun with Socrates in
a generation that was already grown up in 431 B.C., when the
Hellenic Civilization broke down. To retrieve, or at any rate
to mitigate, the tragic consequences of that breakdown was
the Greek philosopher's, as well as the Roman administrator's,
life work; and the philosopher's labours produced a more valuable and more durable result than the administrator's, just
because they were less closely woven into the material texture
of the disintegrating society's life. While the Roman adminis-
trators built a Hellenic universal state, the philosophers endowed Posterity with a *ktema eis aei* in the Academy and the
Peripatus, the Stoa and the Garden, the Cynic's freedom of
the highways and hedges, and the Neoplatonist's unearthly
Land of Heart's Desire.   ——*A Study of History* (New York
and London, 1939), V, 39-40.

The military overthrow of Athens in 404 B.C. and the greater   2
moral defeat which the restored Athenian democracy inflicted
upon itself in 399 B.C. by the judicial murder of Socrates. . . .
——*Ibid.*, IV, 264. See also V, 395 (note), and VI, 39-40.

. . . The martyrdom of the Athenian citizen Socrates, who   3
refused to elude a death-sentence by condescending either to
abscond from the prison where he was awaiting trial or to

prevaricate at the trial when this duly took place.   —*Ibid.*,
V, 404.

4   It may . . . be doubted whether Socrates would have suffered
the death-penalty that Anaxagoras escaped if Socrates' attitude
towards religion had been all that his enemies had had against
him. . . . Socrates was the victim, not so much of conservative
Athenian religious fanaticism, as of democratic Athenian resentment over the final defeat of Athens in the long-drawn-out
Atheno-Peloponnesian war and democratic Athenian vindic-
tiveness towards a fascist-minded Athenian minority who had
seized the opportunity opened to them then by the discredit-
ing of the democratic regime through military defeat in order
to overthrow the democratic constitution. Socrates' past personal association with Critias, the moving spirit among "the
Thirty Tyrants," was the offence that the restored democratic
regime could neither forget nor forgive. It was Politics, not
Religion, that cost Socrates his life.   —*Ibid.*, VII, 472.

5   The exercise of humility that was required of a Modern
Western Science, was not to lose confidence in her prowess
within her own field, but to recognize the bitter truth that,
in spite of all her intellectual achievements—past, present, and
future—she was spiritually impotent, and that Socrates had
taken the right turning at that critical point in his life at
which he had abandoned the study of Physical Science in
order to seek communion with the spiritual power that in-
forms and governs the Universe.   —*Ibid.*, VII, 488. See also
IX, 626.

6   The saint is not paralysed by a horror of seeking unguar-
anteed rewards at the cost of irrevocable sacrifices, because he
is convinced that the standpoint from which human action
appears to be unprofitable pursuit of a will-o'-the-wisp is one
that gives a falsifyingly fragmentary vision of Reality. Such
godlike enlightenment inspired the confidence and fortitude
that Jesus and Socrates and More displayed when they for-

bore to embrace opportunities held out to them for saving their lives at the price of compromising the truth which it was their mission to proclaim. ——*Ibid.,* VII, 522.

Blessed Socrates, also a martyr, show us, like Stephen, how 7 to suffer death in perfect charity towards those that despitefully use us. "London, 1951, 6.25 p.m., after looking once more, this afternoon, at Fra Angelico's picture of the Beatific Vision." ——*Ibid.,* X, 144 (expansion of the "Litany of the Saints" after the passage *"Sancte Stephane, intercede pro nobis"*).

KARL R. POPPER (1902——)

Socrates was a moralist and an enthusiast. He was the type 1 of man who would criticize any type of government for its shortcomings . . . but he recognized the importance of being loyal to the laws of the state. As it happened, he spent his life largely under a democratic form of government, and as a good democrat he found it his duty to expose the incompetence and windbaggery of some of the democratic leaders of his time. At the same time he opposed any form of tyranny; and if we consider his courageous behavior under the Thirty Tyrants, then we have no reason to assume that his criticism of democratic leaders was inspired by anti-democratic leanings. He only demanded that the moral level both of the citizens and of their leaders should be improved by education and enlightenment. It is not unlikely that he also demanded (like Plato) that the best should rule, which would have meant, in his view, the wisest, or those who knew something about justice. But we must remember that by justice he meant equalitarian justice . . . and that he was not only an equalitarian but also an individualist—perhaps the greatest apostle of an individualistic ethics of all times. And we must also be clear that if he demanded that the wisest should rule, he clearly stressed that he did not mean the learned men; in fact,

he was sceptical of all professional learnedness, whether it was
that of the philosophers of the past or of the learned men of
his own generation, the Sophists. The wisdom he meant was
of a different kind. It was simply the realization: how little
do I know! Those who do not know this, he taught, know
nothing at all. This is the true scientific spirit.   ——*The Open
Society and its Enemies* (London, 1945), I, 112.

2   It is important to see that this Socratic intellectualism is
decidedly equalitarian. Socrates believed that everyone can be
taught. . . . And this intellectualism is also anti-authoritarian.
. . . In view of such teaching, it is clear how much the Socratic
demand (if he ever raised this demand) that the best, i.e., the
intellectually honest, should rule, differs from the authoritarian demand that the most learned, or from the aristocratic
demand that the best, i.e., the most noble, should rule. . . .
But this moral intellectualism of Socrates is a two-edged sword.
It has its equalitarian and democratic aspect, which was later
developed by Antisthenes. But it has also an aspect which may
give rise to strongly anti-democratic tendencies. Its stress upon
the need for enlightenment, for education, might easily be interpreted as a demand for *authoritarianism*. . . . The uneducated seems thus to be in need of an authority to wake him
up, since he cannot be expected to be self-critical. But this
one element of authoritarianism was wonderfully balanced in
Socrates' teaching by the emphasis that the authority must
not claim more than that. The true teacher can prove himself only by exhibiting that self-criticism which the uneducated
lacks.   ——*Ibid.*, pp. 113-14.

3   There was [among the generation which I would like to call
the Great Generation] perhaps the greatest of all, Socrates,
who taught the lesson that we must have faith in human reason, but beware of dogmatism; that we must keep away both
from misology, the distrust of theory and of reason, and from
the magical attitude of making an idol of wisdom; who taught,

in other words, that the spirit of science is criticism. ——*Ibid.*, p. 162.

The new faith of the open society, the faith in man, in   4
equalitarian justice, and in human reason, was perhaps beginning to take shape, but it was not yet formulated.

The greatest contribution to this faith was to be made by
Socrates, who died for it. Socrates was not a leader of Athenian
democracy, like Pericles, or a theorist of the open society, like
Protagoras. He was, rather, a critic of Athens and of her democratic institutions, and in this he may have borne a superficial
resemblance to some of the leaders of the reaction. . . . Socrates' criticism was a democratic one, and indeed of the kind
that is the very life of democracy. . . . I have already mentioned some features of Socrates' teaching; his intellectualism,
i.e., his equalitarian theory of human reason as a universal
medium of communication; his stress on intellectual honesty
and self-criticism; his equalitarian theory of justice, and his
doctrine that it is better to be a victim of injustice than to
inflict it upon others. I think it is this last doctrine which can
help us best to understand the core of his teaching, his creed
of individualism, his belief in the human individual as an end
in himself.

The closed society, and with it its creed that the tribe is
everything and the individual nothing, had broken down. . . .
But the philosophy of man began only with Protagoras; and
the creed that there is nothing more important in our life
than other individual men, the appeal to men to respect one
another, and themselves, is due to Socrates. ——*Ibid.*, pp.
165-66.

That he [i.e., Socrates] wanted to die, or that he enjoyed the   5
role of a martyr, I do not believe. He simply fought for what
he believed to be right, and for his life's work. He had never
intended to undermine democracy. In fact, he had tried to
give it the faith it needed. This had been the work of his life.

It was, he felt, seriously threatened. The betrayal of his former companions let his work and himself appear in a light which must have disturbed him deeply. He may have welcomed the trial as an opportunity to prove that his loyalty to his city was unbounded.

Socrates explained this attitude most carefully when he was given an opportunity to escape. Had he seized it, and become an exile, everybody would have thought him an opponent of democracy. So he stayed and stated his reasons. . . .

Socrates' death is the ultimate proof of his sincerity. His fearlessness, his simplicity, his modesty, his sense of proportion, his humor never deserted him. . . . He showed that a man could die, not only for fate and fame and other grand things of this kind, but also for the freedom of critical thought, and for a self-respect which has nothing to do with self-importance or sentimentality.

Socrates had only *one* worthy successor, his old friend Antisthenes, the last of the Great Generation. Plato, his most gifted disciple, was soon to prove the least faithful. He betrayed Socrates, just as his uncles had done. ——*Ibid.*, pp. 170-71.

RICHARD HOWARD CROSSMAN (1907——)

1   Who was this individual whose personality has endured when all the famous men of the period have become thin and ghostly shades, mere names appended to great events? Socrates was not a famous politician, but an ordinary Athenian citizen who served his city in the normal routine of peace and war. He was not a great artist or poet: though he wrote poems, they are not preserved. He was not even a scientist or philosopher, in the usual sense; for he made no discoveries, and, if he wrote any philosophy, not a word of his writings survives.

Socrates was not famous for anything—except for being Socrates. In a sense he did nothing, and yet he was and is one of the greatest figures of Western civilization. Of him and of a

few others—Jesus and St. Francis for instance—it can truly be
said that their lives and individualities have moulded the
shape of our innermost being and are still the inspiration of
the best that is in us.   ——*Plato Today* (New York, 1939), pp.
38-39.

We have said that it is the personality of Socrates, not his   2
actions or teaching, which is really important. That he was
justifiably condemned to death is true; but it is irrelevant to
his greatness. That he made no important discoveries is also
true and also irrelevant. What mattered to Plato and what
matters to us is his life and death. In them he showed that a
man could be found who believed so passionately in the cause
of truth that he would follow it whatever its political or social
effects. Such people there must always be if civilization is to
be preserved. They are so uncompromising that they are quite
unpractical: so simple that they make wise men look like
fools. Oblivious of the disastrous results of their idealism, they
demand truth even where it may ruin a class or a city or a
nation: and if their wickedness is pointed out to them, they
merely reply, "where truth is concerned, compromise is impossible." All that is good in our Western culture has sprung
from this spirit, whether it is found in scientists, or priests,
or politicians, or quite ordinary men and women who have
refused to prefer politic falsehoods to the simple truth. In
the short term, they often do great harm: but in the end
their example is the only force which can break the dictator-
ship of force and greed. Socrates was the first of these men
and women of whose personality history has preserved a
record.

For he was the first man who really saw what intellectual
integrity implied and yet preferred it to everything else. He
was the spirit of research, incorruptible, intolerant of sham,
greedy for every variety of human experience, insatiable in
discussion, ironic and yet serious. Such a spirit is generally
intolerable to any well-organized community. The statesman
who is responsible for "carrying-on," the priest who preaches

the orthodox faith, the professor who repeats the traditional dogmas, will all unite to suppress the free spirit of reason which respects no authority save that of truth. In the face of completely candid criticism every established authority must resort to the most irrational of defences—force. There is no other weapon against the conscientious objector: and Socrates showed that philosophy is nothing else than conscientious objection to prejudice and unreason. Perhaps in the last resort it cannot solve the problems of human right and wrong, and it will have no simple answer to the questions of the hour. Regarding force as irrational, it will refuse to use it and ceaselessly demand that those who are prepared to do so should ask themselves precisely what their purpose and their motives are. The Athenian democracy had no answer to this question, and so Socrates died.

Socrates will always be compelled to die, his death will always be politically justifiable, and it will always be condemned by succeeding generations, who see so easily in retrospect that truth is ultimately preferable to any established falsehood, however efficient it may appear. Condemning the death of the historical Socrates, each generation kills its own. ——*Ibid.*, pp. 86-88.

3   . . . Democracy is not a mere ideal, mystically envisaged by a few dreamers; for the belief in the infinite value of human *personality* is also the belief in human *reason,* and at this point the ideal of Jesus is fused with that of Socrates. I have tried to show how Plato, in his attempt to re-establish a Greek aristocratic order, departed further and further from the principles of his master, until he turned the Socratic belief in reason into a dogmatic and authoritarian code. But democracy, just as it is tied to no particular institution, is tied to no eternal philosophy. Democratic thought must always remain a searching for truth: and the democrat can never cease to be the man who knows that he knows nothing. . . . The Socratic search for truth is the principle which seeks to undermine this [conservative] dogmatism of inertia, to break down the ra-

tional defenses of prejudice, and so to allow human personality to grow and to adapt itself to new conditions. Denying
that any system of theology or ethics or law or government can
be eternally valid, it appeals against Reason to reason itself,
against this system of justice to justice, against these laws to
law. ——*Ibid.,* pp. 304-05.

[The state of modern democracy in which Fascism is bound   4
to grow] can be cured only if we become urgently aware of
the imminence of the catastrophe, and if, holding fast to our
denial of the infallibility of established dogma, and believing
still in the infinite possibilities latent in human nature, we
try to awaken once more that spirit of conscientious objection
to prejudice and Phariseeism of which Socrates was the first
example. Only when Western civilization has shaken off the
shackles of the past and created a new social order worthy of
the human dignity of the common man, will democracy and
religion be once more realized in human society. Till then
both must remain faiths, filled with a prophetic anger at the
sight of the nations and societies which use their name in
vain, and, because they are grounded in the heart of common
man, powerful enough to remove mountains.

It is Socrates, not Plato, whom we need. ——*Ibid.,* p. 308.

AMERICAN

BENJAMIN FRANKLIN (1706–1790)

1   Soon after I procur'd Xenophon's Memorable Things of
Socrates wherein there are many instances of the same [Socratic]
method. I was charm'd with it, adopted it, dropt my abrupt
contradictions and positive argumentation, and put on the
humble inquirer and doubter.   —*Autobiography* (1791), in
The Writings of Benjamin Franklin, ed. A. H. Smyth (New
York, 1905 ff.), I, 244.

Last item on Franklin's list of thirteen virtues:

2   13. Humility: Imitate Jesus and Socrates.   —*Ibid.*, p. 328.

THOMAS PAINE (1737–1809)

Defending his Age of Reason *(1794) against the charge of
blasphemy:*
Socrates, who lived more than four hundred years before the
Christian era, was convicted of blasphemy for preaching
against the belief of a plurality of gods, and for preaching
the belief of one god, and was condemned to suffer death by
poison. . . . We see that in the case of Socrates truth was condemned as blasphemy. Are we so sure that truth is not blasphemy in the present day?   —From a letter to Mr. Thomas
Erskine, counsel for the prosecution of the bookseller Wil-
liams in London for publishing the *Age of Reason* (1797), in
The Life and Writings of Thomas Paine (New York, 1915),
VI, 310.

THOMAS JEFFERSON (1743–1826)

1   The superlative wisdom of Socrates is testified by all antiquity, and placed on ground not to be questioned. When,

therefore, Plato puts into his mouth such paralogisms, such quibbles on words, and sophisms as a schoolboy would be ashamed of, we conclude that they were the whimsies of Plato's own foggy brain, and acquit Socrates of puerilities so unlike his character. ——From a letter to William Short (August 4, 1820), in *The Writings of Thomas Jefferson,* ed. H. A. Washington (Washington, 1854), XV, 258.

... This belief [of the Jews in Jesus' time] carried no more **2** personal imputation, than the belief of Socrates, that himself was under the care and admonitions of a guardian Daemon. And how many of our wisest men still believe in the reality of these inspirations, while perfectly sane in all other subjects. ——*Ibid.,* pp. 261-62.

I should first take a general view of the moral doctrine of **3** the most remarkable of the antient philosophers . . . say of Pythagoras, Epicurus, Epictetus, Socrates, Cicero, Seneca, Antoninus. . . . In this branch of philosophy [relating to ourselves] they were really great. In developing our duties to others, they were short and defective. They embraced, indeed, the circles of kindred and friends, and inculcated patriotism, or the love of our country in the aggregate, as a primary obligation: toward our neighbors and countrymen they taught justice, but scarcely viewed them as within the circle of benevolence. Still less have they inculcated peace, charity and love to our fellowmen, or embraced with benevolence the whole family of mankind. ——"Syllabus of an Estimate of the Merit of the Doctrines of Jesus, Compared with Those of Others" (April, 1803), in *The Writings of Thomas Jefferson,* ed. P. L. Ford (New York, 1897), VIII, 224 ff.

JOHN QUINCY ADAMS (1767–1848)

It is not easy to say whether this [Socrates' account of his **1** daemon or familiar spirit] was the effect of superstition or

whether he spoke in figure. It is still more difficult to impute
it to deliberate deception. The instances which he gives of the
occasions when he heard the voice, make it hardly possible to
consider him as having intended only Prudence or Conscience.
——(October 13, 1811). *Memoirs of John Quincy Adams,* ed.
Charles Francis Adams (Philadelphia, 1874–1877), II, 316.

2   Socrates here [in the *Euthyphro*] mentions that he himself
was accused by Melitus of disbelieving the established gods
and attempting to introduce new ones. He certainly does
ridicule the popular creed about the gods then in repute, and
shows that holiness cannot be defined [as] that which pleases
them. . . . [In the *Apology*] the mildness of his tone and manner, the firmness and intrepidity of his adherence to his principles, the sportive playfulness of his satire, and the exalted
purity of his doctrines, are all but divine. He repeats here the
assurance that he is accompanied by a demon; but there is
no substantial defense against the accusation of Melitus. He
has no defense to make: the charges were substantially
true. . . .

The *Crito* is the exposition of his motives for refusing to
make his escape from prison when under sentence of death—
sublime morality. ——*Ibid.,* pp. 316-17.

WILLIAM ELLERY CHANNING (1780–1842)

When a people shall learn, that its greatest benefactors and
most important members are men devoted to the liberal instruction of all its classes, to the work of raising to life its
buried intellect, it will have opened to itself the path of true
glory. This truth is making its way. Socrates is now regarded
as the greatest man in an age of great men. The name of
King has grown dim before that of Apostle. To teach, whether
by word or action, is the highest function on earth. ——"An
Address on Temperance," in *Works of William E. Channing*
(Boston, 1848), II, 324.

RALPH WALDO EMERSON (1803–1882) [1]

"Emerson was writing a dissertation on the character of Soc-   1
rates for which he received a Bowdoin Prize. . . . The following pages from a study for the paper on Socrates . . . seem
worth while printing."—*From the introductory remarks of the
editor, Edward Waldo Emerson.*

Socrates has little to do with these [the ostentatious rituals
of India], and perhaps his information on the subject was very
limited. He was not distinguished for knowledge or general
information, but for acquaintance with the mind and its false
and fond propensities, its springs of action, its assailable parts;
in short, his art laid open its deepest recesses, and he handled
and moulded it at will. Indeed we do not have reason to suppose that he was intimately versed in his own national literature, Herodotus, Homer, Thucydides, Pindar, etc.—His profession in early life had perhaps imparted a little of poetic
inspiration, but his leading feature seems to have been sagacity—little refinement, little erudition. His genius resembled
Aesop.

The greatness of the philosopher shines forth in its fullest
lustre when we examine the originality, the bold and un-
equalled sublimity of his conceptions. His powerful mind had
surmounted the errours of education and had retained useful
acquisitions, whilst it discarded what was absurd or unprofitable. He studied Nature with a chastised enthusiasm, and
the constant activity of his mind endowed him with an energy
of thought little short of inspiration. When he speaks of the
immortality of the soul, or when he enters on considerations
of the attributes or nature of the deity, he leaves the little
quibblings of the Sophists, and his own inferiour strains of
irony, and his soul warms and expands with his subject; we
forget that he is man—he seems seated like Jupiter Creator

[1] For Emerson's reaction to Carlyle's and Landor's animosity against
Socrates, see under CARLYLE (p. 95, no. 2) and LANDOR (p. 90, no. 3).

moulding magnificent forms and clothing them with beauty
and grandeur. . . . ——*Journals of Ralph Waldo Emerson*
(Boston, 1909), I, 5-6. [Emerson was sixteen when he wrote
his "dissertation."]

2   . . . I read with pleasure every considered expression of
praise of him [Jesus]. But perfect in the sense of complete man
he seems not to me to be, but a very exclusive and partial development of the moral such as the great Compensation that balances the universe provides to repair accumulated depravity.
The weight of his ethical sentences deserves more than all the
consideration they have, and his life is one original pure beam
of truth but a perfect man should exhibit all the traits of
humanity and should expressly recognize the intellectual
nature. Socrates I call a complete universal man fulfilling all
the conditions of man's existence. Sublime as he is, I compare
him not as an ethical teacher to Christ, but his life is more
humane.[2] ——From a letter to Elizabeth Palmer Peabody
(Concord, August 3, 1835), in *The Letters of Ralph Waldo
Emerson* (New York, 1939), I, 451.

3   Pythagoras was misunderstood, and Socrates, and Jesus, and
Luther, and Copernicus, and Galileo, and Newton, and every
pure and wise spirit that ever took flesh. To be great is to be
misunderstood. ——"Self-Reliance," in *Essays* (1841), in *The
Complete Works* (Riverside edn.; Boston, 1883–1906), II,
57-58.

4   Socrates kept all his virtues as well as all his faculties well
in hand. He was sincerely humble, but he utilized his humanity chiefly as a better eye-glass to penetrate the vapors that
baffled the vision of the other men. ——"Powers and Laws of

    2 See also *Journals*, III, 518: "I do not see in him [Jesus] cheerfulness: I
do not see in him the love of natural science; I see in him no kindness for
art; I see in him nothing of Socrates, of Laplace, of Shakespeare. The
perfect man should remind us of all great men."

Thought," London Lectures (1848), in *The Complete Works,* XII, 63.

Socrates and Plato are the double star which the most power- 5 ful instruments will not entirely separate. Socrates . . . in his traits and genius, is the best example of that synthesis which constitutes Plato's extraordinary power. Socrates, a man of humble stem, but honest enough; of the commonest history; of a personal homeliness so remarkable as to be a cause of wit in others—the rather that his broad good nature and exquisite taste for a joke invited the sally, which was sure to be paid. The players personated him on the stage; the potters copied his ugly face on their stone jugs. He was a cool fellow, adding to his humor a perfect temper and a knowledge of his man, be he who he might whom he talked with, which laid the companion open to certain defeat in any debate—and in debate he immoderately delighted. The young men are prodigiously fond of him and invite him to their feasts, whither he goes for conversation. He can drink, too; has the strongest head in Athens; and after leaving the whole party under the table, goes away as if nothing had happened, to begin new dialogues with somebody that is sober. In short, he was what our country people call *an old one.*

He affected a good many citizen-like tastes, was monstrously fond of Athens, hated trees, never willingly went beyond the walls, knew the old characters, valued the bores and philistines, thought every thing in Athens a little better than anything in any other place. He was plain as a Quaker in habit and speech, affected low phrases, and illustrations from cocks and quails, soup-pans and sycamore-spoons, grooms and farriers, and unnameable offices—especially if he talked with any superfine person. He had a Franklin-like wisdom. Thus he showed one who was afraid to go on foot to Olympia, that it was no more than the daily walk within doors, if continuously extended, would easily reach.

Plain old uncle as he was, with his great ears, an immense

talker—the rumor ran that on one or two occasions, in the war
with Boeotia, he had shown a determination which had covered the retreat of a troop; and there was some story that under cover of folly, he had, in the city government, when one
day he chanced to hold a seat there, evinced a courage in opposing singly the popular voice, which had well-nigh ruined
him. He is very poor; but then he is hardy as a soldier, and
can live on a few olives; usually, in the strictest sense, on bread
and water, except when entertained by his friends. His necessary expenses were exceedingly small, and no one could live
as he did. He wore no under-garment; his upper garment was
the same for summer and winter, and he went barefooted; and
it is said that to procure the pleasure, which he loves, of talking at his ease all day with the most elegant and cultivated
young men, he will now and then return to his shop and
carve statues, good or bad, for sale. However that be, it is certain that he had grown to delight in nothing else than this—
conversation; and that, under his hypocritical pretence of
knowing nothing, he attacks and brings down all the fine
speakers, all the fine philosophers of Athens, whether natives
or strangers from Asia Minor and the islands. Nobody can refuse to talk with him, he is so honest and really curious to
know; a man who was willingly confuted if he did not speak
the truth, and who willingly confuted others asserting what
was false; and not less pleased when confuted than when
confuting; for he thought not any evil happened to men of
such a magnitude as false opinion respecting the just and unjust. A pitiless disputant, who knows nothing, but the bounds
of whose conquering intelligence no man had ever reached;
whose temper was imperturbable; whose dreadful logic was always leisurely and sportive; so careless and ignorant as to disarm the wariest and draw them, in the pleasantest manner,
into horrible doubts and confusion. But he always knew the
way out; knew it, yet would not tell it. No escape; he drives
them to terrible choices by his dilemmas, and tosses the Hip-
piases and Gorgiases with their grand reputations, as a boy

tosses his balls. The tyrannous realist!—Meno has discoursed a thousand times, at length, on virtue, before many companies, and very well, as it appeared to him; but at this moment he cannot even tell what it is—this cramp-fish of a Socrates has so bewitched him.

This hard-headed humorist, whose strange conceits, drollery, and *bonhommie* diverted the young patricians, whilst the rumor of his sayings and quibbles gets abroad every day— turns out, in the sequel, to have a probity as invincible as his logic, and to be either insane, or at least, under cover of his play, enthusiastic in his religion. When accused before the judges of subverting the popular creed, he affirms the immortality of the soul, the future reward and punishment: and refusing to recant, in a caprice of the popular government was condemned to die, and sent to the prison. Socrates entered the prison and took away all ignominy from the place, which could not be a prison whilst he was there. Crito bribed the jailer; but Socrates would not go out by treachery. "Whatever inconvenience ensue, nothing is to be preferred before justice. These things I hear like pipes and drums, whose sound makes me deaf to every thing you say." The fame of this prison, the fame of the discourses there and the drinking of the hemlock are one of the most precious passages in the history of the world.

The rare coincidence, in one ugly body, of the droll and the martyr, the keen street and market debater with the sweetest saint known to any history at that time, had forcibly struck the mind of Plato, so capacious of these contrasts; and the figure of Socrates by a necessity placed itself in the foreground of the scene, as the fittest dispenser of the intellectual treasures he had to communicate. It was a rare fortune that this Aesop of the mob and this robed scholar should meet, to make each other immortal in their mutual faculty. The strange synthesis in the character of Socrates capped the synthesis in the mind of Plato. Moreover by this means he was able, in the direct way and without envy to avail himself of the wit and weight of Socrates, to which unquestionably his own debt was great; and these derived again their principal advantage from the perfect art of Plato.[3] ——"Plato, or the Philosopher," in *Representative Men* (1850), in *The Complete Works*, IV, 70-74.

6   Let none presume to measure the irregularities of Michael Angelo and Socrates by village scales. ——"Plato, New Readings," in *Representative Men,* in *The Complete Works,* IV, 87.

7   . . . He who is to be wise for many must not be protected. He must know the huts where the poor men lie, and the chores which poor men do. The first class minds, Aesop, Socrates, Cervantes, Shakespeare, Franklin had the poor man's feeling and mortification. ——"Considerations by the Way," in *The Conduct of Life* (1860), in *The Complete Works,* VI, 260-61.

WALT WHITMAN (1819–1892)

Having studied the new and antique, the Greek and Germanic systems,
Kant having studied and stated, Fichte and Schelling and Hegel,
Stated the lore of Plato, and Socrates greater than Plato,
And greater than Socrates sought and stated, Christ divine having studied long,
I see reminiscent to-day those Greek and Germanic systems,
See the philosophies all, Christian churches and tenets see,

---

[3] Carlyle, acknowledging his gift copy of *Representative Men* in a letter to Emerson, written July 19, 1850, makes this comment about the Plato essay: "Plato, I think, though he is the most admired by many, did the least for me; little save Socrates with his clogs and big ears remains alive with me from it." (*Representative Men,* Notes, in *The Complete Works,* IV, 296.)

Yet underneath Socrates clearly see, and underneath
  Christ the divine I see,
The dear love of man for his comrade, the attraction of
  friend to friend,
Of the well-married husband and wife, of children and
  parents,
Of city for city and land for land.

       ——"The Base of All Metaphysics," in *Leaves
         of Grass* (New York, 1951), pp. 124-25.

HERMAN MELVILLE (1819–1891) [4]

Though the Christian era had not yet begun, Socrates died 1
the death of a Christian. ——*Redburn* (London, 1922), p. 377.

Oh brave cock! . . . . Oh, bird rightly offered up by the in- 2
vincible Socrates, in testimony of his final victory over life . . .
this bird of cheerful Socrates, the game-fowl Greek who died
unappalled. ——"Cock-A-Doodle-Doo," in *Billy Budd and
Other Prose Pieces* (London, 1924), pp. 152, 154.

    And Socrates a spirit divine, 3
      not alien held to cheerful wine.
  ——"At the Hostelry," in *Poems* (London, 1924), p. 374.

"You are undermining the laws, and are dangerous to the 4
young," said the judges to Socrates. They said the truth,
and from this point of view were just in condemning him.
——Quoted from Melville's annotation in his copy of Mme. de
Staël's *Germany* (New York, 1859), I, 26. [This and the following passage are printed here by permission of the Committee on Higher Degrees in the History of American Civilization, Harvard University.]

  [4] The references in this entry were provided by Professor Merton Sealts,
of the Department of English of Lawrence College.

5   The "volumes" exclaims the master critic.[5] What could a
sage of the nineteenth century teach Socrates? Why, nothing
more than something about Cyrus Fields and the ocean tele-
graph, and the sewing machine, etc.   ——Quoted from Melville's annotation in his copy of Matthew Arnold's *New Poems*
(Boston, 1867), p. 28.

PHILLIPS BROOKS (1835–1893)

I can almost dream what Socrates would say to any man who
said there was no difference between Jesus and him. But how
shall we state the difference? One is divine and human; the
other is human only. One is Redeemer; the other is philosopher. One is inspired, and the other questions. One reveals,
and the other argues. These statements, doubtless, are all true.
And in them all there is wrapped up this, which is the truth
of all the influence of Jesus over men's minds, that where
Socrates brings an argument to meet an objection, Jesus always brings a nature to meet a nature,—a whole being which
the truth has filled with strength, to meet another whole being which error has filled with feebleness.   ——*The Influence
of Jesus* (New York, 1879), p. 245.

HENRY ADAMS (1838–1918)

1   The contrast between the shop-keeping bourgeoisie of
Athens, with their so-called wit, and their damnable scepticism and their idiotic Socratic method, on the one side; and
the dignity, grace, decorative elegance, and almost complete

---

[5] The reference is to lines 332-34 from Matthew Arnold's "Empedocles
on Etna":

> But still, as we proceed,
> The mass swells more and more
> Of volumes yet to read.

want of religious depth or intensity of Eleusis, Delphi, and
their symbol the Parthenon, on the other, is what I felt most
strongly on the Acropolis. Aristophanes and Euripides are perfectly intelligible there, and alive still. Under these influences
I should certainly have voted to hang Socrates.   ——Letter to
his brother Brooks Adams (Sept. 10, 1899), in Harold Dean
Cater, *Henry Adams and His Friends* (Boston, 1947), p. 479.

The form of logic most fascinating to youthful minds, as   2
well as to some minds that are only too acute, is the *reductio
ad absurdum;* the forcing an opponent into an absurd alterna-
tive or admission; and the syllogism lent itself happily to this
use. Socrates abused the weapon and Abélard was the first
French master of the art; but neither State nor Church likes
to be reduced to an absurdity, and, on the whole, both Socrates and Abélard fared ill in the result.   ——*Mont-Saint-
Michel and Chartres* (privately printed in 1904; Boston, 1924),
p. 291.

CHARLES SANDERS PEIRCE (1839–1914)

[Pragmatism] appears to have been virtually the philosophy   1
of Socrates. The rivulets at the head of the river of pragmatism are easily traced back to almost any desired antiquity.
Socrates bathed in these waters.   ——*Collected Papers,* ed.
Charles Hartshorne and Paul Weiss (Cambridge, Mass., 1931),
6.490, p. 335, and 5.11.

When Scotus Erigena is commenting upon a poetical pas-   2
sage in which Hellebore is spoken of as having caused the
death of Socrates, he does not hesitate to inform the inquir-
ing reader that Helleborus and Socrates were two eminent
Greek philosophers, and that the latter, having been overcome
in argument by the former, took the matter to heart and died
of it.[6] What sort of an idea of truth could a man have who

[6] We have been unable to trace the source of this reference.

could adopt and teach, without the qualification of a perhaps, an opinion taken so entirely at random? The real spirit of Socrates, who I hope would have been delighted to have been "overcome in argument," because he would have learned something by it, is in curious contrast with the naïve idea of the glossist, for whom . . . discussion would seem to have been simply a struggle. ——*Ibid.*, 5. 406.

OLIVER WENDELL HOLMES (1841–1935)

I don't retain an impression that the cross-examinations of Socrates were so ineluctable as convention avers. My impression—mostly from youth—is of postulates that oughtn't to have been granted and of consequences that do not follow. ——Letter to Sir Frederick Pollock (July 2, 1919), in *Holmes-Pollock Letters*, ed. Mark DeWolfe Howe (Cambridge, Mass., 1941), II, 19-20.

WILLIAM JAMES (1842–1910)

1   There is absolutely nothing new in the pragmatic method. Socrates was an adept at it. . . . But these forerunners of pragmatism used it in fragments; they were preluders only. ——*Pragmatism* (New York, 1946), p. 50.

2   The temper of finality is foreign to empiricist minds. They may be dogmatic about their method of building on "hard facts," but they are willing to be sceptical about any conclusions reached by the method at a given time. They aim at accuracy of detail rather than at completeness; are contented to be fragmentary; are less inspiring than the rationalists, often treating the high as a case of "nothing but" the low ("nothing but" self-interest well understood, etc.), but they usually keep more in touch with actual life, are less subjective, and their spirit is obviously more "scientific" in the hackneyed sense of that term. Socrates, Locke, Berkeley, Hume, the Mills,

F. A. Lange, J. Dewey, F. C. S. Schiller, Bergson, and other contemporaries are specimens of this type. —*Some Problems of Philosophy* (New York, 1911), pp. 36-37.

JOSIAH ROYCE (1855-1916)

That the ultimate moral authority for each of us is determined by our own rational will, is admitted even by apparently extreme partisans of authority. Socrates long ago announced the principle in question when he taught that no man is willingly base. —*The Philosophy of Loyalty* (New York, 1908), p. 26.

1

. . . Every science, in dealing with the facts of experience, employs *Methods of Classification,* and is so far still making its own use of the lessons that Socrates taught. —"The Principles of Logic," in *Encyclopaedia of the Philosophical Sciences,* ed. Wilhelm Windelband and Arnold Ruge (London, 1913), I, 74.

2

WILLIAM HERBERT CARRUTH (1859-1924)

Socrates drinking the hemlock,
  And Jesus on the rood;
. . . .
Some call it Consecration,
  And others call it God.
—*Each in His Own Tongue and Other
  Poems* (New York, 1909), pp. 2-3.

JOHN DEWEY (1859-1952)

For any act (as distinct from mere impulse) there must be "theory," and the wider the act, the greater its import, the more exigent the demand for theory. It is not likely that the

1

wheels of moral movement are to be reversed after two thousand and more years. It was Socrates who initiated the movement, when he said that "an unexamined life is not one to be
led by man." Whatever may be the case with savages and
babes, the beginning of every ethical advance, under conditions of civilized existence, must be in a further "examination
of life." Not even customary morality, that of respectability
and of convention, is freed from dependence upon theory; it
simply lives off the funded results of some once-moving examination of life.   ——"Moral Theory and Practice," in *International Journal of Ethics,* I (1892); reprinted in Joseph Ratner, *The Philosophy of John Dewey* (New York, 1928), pp.
311-12.

2   To question the old must inevitably seem irreverent and
anarchical. Some questioned merely to doubt; others, and of
these Socrates was the leader, questioned in order to find a
firmer basis, a more authoritative standard. But naturally the
popular mind did not distinguish between these two classes of
questioners, and so Socrates perished, not merely as the victim of unjust popular calumny, but as the victim of the tragedy of moral progress, of the change from the established to
the new.   ——J. Dewey and J. Tufts, *Ethics* (New York, 1908),
pp. 118-19.

3   We present to ourselves the epoch when philosophy was still
consciously, and not simply by implication, human, when reflective thought had not developed its own technique of
method, and was in no danger of being caught in its own machinery—the time of Socrates. What does the assertion of Socrates that an unexamined life is not one fit to be led by man;
what does this injunction "Know thyself" mean? It means that
the corporate motives and guarantees of conduct are breaking
down. . . . The "Know thyself" of Socrates is the reply to the
practical problem which confronted Athens in his day. Investigation into the true ends and worths of human life, sifting
and testing of all competing ends, the discovery of a method

which should validate the genuine and dismiss the spurious, had henceforth to do for man what consolidated and incorporate custom had hitherto presented as a free and precious gift.

With Socrates the question is as direct and practical as the question of making one's living or of governing the state; it is indeed the same question put in its general form. It is a question that the flute player, the cobbler, and the politician must face no more and no less than the reflective philosopher. The question is addressed by Socrates to every individual and to every group with which he comes into contact. Because the question is practical it is individual and direct. It is a question which every one must face and answer for himself, just as in the Protestant scheme every individual must face and solve for himself the question of his final destiny.

Yet the very attitude of Socrates carried with it the elements of its own destruction. Socrates could not raise the question, or rather demand of every individual that he raise it for himself. Of the answer he declared himself to be as ignorant as was any one. The result could only be a shifting of the center of interest. If the question is so all-important, and yet the wisest of all men must confess that he only knows his own ignorance as to its answer, the inevitable point of further consideration is the discovery of a method which shall enable the question to be answered. This is the significance of Plato. . . . If the Socratic command, "Know thyself," runs against the dead wall of inability to conduct this knowledge, some one must take upon himself the discovery of how the requisite knowledge may be obtained. ——"The Significance of the Problem of Knowledge," in *The Influence of Darwin on Philosophy* (New York, 1910), pp. 275 ff.

The Socratic contention is the need of compelling the com- 4 mon denominator, the common subject, underlying the diversity of views, to exhibit itself. It alone gives a sure standard by which the claims of all assertions may be measured. Until this need is met, discussion is a self-deceiving play with unjudged, unexamined matters, which, confused and shifting, impose themselves upon us.—We are familiar enough with the theory that the Socratic universal, the Platonic idea, was generated by an ignorant transformation of psychological abstractions into self-existent entities. To insist upon this as the key to the Socratic logic is mere caricature. The objectivity of the universal stood for the sense of something decisive and controlling in all reflection, which otherwise is just manipulation of personal prejudices. This sense is as active in modern science as it was in the Platonic dialectic. What Socrates felt was the opinionated, conceited quality of the terms used in the moral and political discussion of his day, as that contrasted with the subject-matter, which, if rightly grasped, would put an end to mere views and argumentations. ——*Essays in Experimental Logic* (Chicago, 1916), pp. 200-01.

5   Although Socrates was doubtless sincerely interested in the reconciliation of the two sides [moral rules and ideals embodied in the traditional code and the matter-of-fact positivistic knowledge which gradually grows up], yet the fact that he approached the matter from the side of matter-of-fact method, giving its canons and criteria primacy, was enough to bring him to the condemnation of death as a contemner of the gods and a corrupter of youth. ——*Reconstruction in Philosophy* (New York, 1920), p. 14.

6   That current customs contradict one another, that many of them are unjust, and that without criticism none of them is fit to be the guide of life was the discovery with which the Athenian Socrates initiated conscious moral theorizing. ——*Human Nature and Conduct* (New York, 1922), p. 78.

7   Present-day philosophy cannot desire a better work than to engage in the act of midwifery that was assigned to it by Socrates twenty-five hundred years ago. ——*Problems of Men* (New York, 1946), p. 20.

RUFUS JONES (1863–1948)

The mysticism of the Platonic movement in reality goes back behind Plato himself and had its creative source in Socrates. . . . Socrates belongs to the order of the prophets. He is in that class of persons, appearing in all ages, who *feel* their connection with the Divine, and who speak and act with an insight far beyond the range of their own account of it. During his entire life he was conscious of an inner guide which he called "the divine something in his breast." Intimation, upon numerous occasions of his life, came to him with an inward compelling power, and he had direct revelations of the suitable course for him to pursue, and these experiences made him feel that he was in an unusual sense under divine care and under divine orders. Feelings, suggestions, incursions, whose origin he could not trace or discover, exercised over him irresistible control. ——*Studies in Mystical Religion* (London, 1919), p. 58.

GEORGE SANTAYANA (1863–1952)

If the happy freedom of the Greeks from religious dogma made them the first natural philosophers, their happy political freedom made them the first moralists. It was no accident that Socrates walked the Athenian agora; it was no petty patriotism that made him shrink from any other scene. His science had its roots there, in the personal independence, intellectual vivacity, and clever dialectic of his countrymen. . . . Having developed in the spirit the consciousness of its meanings and purposes, Socrates rescued logic and ethics for ever from authority. With his friends the Sophists, he made man the measure of all things, after bidding him measure himself, as they neglected to do, by his own ideal. That brave humanity which had first raised its head in Hellas and had endowed so many things in heaven and earth, where everything was hitherto monstrous, with proportion and use, so that man's works might justify themselves to his mind, now found in Socrates its precise definition; and it was naturally where the Life of Reason had been long cultivated that it came finally to be conceived.— Socrates had, however, a plebeian strain in his humanity, and his utilitarianism, at least in its expression, hardly did justice to what gives utility to life. His condemnation for atheism— if we choose to take it symbolically—was not altogether unjust; the gods of Greece were not honoured explicitly enough in his philosophy. Human good appeared there in its principle; you would not set a pilot to mend shoes, because you knew your own purpose; but what purposes a civilised soul might harbour, and in what highest shapes the good might appear, was a problem that seems not to have attracted his genius. ——*The Life of Reason. Reason in Common Sense* (New York, 1905), pp. 18-19.

2   When Socrates and his two great disciples composed a system of rational ethics they were hardly proposing practical legislation for mankind. One by his irony, another by his frank idealism, and the third by his preponderating interest in history and analysis, showed clearly enough how little they dared to hope. They were merely writing an eloquent epitaph on their country. They were publishing the principles of what had been its life, gathering piously its broken ideals, and interpreting its momentary achievement. ——*The Life of Reason. Reason in Science* (New York, 1905), p. 262.

3   Having become Socratic, the thinking part of mankind devoted all its energies henceforward to defining good and evil in all their grades, and in their ultimate essence; a task which Dante brings to a perfect conclusion. ——*Three Philosophical Poets* (Cambridge, Mass., 1910), p. 77.

4   Several great philosophers, like Socrates and Hume, have come very near to avoiding heresy. . . . But they have not quite

avoided it, for they have assigned to their introspection a public value which it did not have, and have denied the validity
of some of the sciences or of all of them. Had they reported
ingenuously what they perceived (as sometimes they affected
to do), . . . had . . . the ethics of Socrates [not been] intolerant, all their profound radicalism might have left them orthodox. —"Philosophical Heresy" (1915), in *Obiter Scripta*
(New York, 1936), p. 101.

We must remember that ever since the days of Socrates, and 5
especially after the days of Christianity, the dice of thought
have been loaded. Certain pledges have preceded inquiry and
divided the possible conclusions beforehand into the acceptable and the inacceptable, the edifying and the shocking, the
noble and the base. Wonder has no longer been the root of
philosophy, but sometimes impatience at having been cheated
and sometimes fear of being undeceived. The marvel of existence, in which the luminous and the opaque are so romanti-
cally mingled, no longer lay like the sea open to intellectual
adventure, tempting the mind to conceive some bold and curious system of the universe on the analogy of what had been so
far discovered. —*Character and Opinion in the United
States* (New York, 1910), pp. 10-11.

The Sophists and Socrates affected to care nothing about 6
natural science, unless it could make their pot boil. This utilitarianism was humorous in Socrates, and in some of the Sophists unprincipled; but the habit of treating opinions about
nature as rhetorical themes, or as more or less edifying myths,
had disastrous consequences for philosophy. It created metaphysics. . . . After Socrates a theory constructed by reasoning,
in terms of logic, ethics, and a sort of poetic propriety, was
put in the place of physics; the economy of the human mind
was projected into the universe; and nature, in the works of
the metaphysicians, held the mirror up to man. —*Solilo-
quies in England* (London, 1924), pp. 214-5.

7   The wisdom of Socrates was enough for living and judging
rightly in any world, the most magical or the most mechanical,
the best or the worst. I had no need to adopt the cosmology
of Plato—a mythical and metaphysical creation, more or less
playful and desperate, designed to buttress his moral philosophy. I was old enough, when I came under his influence, to
discount this sort of priestcraft in thought, so familiar in
Christian apologists.   ——Preface to the second edition of *The
Life of Reason* (1922), p. xii.

8   Socrates may humorously eschew all science that is useless
to cobblers; he thereby expresses his plebeian hard sense, and
his Hellenic joy in discourse and in moral apologues; but if
he allows this pleasant prejudice to blind him to the possibility of physical discoveries, or of cogent mathematics, he becomes a simple sophist. The moralist needs true knowledge of
nature—even a little astronomy—in order to practice the art of
life in a becoming spirit; and an agnosticism which was not
merely personal, provisional, and humble would be the worst
of dogmas. ——*Scepticism and Animal Faith* (New York,
1923), p. 307.

9   The earliest and noblest form of this idealism [i.e., a gnostic
physics in which chosen ideas pass for facts and felt values for
powers, and not the pure study and love of essence] was the
doctrine of the Platonic Socrates. In somewhat playfully defining the current terms of speech, he very earnestly disen-
tangled the types of moral excellence and the goals of political wisdom. . . .
        This initial phase of Platonism is pregnant with several dif-
ferent possibilities, all of which, perhaps, have not been noticed or developed. In one direction, for instance, it points to
supernaturalism, to the conviction that the soul would never
find her true good until she was disembodied and identified
in contemplation with the ideas which were her natural food.
. . . This view was actually recommended by the Platonic
Socrates in his last hours; probably at any other time it would

have proved embarrassing, and we need not wonder that it remained in abeyance. Had it been pressed, what would have become of that sane plebeian wisdom of Socrates, austerely reducing all beauty to health, all virtue to circumspect knowledge, and all good to utility for pleasure? Evidently in heaven there would be no place any longer for beds and bridles, for ogling love, or for the restless yearning to bring all things to birth in beauty. ——*The Realm of Matter* (New York, 1930), Bk. II of *Realms of Being*, pp. 191-93.

If we wish to make a religion of love, after the manner of 10
Socrates, we must take universal good, not universal power, for the object of our religion. . . . God, according to the Socratic tradition, was the good to which all creation moved; so that any one who loved deeply, and loved God, could not fail, by a necessary inclusion, to love the good which all creatures lived by pursuing, no matter how repulsive these creatures might be to natural human feeling. ——"Ultimate Religion" (1932), in *Obiter Scripta* (New York, 1936), pp. 293-94.

We must be prepared for surprises in morals, no less than 11
in physics, as investigation and analysis proceed. As the blue vault vanishes under the telescope, so moral conventions might dissolve in an enlightened conscience, and we might be abashed to perceive how disconcerting, how revolutionary, how ascetic the inmost oracle of the heart would prove, if only we had ears to hear it. Perhaps a premonition of this ultimate moral disillusion renders Socrates so endlessly patient, diffident, and ironical, so impossible to corrupt and so impossible to deceive.

I think, however, that there was one ethical illusion . . . that warped the moral impartiality of his precepts and rendered him partisan and dogmatic in spite of his intention to be absolutely courteous and fair. He assumed that human nature was simple and immutable. . . . The good that glimmered like buried gold in his own heart must lie also in the hearts of others, and only ignorance or sophistry could keep them

from seeing it. ——*The Realm of Truth* (New York, 1938),
Bk. III of *Realms of Being,* pp. 74-75.

12   [To reserve the moral sphere as a private retreat, a humorous or sarcastic or poetical oasis for the spirit in the environ-
ing desert] was, at heart, the path chosen by Socrates and his
less metaphysical followers, who were not also followers of
Plato. Cynics and Cyrenaics, like Confucians and skeptics elsewhere, summoned the spirit to live on its own resources, in
studious or domestic peace, dominating the world only intellectually, describing it sometimes scientifically, sometimes satir-
ically, and cultivating abstention from passion and war, and
from excessive confidence in fortune or in human virtue. The
spirit, as these men saw, was invulnerable in its idyllic modesty, and far more divine than the thundering gods; yet the
authority of this spirit over the rest of the human soul remained precarious, and philosophy when honest had to be
composed in a minor key. Minor, that is, in its philosophical
pretensions, yet often merry and running into *scherzo;* for in
fact this homely strain in Socratic wisdom has flowed ever
since through all the pleasant fields of literature and worldly
wisdom, while religion and science, not always more spiritually, frowned from the heights. For can it be regarded as a
triumph of spirit to live, artificially exalted, on its own illusions? The zeal, the trembling anxiety, the fanaticism with
which these illusions are sometimes defended betray their
non-spiritual source. They represent psychic and political
forces struggling to maintain a particular form of life, and
dragging the spirit into their vortex, which is by no means
identical with the free and natural organ of spirit.

No doubt the metaphysical side of Socratic philosophy, the
hypostasis of language and morals into cosmic powers, expressed spiritual enthusiasm, and seemed to support it; yet in
the end we find that it contaminated and betrayed the spirit.
Earthly warfare against the world is an earthly and worldly
business; it impoverishes its own side by condemning too large
a part of nature and of human nature, which might also have

served the spirit; and it constrains such spirit as it fosters into a false alliance with particular opinions and moralities. Spirit soon has to cry aloud to be saved from such salvation. — *The Realm of Spirit* (New York, 1940), Bk. IV of *Realms of Being,* pp. 198-200.

Socrates . . . was an austere moralist, what we should call a 13 reactionary and a man of the Right, inveighing against the sophistry and luxury of the age, and idealizing the principles of simpler, harsher, and more religious times. But like all reactionaries that found a new order he was a man of the people, with the tone and manners of that corrupt society which he condemned; and though occasionally he seems to have reached extremes of asceticism and mystic abstraction, which made him the precursor of the Cynics and the monks, he ordinarily passed his days eating and drinking, reasoning and joking, and pushing a plebeian utilitarianism to its most comical consequences. Thus he maintained that his own popeyes, upturned nostrils, and voluminous gross mouth were better and more beautiful than regular features, because they served and expressed better the uses of those organs. Such paradoxes, in raising a laugh, were meant to awaken the conscience. Away, they suggested, with all prejudices, all whims, all empty pleasures. There is a true, a perfect, a sublime Good within reach, to which it would be a joy and a deliverance to sacrifice everything else. —*Ibid.,* pp. 215-16.

If Plato, or Socrates himself, found comfort in this tautology 14 (that the life of Socrates can never be identical with his non-life or non-existence), he is to be congratulated on the degree to which respect for the *truth*, essentially eternal, has overcome in his mind the animal impulse to go on living: an impulse which, after triumphing in a complete human life, is necessarily defeated. A timely and noble death, like that of Socrates, eternally crowns, far from destroying, his appointed existence. —*The Idea of Christ in the Gospels. A Critical Essay* (New York, 1946), p. 64.

15   It was a sad misfortune for Christian theory that it drew its
philosophy from the disciples of Socrates rather than from his
predecessors, who had faced the world bravely and without
prejudice; for Socrates and his followers, in the interests of
morals and politics, which in their time were in a parlous
state, had thought to save ancient society by attributing to the
universe, quite falsely, a political and moral constitution. This
unhappy method not only verbalised natural science but represented morality and holiness as hanging on imaginary physical sections, and not on the inherent vocation of human life
and mind.   —*Ibid.*, p. 237.

16   Without any pretence to classical or historical learning I
imagined myself intruding into the company of those ancient
sages Democritus and Socrates, whom I recognized to be my
real masters, above the heads of all the moderns. I returned to
them as a sort of prodigal son, yet also as a secret critic . . .
Socrates, supreme in ideal morality, would have imposed on
all mankind for ever his archaic ideal of a Greek City.
—*Dialogues in Limbo* (New York, 1949), Preface to the new
edition, p. vii.

17   THE STRANGER [i.e., Santayana]: I suspect, for instance, that
what you [Alcibiades] did to the Hermae secretly delighted
him [Socrates].
    ALCIBIADES: What an extraordinary notion! He, so pious a
man!
    THE STRANGER: I mean it seriously. That which was ribaldry
and sacrilege in you fell in with the beginnings of iconoclasm
and prudery in him; he thinks even old thrice-chastened
Homer immoral; and knavery and vice, if only they confess
that they are such, are more interesting to him and more congenial than an unconcerned and fearless liberty. He combines
the illusions of a paederast with the self-immolating zeal of a
missionary.   —*Ibid.*, p. 179.

18   THE STRANGER: Rational beauty he [Socrates] describes perfectly, only he overlooks and even denies this little fact: that it

is not reason that rules the world. What ought to be, according to human reason, never will be according to the course of nature. Nonetheless, to see and proclaim what ought to be according to human reason is of the greatest importance, not because we can make it happen except in trifles and ironically, but because thereby we uncover the heart and the mind of man, and enable him to live knowingly and undeceived. The gods made us, but Socrates reveals to us what the gods have made. That is why I say that he has taught us a more precious lesson than Prometheus, or any other material benefactor of mankind. He has taught us to distinguish arts that are truly profitable from those that are at once irksome and vain.

ALCIBIADES: Why then was he unfortunate in being right . . . ?

THE STRANGER: Because all true goods are not compatible in human life. Good fortune lies in having the gifts and virtues appropriate to your time and country, so that you need not pine for those that then and there are out of season. Both you [Alcibiades] and Socrates, it seems to me, though apparently very much in the fashion of your day, were at heart strangers in it, as I have been in mine: not spring flowers or summer fruits, but only autumn leaves. No chance for you to play the hero like Achilles or Theseus; no chance for Socrates to restore the virtues proper to an archaic city. Yet you each had an autumnal beauty or wisdom of your own. ——*Ibid.*, pp. 185-86.

ALCIBIADES: There he goes, the brave old fellow. Never was   19
there anyone like him, and there never will be. What a hero
he is!

THE STRANGER: And how unfortunate!

ALCIBIADES: I know; but what can you expect when superior people must submit to be judged by mobs? After all, we must all die in the end, and Socrates lived to a ripe old age. What matters it whether a cup of hemlock carries you off, or a sluggish liver?

THE STRANGER: I was not thinking of his death, which was

magnificent, but of his philosophy. His work was perhaps the most important and the most generally praised that anyone ever accomplished in moral philosophy; and yet how profoundly disappointing! . . . You see how intrepid he is in the pursuit of truth and how untiring; but do you think he has ever found it? On this very point which we have been discussing [that in no form of true beauty can there be anything sinister or sensuous or ethereal], has he grasped more than a thin ghost of the truth?

ALCIBIADES: You were obliged to admit that he was right.

THE STRANGER: Yes, verbally. . . . His philosophy is all a play of words or logic of concepts, backed in his person by a heroic ascetic discipline, yet in itself arid and verbal, and fit to defend any fanaticism or superstition. If he were interested in nature and in the miscellaneous budding and joys of life, what would be the need of arguments and reasonings, and how could he ever have thought it an excellent method to squeeze the conventional language of ignorant people in order to distil the pure essence of the beautiful?

.   .   .   .

THE STRANGER: Socrates and you, though thinking you still worshipped the gods of Hellas, really were forerunners of very un-Greek loves and very romantic rebellions.

ALCIBIADES: So that according to you the judges who condemned Socrates were guided by a true though hopeless allegiance to the gods and to the laws of Athens. . . . Socrates, if he heard you, would roll his popeyes in a terrific passion and transfix you with six questions like six Homeric Spears.

THE STRANGER: His wrath would not be philosophical; for here [in limbo], where the harvests of every season are garnered together, what matters it whether, while we lived, we worked at sowing, or reaping, or winter plowing? ——*Ibid.*, pp. 214-17.

20   If the wisest man of Greece—Socrates—had been asked to pronounce on the same political or military alternatives [as the Greek oracle] would his advice have been better than that

of the Pythoness and her tripos? I am afraid that the decisions
of oracles or of philosophers at best divert the course of very
slender streams. . . . Socrates resisted the Thirty Tyrants with
heroic courage; but his example, like that of Phocion, was
powerless to arrest the general decay. ——*Dominations and
Powers* (New York, 1951), pp. 234-35.

What Socrates seems to have forgotten to say [in his doc- 21
trine that it is knowledge, not accidental desires and opinions,
that makes conduct rational and right] is that the knowledge
requisite to make action rational in this sense lies entirely beyond the reach of mankind. . . .
Socrates . . . was providentially inspired as a prophet of his
time, which was the turning point in the fortunes of ancient
Greece. The age of political and plastic arts was over, and
that of private moral reflection and conversion had begun. His
imagination, if we may trust the Utopia that Plato puts into
his mouth, was archaically political. ——*Ibid.*, pp. 300-301.

Socrates had been stunned by the same tragedy of his coun- 22
try [as the early Greek philosophers]—very much as Europe
is stunned today—and the refuge he took in the inner man
gave the signal for the current of Greek philosophy to turn
away from its honest naturalism and merge in the turbid but
impetuous flood of supernatural revelations. ——*Ibid.*, pp.
336-37.

PAUL ELMER MORE (1864–1937)

I can speak only of what I know, and as for me, as one de- 1
ceptive hope after another has fallen away, I go back to the
life of Socrates and the reasoning of Plato and am never deceived. I am assured that they were seeking what I seek, and
that they attained what hardly and with their borrowed
strength I may at last attain. ——"Socrates," in *Shelburne
Essays* (6th series; New York, 1909), p. 247.

2   Socrates, dearly as he loved his native city, belonged not to
a city or country, but to the world. . . .
       Socrates gave the impulse to a new way of approaching the
perennial questions that interest and trouble man's soul. By
his life and death he gave to doubting men renewed assurance
that virtue is the only real happiness, more to be desired than
riches or honour or power or life itself, and that there is a
lamp of truth to guide us in virtue's path.   —*Ibid.,* p. 267.

3   The heroic struggle of Socrates with the Athenian people
may be regarded as typical of the long contest that was to
follow. . . . A few men, handing on the new ideal of the master and developing its latent philosophy, prepared the way
for the more efficient and in some respects antagonistic revelation of Christianity, and for the Platonism that has united
in one family all the spiritually minded inquirers of the ages.
Yet we must never forget that the teaching of the Athenian
sage still in its simplest form persists through all its later developments, and still is one of the powers working for truth
and righteousness in the world.   —*Ibid.,* p. 272.

IRVING BABBITT (1865–1933)

1   Socrates, according to Rousseau, praises ignorance. Rousseau does not often indulge in such an unblushing sophism.
What Socrates actually asserted, of course, was, that though
men imagine they know something they are in reality ignorant. The American scientist who complained only the other
day that nobody knows more than seven billionths of one
percent about anything was merely echoing what Socrates
said many centuries ago at Athens. But Socrates would have
men cherish precisely this fraction of knowledge, however in-
finitesimal, and the faculties by which they have attained it,
in the hope that they may ultimately add to it a few more
billionths of a percent. We can imagine with what irony he

would have greeted any Wordsworthian or Rousseauistic talk about "the false secondary power by which we multiply distinctions." On the contrary he spent his whole life in multiplying distinctions, and may indeed be regarded as the founder of formal logic. —"The Romantic Confusion of the Arts," in *The New Laokoön* (Boston, 1919), pp. 91-92.

The irony of Socrates . . . is not of the centrifugal character. Socrates professes ignorance, and this profession seems very ironical, for it turns out that his ignorance is more enlightened, that is, more central than other men's swelling conceit of knowledge. It does not follow that Socrates is insincere in his profession of ignorance; for though his knowledge may be as light as that of the ordinary Athenian, he sees that in comparison with true and perfect knowledge it is only darkness. For Socrates was no mere rationalist; he was a man of insight, one would even be tempted to say a mystic were it not for the corruption of the term mystic by the romanticists. This being the case he saw that man is by his very nature precluded from true and perfect knowledge. A path, however, opens up before him towards this knowledge, and this path he should seek to follow even though it is in a sense endless, even though beyond any centre he can attain within the bounds of his finite experience there is destined always to be something more central. Towards the mere dogmatist, the man who thinks he has achieved some fixed and final centre, the attitude of Socrates is that of scepticism. This attitude implies a certain degree of detachment from the received beliefs and conventions of his time, and it is all the more important to distinguish here between Socrates and the romanticists because of the superficial likeness. . . . Socrates himself was perhaps needlessly unconventional and also unduly inclined to paradox—as when he suggested to the jury who tried him that as an appropriate punishment he should be supported at the public expense in the prytaneum. Yet in his inner spirit and in spite of certain minor eccentricities,

2

Socrates was neither a superman nor a Bohemian, but a humanist. Now that the critical spirit was abroad and the traditional basis for conduct was failing, he was chiefly concerned with putting conduct on a positive and critical basis. In establishing this basis his constant appeal is to actual experience, and the more homely this experience the more it seems to please him. While working out the new basis for conduct he continues to observe the existing laws and customs; or if he gets away from the traditional discipline it is towards a stricter discipline: if he repudiates in aught the common sense of his day, it is in favor of a commoner sense. One may say indeed that Socrates and the Rousseauists (who are in this respect like some of the Sophists) are both moving away from convention but in opposite directions. What the romanticist opposes to convention is his "genius," that is his unique and private self. What Socrates opposes to convention is his universal and ethical self. ——*Rousseau and Romanticism* (Boston, 1919), pp. 243 ff.

3   I have been dwelling . . . on the indispensableness of a keen Socratic dialectic and of the right knowledge it brings for those who aspire to be critical humanists. ——*Ibid.*, p. 385.

4   The outstanding fact of the present period . . . has been the weakening of traditional standards. An emergency has arisen not unlike that with which Socrates sought to cope in ancient Athens. Anyone who is untraditional and seeks at the same time to be discriminating must almost necessarily own Socrates as his master. As is well known, Socrates sought above all to be discriminating in his use of general terms. Before allowing one's imagination and finally one's conduct to be controlled by a general term, it would seem wise to submit it to a Socratic scrutiny. It is, therefore, unfortunate that at a time like the present, which plainly calls for a Socrates, we should instead have got a Mencken. ——"The Critic and American Life," in *On Being Creative and Other Essays* (Boston, 1932), p. 205.

MADISON GRANT (1865–1937)

Socrates and Diogenes were apparently un-Greek and represent remnants of some early race, perhaps of Paleolithic man [cf. their busts with other Greek statues]. The history of their lives indicates that each was recognized by his fellow countrymen as in some degree alien, just as the Jews apparently regarded Christ as, in some indefinite way, non-Jewish. ——*The Passing of the Great Race* (New York, 1931), p. 227.

HARRY ALLEN OVERSTREET (1875——)

The ordinary Athenian could not comprehend that queer   1
fellow, Socrates, who insisted upon pestering everybody with embarrassing questions. Why did he not stick to his work, make a decent living for his Xantippe, and leave respectable folk to go undisturbed about their business? They could not see that Socrates was loyal to a new kind of loyalty. Today that new kind of loyalty is both understood and respected. Every true scientist is a Socrates who spends his life putting questions to the stubborn realities that he confronts. We honor Socrates today because we are now able to see that what he perceived as the true way of life is the true way of life—in short, we have moved up to Socrates. ——*The Enduring Quest* (New York, 1931), p. 229.

We might say that Socrates' thoughts continue to endure.   2
They have been woven into the processes of life. Here in the twentieth century is a young man who has suddenly taken on a new lease of life after reading the account of Socrates' challenge to his jurors. The value, then, that Socrates generated over two thousand years ago still endures and is actually operating in the living world. ——*Ibid.*, pp. 249-50.

Socrates spent a lifetime revealing to his fellow Athenians   3
that what they thought was the exercise of reason was actually

the exercise of unreason. Therefore—as though, perversely, to prove themselves as unreasonable as he said they were—they put him to death. ——*The Mature Mind* (New York, 1948), p. 105.

WILLIAM ELLERY LEONARD (1876–1944)

1   Socrates, in a sense that would justify honorable mention of his name and fame in any work on religious leaders, proclaimed long before Paul the unknown God unto the Athenians. ——*Socrates, Master of Life* (Chicago, 1929), p. 2.

2   He was, I believe, an incorrigible utilitarian. The measure of any thing's worth was to him in its adaptation to use. But after all, the crux is in the content of the use; and Socrates recognized only noble uses. Reason as we will, we cannot reason away his implicit idealism. ——*Ibid.*, pp. 85-86.

3   Socrates is more than the facts of his life and more than the Socratic teaching. . . . His moral grandeur still towers over Athens and her shattered temples to rebuke the world. . . . This is a true superman. . . . But, like the rest of the world's eminent, he falls short of epitomizing humanity. Some qualities he had not. . . . Truly, he lacked humanity's worst passions and vices and shared apparently in few of its blunders. And on the other hand, though a Greek, he had little joy in the glory and the charm of nature or of art. . . . He had not the creative imagination. He was no poet, like Jesus and Mohammed, each in his way. His kindliness had yet none of the plangent pity for the sorrow of life, naught of the throbbing love and enfolding arms. His righteousness . . . burned with no fiery imprecation, entreaty, or command, and rose, cool, observing, undepressed, assistant, before his own shortcomings or the sins of the world . . . as a mode of thinking and acting among men, not in prostration or in ecstasy: he was

neither a god-smitten nor a god-intoxicated man. —*Ibid.*, pp. 105 ff.

WALTER BOUGHTON PITKIN (1878–1953)

Were I to set down faithfully here the details of my first meetings with Socrates, and were I to add nothing else, you would get a false picture. As you read on, keep in mind then that in these few hundred words are telescoped intellectual events which spread over a quarter-century.

Lloyd [7] started it all. . . . The art of intellectual cross-examination came to life in Lloyd. As he went on thinking, he would pause to put a question to one of us. In a few minutes he had us in a frightful mess. We had walked into a trap. Lloyd smiled gently, then went on with his thinking. After class a few of us would argue the way out of the trap. As we strove, we deepened our respect for both Socrates and Lloyd.

We were beginning to discover the terrible power of a presupposition. We saw, then all too unsurely, that most men did not know which presuppositions they were holding as they went on thinking. To find the substratum was Socrates' deepest urge. He did not realize what he was doing. He thought he was merely trying to find somebody who truly knew something. Yet he was forever working backward, in his quizzing, toward the unconscious propositions a man entertained. To this extent he was pioneering toward modern logic.

Dry as dust? Yes, so it was then. But under desert sands he who knows the desert digs and strikes cool water. So beneath all the weavings of inner logic which Lloyd carried on, as he led us slowly through the history of Western philosophy, beginning as usual with Thales. In time he had finished with the dry surface dust of Plato and Socrates. And then. . . .

He told us, in his own manner and words, the story of ugly

[7] Alfred H. Lloyd (1864–1927), Professor of Philosophy at the University of Michigan from 1891 to 1927.

old Socrates. The mood changed. The lights went down. A
strange wind blew. . . . A great rabble stood in silence around
an old man. The old man smiled calmly as he talked. . . .

"So I bear no resentment against those who have condemned
me. But this much I do beg of them. Punish my sons, when
they grow up. Hurt them as I have hurt you, if they seem to
care for riches or anything else before virtue, and if they
think themselves to be something when they are nothing. Reproach them . . . for conceiving themselves to be something
when they are worth nothing. . . ."

Somebody was weeping. We looked around. What? Lloyd?
How did he get here? He was hurrying from the room. . . .

The Athenian rabble had melted into thin air. Socrates had
gone too. We tiptoed from the room, back into the brisk early
winter air of Michigan. . . .

That night we sat around wondering. Lloyd, this twanging
old Yankee, had been teaching this course for years . . . and
yet he cried as he told us about Socrates.

. . . . I went on wondering. And still I wonder. . . . Yes, the
Athenians condemned this old codger to death on two counts.
He was impious. And he adopted new ways of living. These
new ways ran counter to the old ways, the approved ways, the
ways of the ancient culture. Hence the fellow outraged things
holy. For the holy is the hallowed; the hallowed is the old, the
accepted, the habitual.

Yes, I began to see. This Socrates was the world's most
magnificent Social Misfit. He lacked all respect for the ways
of the herd. He dared question men about the most sacred
beliefs and customs. Thus he brought into disrepute both the
priests and the politicians, the two eternal racketeers of culture.

The crowning infamy, however, was Socrates' cold exposure
of the abject ignorance of the priests and the politicians. His
cross-examining laid bare their tiny souls and their midget
minds. So it was war to the death. Socrates and Athenian culture could not exist in the same place and time. Darwin was
right; it was the struggle for survival. And in this struggle

Socrates proved himself to be greater than the animal that laughs.

He was the first thinker on record who knew that he knew nothing. He was the first to realize that he was worth nothing. And he begged his judges to punish his sons if ever they slipped into the commonplace paranoid delusion of thinking themselves of some consequence. In Socrates' day nobody knew about paranoia, yet a few like him recognized the mental disease even in its mild form of conceit. Socrates alone understood that this paranoid trend was the blight of the human race. Today's thinkers still have this to learn. They have not caught up with the ugly old codger.

Yes, I began to see. This fellow understood his own complete unimportance, and that made him the most important man in the history of our race. Here was a man so unimportant in his own esteem that he would not fight for his life, as all healthy apes and farmers and ministers and politicians do. Hence he alone was deathless. Thousands of years after the last mighty war hero has been forgotten, men wiser than any of us will be talking of Socrates.

Here was a queer chap born out of his time and place, in a small society blighted with the usual frozen culture whose racketeers had to kill everybody who cast doubt upon the system. He was a man without a culture, a man beyond all cultures. He belonged to a world which may not come into being for another thousand years. He sought precise knowledge. So, though he never knew it, he was the forerunner of all scientists. He sought insight into man's nature, so he was the forerunner of all psychologists in particular.

And he knew human nature well enough, even in his day, to understand and to forgive his accusers and those who killed him. He also came closer to knowing himself than did any later philosopher or psychologist I know. . . .

Forty-seven years have passed since I began reading the history of philosophy. As I now look at myself, I see that the only influence of the first magnitude between Thales and Dewey was this tough, ugly, ill-mannered and shiftless fellow who so

overwhelmed the rich olive merchant, Plato, that Plato made
him the hero of the world's greatest drama, *Man Against the
Herd*. ——"Then came Socrates," chap. 46 in *On My Own*
(New York, 1944), pp. 235 ff.

DON MARQUIS (1878–1937)

1   Who storms the moss-grown walls of eld
                 And beats some falsehood down
            Shall pass the pallid gates of death
                 Sans laurel, love or crown;
            For him who fain would teach the world
                 The world holds hate in fee—
            For Socrates, the hemlock cup;
                 For Christ, Gethsemane.
——"The Wages," in *Dreams and Dust* (New York, 1915), p. 99.

2   How often when they find a sage
                 As sweet as Socrates or Plato
            They hand him hemlock for his wage,
                 Or bake him like a sweet potato!
            ——"Taking the Longer View," in *Noah an' Jonah
            an' Cap'n John Smith* (New York, 1921), p. 133.

MORRIS R. COHEN (1880–1947)

1   The great service of Socrates to humanity was surely not
in his somewhat superficial criticism of the Athenian electoral
machinery of his day, but rather in developing certain intellectual methods, and suggesting to Plato certain doctrines as
to the nature of the soul and ideas—doctrines which in spite
of their impracticality have served for over two thousand
years to raise men above the groveling, clawing existence in
which so much of our life is sunk.   ——*The Faith of a Liberal*
(New York, 1946), p. 88.

In the philosophic tradition, which begins with Socrates 2 and finds its expression in the dialogues of Plato, we have the classic expressions of the well-bred courtesy of free men; and I think that in times of bitter strife between classes and nations men will do well to study these philosophic classics. —*Ibid.,* p. 414.

We see this spirit [of free inquiry] in the teaching of phi- 3 losophy by dialogue. Socrates proves propositions to a slave boy, not by telling him on the authority of his own wisdom but by showing him that this truth is obtainable by clear thinking. —*Ibid.,* p. 457.

Socrates, if Plato's account be right, was a humanist of the 4 type that underestimates purely natural knowledge—as can be seen by his references to Anaxagoras. In that regard Socrates only continued the humanism of Sophocles, that not only made man the center of its interests, but paid little attention to the wider phases of nature which had interested the non-Athenian naturalistic philosophers. —*The Meaning of Human History* (LaSalle, 1947), p. 203.

WALTER LIPPMANN (1889—)

. . . When Socrates faced his accusers, his answer to the 1 accusation of heresy must certainly have sounded unresponsive. "I do believe," he said, "that there are gods, and in a higher sense than that in which my accusers believe in them." That is all very well. But to believe in a "higher sense" is also to believe in a different sense. —*A Preface to Morals* (New York, 1929), pp. 10-11.

There is no doubt that in one form or another, Socrates 2 and Buddha, Jesus and St. Paul, Plotinus and Spinoza, taught that the good life is impossible without asceticism, that without renunciation of many of the ordinary appetites, no man can really live well. Prejudice against the human body and a tendency to be disgusted with its habits, a contempt for the ordinary concerns of daily experience is to be found in all of them. . . . —*Ibid.*, p. 155.

3   Apart from the asceticism of primitive peoples . . . there is a sane and civilized asceticism which presents a quite different face. There is, for example, the argument of Socrates in the *Phaedo* that the body is a nuisance to a philosopher in search of truth. —*Ibid.*, p. 159.

BRAND BLANSHARD (1892——)

1   When we seem to differ about ultimate goods, do we really have the same goods in mind? And if we do have the same goods in mind, do we not always value them in the same way? Socrates, confronting a confusion and relativism strikingly like our own, believed that we did. He believed that the nearer we came to understanding what we meant by the true and the good, the nearer we came to understanding each other, since in the end we all meant the same. What was deepest in each was common to all. And philosophy was the midwife which brought the hidden meanings to light. So teaching, he set the course of Western thought. —"The Opportunity of Philosophy," in *Philosophy in American Education* (New York, 1945), p. 102.

2   Philosophy means philosophizing. It is not truth but the search for truth, a constantly baffled but passionately and stubbornly renewed pursuit of understanding. Socrates declared himself the lover, the wooer, the pursuer of truth, not the bridegroom in complacent possession. So the philosopher remains today. —*Ibid.*, p. 109.

FRENCH AND RELATED

QUEEN MARGUERITE DE NAVARRE (1492–1549)

Socrates received the light [of knowledge about God] when he gently accepted the hemlock, in the right belief that the soul was immortal. ——*Les dernières poésies* (Paris, 1896), p. 209.

FRANÇOIS RABELAIS (*c.* 1495–1553)

Very illustrious drinkers and you, my precious pocky ones—for to you, not others, my writings are dedicated—Alcibiades in Plato's dialog entitled the *Symposion,* praising his teacher Socrates, without dispute the prince of philosophers, says among other things that he is like [the ancient busts of] Silenus. . . . Such a one, he said, was Socrates: because seeing him from the outside and judging him by external appearances you would not have given the skin of an onion for him, so ugly he was in physique and ridiculous in his bearing, with pointed nose, the sidelong gaze of a bull, and the face of a fool, unrefined in manners, rustic in clothing, poor in means, luckless with women, inept for all public duties, always laughing, always holding his own in drinking with anyone, always ridiculing, always concealing his divine wisdom. But on opening that box you would have found inside a heavenly and priceless drug, more than human insight, marvelous virtue, invincible courage, unequaled sobriety, secure contentment, perfect self-assurance, and an incredible contempt of everything for which human beings do so much watching, running, toiling, sailing, and fighting. ——"Prologue de l'auteur," *Gargantua* (1542), in *Oeuvres* (Paris, 1913), I, 3 ff.

MICHEL DE MONTAIGNE (1533–1592) [1]

1   How often does one see well-known personalities, when led
off to death—and not just a simple death but one connected
with disgrace and perhaps even with severe torture—bring to
it such self-assurance, now derived from strong convictions,
now from natural simplicity, that one does not notice any
change from their ordinary condition; settling their domestic
affairs, commending themselves to their friends, singing,
preaching, and entertaining the people, even bringing in an
occasional word of humor and drinking to their acquaintances,
as well as Socrates did? (A) —"That the Sense of Good and
Evil Things Depends Largely on the Opinion We Have of
Them," I, 14, in *Les essais* (1580–95), ed. Pierre Villey (Paris,
1922), I, 60.

2   Socrates was asked from where he came. He did not answer, "from Athens," but "from the world." He, who had an
unusually open and wide imagination, embraced the universe
as his city, assigned his acquaintances, his associations, and
his affections to all the human race, not like us, who do not
heed anyone but ourselves (A). —"On the Education of
Children," I, 26, in *Les essais,* I, 202.

3   The prize and height of virtue lies in the ease, the usefulness, and the pleasure of its exercise, so far removed from
difficulty that children can attain it as well as adults, simple-
minded as well as refined people. Regulation is its tool, not
compulsion. Socrates, virtue's prime favorite, gives up its force
deliberately in order to glide into his progress (C). —*Ibid.,*
p. 208.

  [1] The letters A, B, and C following the quotations or parts of them
refer to the editions of the *Essays* of 1580, 1588, and 1595 respectively,
thus indicating the development of Montaigne's estimate of Socrates.

Because Socrates alone had seriously absorbed the precept 4
of his God to know himself, and by his study had arrived at
despising himself, he alone was considered worthy of being
called a sage. If any man knows himself like this, he should
make himself known boldly by his words (C).   ——"Of Exercise," II, 16, in *Les essais,* II, 68.

Thus far I got along fairly to my satisfaction. But at the 5
end of this discourse [that the name of virtue presupposes
difficulty and opposition and cannot be exercised without an
adversary] it occurs to my imagination that the soul of Socrates, which is the most perfect that has come to my attention,
would in my account deserve little commendation. For I
cannot conceive in his personality any stirring of a vicious
concupiscence. I cannot imagine that there should be any difficulty or any constraint in the course of his virtue: I know
that reason was so powerful and so supreme in him that he
would never have allowed a vicious appetite strength enough
to be born. I have nothing to set over against a virtue so sublime. I think I can see him marching at a victorious and tri-
umphant pace, in pomp and at his ease, without opposition or
disturbance (A).   ——"On Cruelty," II, 11, in *Les essais,* II,
126.

Who among those whose brain has been colored—however 6
little—by the true philosophy can be content to imagine Socrates merely free of fear and passion in the accident of his
prison, of his chains, and of his condemnation? And who
does not recognize in him, beyond firmness and constancy
(that was his ordinary attitude), also I know not what new
contentment and conscious gaiety in his ideas and last conduct? (A) When he quivers, at the pleasant sensation of
scratching his leg after the irons have been taken off, does
he not proclaim an equal sweetness and joy in his soul at
being unshackled from the past inconveniences and at enter-
ing into the knowledge of the things to come? (C) I beg

Cato to forgive me: His death was more tragic and more exalted. But *this* death, though I cannot say how, is even more beautiful (A). ——"On Cruelty," III, 2, in *Les essais*, II, 128-29.

7   The virtuous actions of Socrates and of Cato remain vain and unprofitable, since they had no end and had no regard for the love of and obedience to the true creator, and ignored God (A). ——"Apology for Raymond Sebonde," II, 12, in *Les essais*, II, 158.

8   To me there is nothing more illustrious in the life of Socrates than the way in which, when he had thirty whole days to ponder on his death sentence, he assimilated it during all that time with a most certain hope, without commotion, without inner change, and with a manner of acting and speaking toned down and expressing indifference, rather than affected and raised by the weight of such thought (C). ——"How to Judge of the Death of Others," II, 13, in *Les essais*, II, 377.

9   The virtue of Alexander on his stage seems to me to represent much less strength than that of Socrates in his lowly and obscure sphere of action. I can easily conceive of Socrates in the place of Alexander; to conceive of Alexander in that of Socrates I cannot. To him who would ask the former what he knows how to do, the answer would be: to subjugate the world; to him who would ask the latter, it would be: to live a human life in accordance with its natural condition, a knowledge much more comprehensive, more weighty and legitimate. The highest condition of the soul does not consist in striding high, but in good order (B). ——"On Repentance," III, 2, in *Les essais*, III, 33.

10   The other lesson [compared with evading evil] is too high and too difficult. That is, it is reserved for superior men to concentrate purely on the matter before us, to consider and evaluate it. It is the unique property of a Socrates to approach

death with his usual expression, to be familiar with it and play with it. He does not look for any comfort outside the situation. Death seems to him a natural and indifferent accident. He focusses it clearly and is ready for it without looking elsewhere (B). ——"On Diversions," III, 4, in *Les essais,* III, 65.

Socrates was human; and he did not want to be or to seem   11
anything else (C). ——"On Verses from Virgil," III, 5, in *Les essais,* III, 193.

Socrates makes his soul move with what is natural and   12
common: a peasant said this; a woman said that (B). He never talks about anyone but carters, carpenters, cobblers, and masons (C). Here are inductions and analogies drawn from the most common and familiar actions of men; everyone understands him. We should never have discovered the nobility and splendor of his admirable conceptions under so vulgar a form: we (B), who think everything flat and low that is not exalted by learning (C) and who do not notice riches save in pomp and showiness. . . . He proposed to himself no vain fancies; his design was to furnish us with real things and precepts that really and immediately serve life. . . . He was also always one and the same and raised himself not by spurts but by temperament to the highest pitch of vigor; or, to say it better, he did not rise at all, but rather brought down and reduced to its original and natural level, and subjected to it, all the asperities and difficulties; for in Cato one can see quite clearly that this is a gesture strained far beyond the common level; in the brave exploits of his life and in his death we find him always mounted upon high horses. The other marches always on the ground, at a soft and ordinary pace, treats the most useful subjects and conducts himself both in death and in the roughest straits that present themselves in the ordinary manner of human life.

It has been our good fortune that the man most worthy to be known and to be presented to the world as an example should also be the one of whom we have the most certain knowledge; he has been explored by the most clear-sighted men who ever were; the testimonies we have of him are admirable both in fidelity and completeness.

It is a great thing that he was able so to guide the pure imagination of a child that, without altering or stretching, he produced the most beautiful effects of our soul. He does not present it as either exalted or rich; he only presents it as healthy, but assuredly with a lively and clean health. By these common and natural resources, by these ordinary and common devices, without being emotional or angry, he set up not only the most orderly, but the most vigorous beliefs, actions, and manners that ever were. It was he who brought human wisdom back from heaven, where she had wasted her time, in order to restore her to man, with whom her most proper, her most laborious and useful business lies. Watch him plead before his judges; see the reasons by which he awakens his courage to the hazards of war; what arguments fortify his patience against slander, tyranny, death, and the bad humor of his wife; there is nothing in all this borrowed from the arts and sciences; the plainest men can recognize in it their own means and strength. It is not possible to go farther and deeper than he. He has done human nature a great favor by showing it how much it can do by itself (B). ——"On Physiognomy," III, 12, in *Les essais,* III, 341-42.

13   We need no special science in order to live at ease. Socrates teaches us that [this knowledge] is within ourselves, and that we have both the way to find it there and to make use of it (B). ——*Ibid.,* p. 343.

14   We shall not be in want of good masters, interpreters of natural simplicity. Socrates will be one of them. For, from what I remember, he speaks about this way to the judges who are to decide over his life and death: [here follows a rather brief free paraphrase of Plato's *Apology,* especially 40 ff., 38, and 36, in order]. This is (B) not cut and dried pleading but,

while here and there naïve and lowly (C), of an unimaginable grandeur (B), truthful, frank, and just, beyond any example (C), and given under such pressure! (B) Verily, he had ample reason to prefer it to the one which the great orator Lysias had prepared for him, excellently phrased in the courtroom manner, but unworthy of such a noble criminal. Had an imploring voice ever been heard out of the mouth of Socrates? Did that superb virtue fail in the face of its supreme opportunity? And had his rich and powerful nature committed its defense to art, and, in its supreme test, renounced truth and simplicity, the ornaments of his speaking, to adorn and deck itself with the embellishments of figures and flourishes of a studied oration? He was very wise, and true to himself, not to corrupt the style of an incorruptible life and such a sacred image of the human form, to prolong by a year his decrepit age, and to betray the immortal memory of that glorious end. He owed his life not to himself but the world as an example. Would it not have been a public loss if he had concluded it in a leisurely and obscure manner? (C) Assuredly, that casual and indifferent way of looking at death deserved that posterity should consider it so much the more, which is exactly what it did. . . . If anyone should think that, with so many examples to choose from for my purpose among the words of Socrates, I had ill chosen this speech, and should consider it far above common thinking, I have done so knowingly. For I think differently and hold that this is a speech which in its rank and genuineness goes behind and is deeper than the common opinions. It represents (B) in an inartificial, natural, and childlike sincerity (C) the pure and first impression (B) and innocence (C) of nature; for it is to be believed that we have naturally a fear of pain but not of death by reason of itself. . . . Besides, is not the way of arguing here applied by Socrates equally admirable for its simplicity and its forcefulness? Truly, it is much easier to talk like Aristotle and to live like Caesar than to talk and to live like Socrates. Here lies the climax of perfection and difficulty. Art cannot attain to it (B). ——*Ibid.*, pp. 362-66.

15   Socrates was a perfect exemplar of all great qualities! I am
vexed that he met with a body and a face as vulgar as his
are said to have been and so unsuited to the beauty of his
soul—himself so amorous of and so smitten with beauty.
Nature did him an injustice. . . . As Socrates said, his physical
unshapeliness would have rightly accused him of a similar
defect in his soul, had he not corrected it by education. But
I believe that in saying so he did but joke, as was his custom.
Never did so excellent a soul form itself (C). —*Ibid.*, p. 369.

16   Universal reason, implanted in every man who is not depraved, which cures Socrates of all inclination to vice, makes
him obey the men and the gods who rule his city and be
courageous in his death, not because his soul is immortal, but
because it is mortal. What a ruinous doctrine for all government, and much more damaging than ingenuous and
subtle, which persuades the people that religious faith is
sufficient by itself, without morals, to satisfy divine justice!
Practice makes us see an enormous difference between devotion and conscience (C). —"On Physiognomy," III, 13, in
Les essais, III, 372.

17   In this matter of knowing oneself, the fact that everyone
seems so relaxed and satisfied, and thinks that he knows himself sufficiently, indicates that no one understands what it
means (B), as Socrates shows to Euthydemus in Xenophon
(C). I myself, who profess nothing else, discover in it such
depth and variety that my apprenticeship has had no other
fruit than to teach me how much more remains for me to
learn. . . . It is by virtue of my own experience that I accuse
the ignorance of man, which is in my opinion the surest part
of the school of the world. Those who do not want to conclude this for themselves, on the strength of as vain an example as mine or theirs, let them recognize it on that of Socrates, the master of masters (B). —"On Experience," III,
13, in *Les essais*, III, 393-94.

Aristippus defended only the body, as if we had no soul; 18
Zeno embraced only the soul, as if we had no body. Both thus
vitiated matters. Pythagoras, they say, followed a philosophy
completely based on contemplation; Socrates [followed] one
based completely on morals and action; and Plato found the
right proportion between the two. But they say so for the
sake of talk, and the true proportion is found in Socrates;
Plato is much more Socratic than Pythagorean, and it suits
him better (C). —*Ibid.*, pp. 438-39.

There is nothing more remarkable about Socrates than the 19
fact that in advanced years he finds the time to take lessons
in dancing and playing instruments, and considers it well
employed. This man stood in ecstasy, for an entire day and
night, in the presence of the whole Greek army, overtaken
and ravished by some deep idea (B). He was also to be the
first to come to the aid of Alcibiades, who had been overwhelmed by his enemies, protecting him with his body and
relieving him from the onslaught with direct force of arms.
He was first among all the people of Athens who, like him,
were revolted by such a disgraceful spectacle, prepared to
rescue Theramenes, when led off to death by the henchmen of
the Thirty Tyrants; and, although not more than two others
had joined him, he only desisted from this bold enterprise
because of the remonstrances of Theramenes himself. He was
seen, when pursued by a beauty which had captivated him,
maintaining a severe self-restraint when needed. He was seen
at the battle of Delium relieving and saving Xenophon, who
had been thrown off his horse (C). He was seen going off to
war again and again (B), walking on ice (C) with his bare
feet, wearing the same garment in winter and summer, ex-
celling all his companions in endurance, and not eating any
differently at a feast than he did ordinarily (B). He was seen
for twenty-seven years wearing the same expression, enduring
hunger, poverty, the unteachableness of his children, the claws
of his wife, and finally slander, tyranny, prison, irons, and

poison (C). But this man—did the obligation to be civil urge him into a drinking bout?—was also the one of the party who held the advantage all the same; one who did not refuse either to play at cobnut with children or to race with them on a hobby horse, and did so in good grace. For all actions, says philosophy, are equally becoming and honorable to the sage. There is good reason for never wearying of holding up the image of this great personality in all patterns and forms of perfection (B). ——*Ibid.,* pp. 441-42.

20   Socrates, its [philosophy's] master and ours, duly values physical pleasure, but he prefers the pleasures of the spirit as having more force, stability, variety, and dignity. The former, for him, never goes by itself alone (he is not that fantastic) but only comes first. For him temperance is the moderator, not the enemy, of physical pleasure (C). ——*Ibid.,* p. 447.

21   Those transcendent moods frighten me, like precipitous and inaccessible places, and nothing is more difficult for me to digest in the life of Socrates than his ecstasies and his dealings with daemons (C). ——*Ibid.,* pp. 449-50.

PIERRE CHARRON (1541–1603)

1   Socrates was considered the wisest of men, not because he was the most learned and the cleverest, or because he had some ability above others, but because he knew himself better than others in keeping to his rank and in acting well the part of a man [*en faisant bien l'homme*]. He was the king of men in the sense of the saying that the one-eyed are kings among the blind—that is, those deprived of their senses—for they are by nature feeble and miserable and, along with that, they are proud and not aware of their defect. Socrates was only one-eyed; but he knew well that he was a man like the others, feeble and miserable, and recognized this true condition in

good faith, ruled himself, and lived accordingly. ——Bk. I,
chap. 1 in *Traité de la sagesse* (1604; Paris, 1827), I, 7-8.

[Those who came after Aristotle with their presumptuous, 2
pedantic minds] do not know that there is a kind of ignorance
and doubt more learned and secure, more noble and generous,
than all their science and certitude; it is this which made
Socrates so renowned and considered the wisest of all; this is
the science of all sciences and the fruit of all our studies: a
modest, candid, innocent, and cheerful recognition of the
mysterious height of the truth and of our poor human condition full of darkness, feebleness, and uncertainty. ——Bk.
II, chap. 2, in *Traité*, I, 49.

Enough has now been said about this perfect freedom of 3
judgment, consisting of these three phases, to judge about
everything [*juger de toutes choses*], not to judge anything [*ne
juger rien*], and to be open-minded [*être universel*], on which
I have dwelt more, since I know that it is not the taste of the
world and opposed to pedantry just as wisdom is. However,
this is the fine flower of wisdom which protects us from the
two opposite reefs on which the vulgar usually founder,
namely, arrogant and opinionated knowledge on the one
hand, and shameful recantations, repentances, and reversals
on the other; thus (by being open-minded) we keep ourselves
in a sweet, peaceable, and secure contentment and great
freedom of spirit, a noble and magnificent universality. This
is the great quality and self-sufficiency of Socrates, the cory-
phaeus of the sages by universal admission, of whom it is said,
as Plutarch reports, that he did not procreate, but, serving as
a midwife, made others procreate. ——*Ibid.*, pp. 63-64.

Socrates was a great master and admirable doctor on what 4
is natural, as Aristotle was on art and science. Socrates, by
the most simple and natural suggestions, by smiles and common inductions, speaking like a peasant or a woman, fur-

nished precepts and rules of the good life and remedies against all evils, of such strength and vigor that all the art and science of the world would not have been able to invent or discover them. ——Bk. II, chap. 3, in *Traité,* II, 88-89.

RENÉ DESCARTES (1596–1650) [2]

I dare to believe that inward joy has a certain power to make Fortune more favorable to it. . . . I have an infinity of experiences and together with them the authority of Socrates to confirm my opinion. . . . What is commonly called the genius of Socrates was undoubtedly something different, unless he should have been accustomed to follow his inner inclinations and believed that the outcome of what he undertook would be lucky when he had a certain secret feeling of gaiety, and conversely unlucky when he was sad. It is true, however, that it would mean being superstitious to believe this as extensively as he is said to have done; for Plato reports that he even remained in his home whenever his genius did not advise him to leave it (*Apology* 31d). ——From a letter to the Princess Elizabeth (November, 1646), in *Oeuvres,* ed. Charles Adam and Paul Tannéry (Paris, 1897 ff.), IV, 529-30.

BLAISE PASCAL (1623–1662)

The conversion of the pagans was reserved only to the grace of the Messiah. . . . Sages like Plato and Socrates were unable to persuade them. ——*Pensées* (1670), ed. Léon Brunschvicg (Paris, 1904), No. 769, III, 215.

[2] For other incidental proof of Descartes' admiration for Socrates, see *Correspondence of Descartes and Constantine Huygens* (1635–1647), ed. Leon Roth (Oxford, 1926), pp. 137, 236.

JACQUES BÉNIGNE BOSSUET (1627-1704)

True, the philosophers had finally recognized that there was a God different from those whom the crown worshiped, but they did not dare to admit it. On the contrary, Socrates stated as his maxim that everyone ought to follow the religion of his country (see *Athenagoras* I. xiii). . . . Philosophers of such weight, who have said such fine things about the divine nature, did not dare oppose the public error and despaired of their power to conquer! When Socrates was accused of denying the existence of the gods whom the public worshiped, he defended himself against the charge as if it [such denial] were a crime. ——*Discours sur l'histoire universelle* (1673), in *Oeuvres complètes* (Nancy, 1862), IV, 174.

BARUCH SPINOZA (1632-1677)

The authority of Plato, Aristotle, and Socrates has not much weight with me. ——From a letter to Hugo Boxel (October, 1674), in *Correspondence of Spinoza,* ed. A. Wolf (London, 1928), p. 290.

NICOLAS BOILEAU (1636-1711)

And what, after all, was Socrates, the prize exhibit of profane Greece, if closely examined, but a mortal, by his own nature dragged toward evil alone, and, in spite of the virtue of which he made a great show, the rather questionable friend of young Alcibiades? ——"Sur l'équivoque," in *Satires* (1705), XII, lines 145-50.

PIERRE BAYLE (1647-1706)

Here [i.e., in Socrates' words from Plato's *Phaedo,* 97 ff., as quoted before] you can well see the good taste of Socrates: He had abandoned the study of physics and had applied himself entirely to morals. This is the reason why he asked for an explanation of all nature by moral reasons, by ideas of order, by ideas of perfection. I venture to say that his censure of Anaxagoras was unwarranted. No philosopher who has once made the assumption that an intelligent being has set matter in motion and has arranged the parts of the universe is any longer under an obligation to give [such] a reason for every effect in nature.   ——"Anaxagoras," in *Dictionnaire historique et critique* (first published in 1697; Paris, 1820), I, 63.

2   Lactantius infers from Socrates' saying, "What is above us is nothing to us" (*Quod supra nos, nihil ad nos*), that he despised religion. . . . Lactantius may forgive me, but the maxim of Socrates which I have reported did not at all commit this philosopher to a neglect of theology. His doctrine, besides, was as noble as one could expect of a pagan; and it seems to me that he did not want anything but to set limits to human curiosity on grounds which even our most pious theologians have adopted; namely that we must want to be ignorant of what God has not wanted us to know, and that there are dangers in these profound studies.   ——"Ariston," in *ibid.*, II, 347.

FRANÇOIS DE SALIGNAC DE LA MOTHE FÉNELON
(1651–1715)

1   SOCRATES: As to myself, I believed that one could not establish the true maxims without ascending to the first principles which can prove them, and without refuting all the prejudices of men.

CONFUCIUS: But in the end, have your first principles enabled you to avoid controversies among your disciples?

SOCRATES: Not at all; Plato and Xenophon, my chief disciples, held entirely different views. The Academy founded by Plato suffered an internal division. These experiences have disillusioned me in my hopes for men. Man has almost no influence over other men. Men have almost no influence over themselves, because of the impotence to which pride and passions reduce them; still less do men have influence over others. —"Confucius et Socrate," in *Dialogues des Morts* (1700–12), VII.

ALCIBIADES: You are angry! It seems to me you were in a   2 better mood when you were on earth; your piquant irony had a quality that was more enjoyable.

. . . .

ALCIBIADES: I see well that Anytus was not wrong to make you drink the hemlock, and that one ought to have feared your politics even more than your new religion.   —"Socrate et Alcibiade," in *Dialogues des Morts*, XVII.

ALCIBIADES: Is there no one whom you would regret to leave   3 [by committing suicide]? Really, no man—without exception? Think it over well before answering.

TIMON: I would regret somewhat to leave Socrates.

ALCIBIADES: Watch out. Don't you know that he is a man?

TIMON: No, I am not quite sure of that: sometimes I doubt it, for he does not at all resemble the others. He seems to me to be disinterested, without ambition, without cunning; I find him just, sincere, unchanging. If there were ten people like him, truly, I believe they would reconcile me with mankind. . . . Although he has always been a little too facile and too sociable, I am not afraid of following his advice. Oh my dear Socrates! when I behold mankind and then turn my eyes upon you, I am tempted to believe that you are Minerva, who has come in the shape of man to instruct the city.   —"Socrate, Alcibiade et Timon," in *Dialogues des Morts*, XVIII.

A virtue as pure as that of Socrates could not fail to elicit   4 our admiration. . . . It is difficult to understand how a man who led everybody to praise the gods and who exhorted young men to flee from vice could have been condemned as impious

and as a corruptor of youth. This crying injustice could have
occurred only in a time of disorders.   ——*Abrégé des vices des
anciens philosophes* (1726), in *Oeuvres complètes* (Versailles,
1820–30), III, 290.

BARON DE MONTESQUIEU (1689–1755)

It was the same error which permeated their [the Greeks']
whole philosophy: bad physics, bad morality, bad metaphysics.
They had no feeling for the difference between positive qualities and relative qualities. . . . Plato and Socrates deceived
themselves with their beauty, their goodness, and their wisdom. . . . The terms "the beautiful," "the good," "the great,"
"the perfect," are attributes of objects which are relative to
the beings who think of them. It is important to get this
principle firmly into one's head. It is the sponge for almost
all the prejudices; it is the flail of ancient philosophy, of Aristotle's physics, of Plato's metaphysics. And if one reads the
dialogues of this philosopher, one discovers that they are
nothing but a tissue of sophisms resulting from the ignorance
of this principle.   ——"Pensées diverses: Des anciens," in
Oeuvres complètes (Paris, 1879), VII, 160.

FRANÇOIS MARIE AROUET VOLTAIRE (1694–1778) [3]

1   All men have received from heaven, together with intelligence, the bridle of justice and of conscience. . . . In a word,
this [conscience] is the felicitous genius of Socrates, that secret
god who directed his whole life, and who presided over his
fate at the very end, when without paling he drank the cup
of death.   ——"Poème sur la loi naturelle" (1752), in *Oeuvres
complètes* (Paris, 1882 ff.), II, 449.

2   If one may dare compare the sacred with the profane and
a God with a man, his [Jesus'] death has much resemblance to

[3] For Voltaire's letter to the Abbé d'Olivet (1767) on Rousseau's estimate of Socrates, see under ROUSSEAU, p. 188*n.*

that of Socrates. The Greek philosopher perished because of the hatred of the sophists, the priests, and the leaders of the people; the legislator of the Christians succumbed to the hatred of the scribes, the pharisees, and the priests. Socrates could have evaded death, but did not wish to; Jesus Christ offered himself voluntarily. The Greek philosopher not only forgave his maligners and his unjust judges, but even asked them to treat his sons like himself some day if they should be lucky enough to deserve such hatred as he had incurred; the legislator of the Christians, infinitely superior, asked his father to pardon his enemies. ——"Traité sur la tolérance à l'occasion de la mort de Jean Calas" (1763), chap. 14, in *Oeuvres,* XXV, pp. 86-87.

Is the mold smashed by those who love virtue for its own 3 sake, such as Confucius, Pythagoras, Thales, Socrates? In the times of those men, multitudes of people were devoted to their pagodas and their divinities with minds stricken by the fear of Cerberus and the Furies, who went in for initiation rites, pilgrimages, and mysteries, who went bankrupt by buying up black sheep for sacrifice. All periods have seen these unfortunates of whom Lucretius speaks: [Here follows *De Rerum Natura* III. 51-54]. Self-mutilations were practiced; the priests of Cybele had themselves castrated in order to preserve their continence. Why is it that among all these martyrs of superstition antiquity does not count one single great man, one sage? It is because fear has never been able to create virtue. Great men have been enthusiastic for the moral good. Wisdom was their commanding passion; they were sages, as Alexander was a warrior, as Homer was a poet, and Apelles a painter, by virtue of a power and a nature of superior character, and perhaps that is all one ought to understand the daemon of Socrates to mean.

One day two citizens of Athens on their return from the chapel of Mercury noticed Socrates in the public square. One said to the other: "Isn't that that criminal who says that one can be virtuous without offering up sheep and geese every day?" "Yes," said the other, "it is that sage who has no religion at all; that atheist who says that there is only one God." Socrates approached them with his plain manner, his daemon, and his irony, which Mme. Dacier [4] has so strongly exalted. "My friends," he told them, "one brief word, please. How would you call a man who prays to the Divinity, who adores it, who tries to resemble it as far as human weakness can, and who does all the good of which he is capable?" "That is a very religious soul," they said. "Very well; one could then adore the Supreme Being and have the highest degree of religion?" "Agreed," said the two Athenians. "But do you believe," continued Socrates, "that when the divine architect arranged all those globes that rotate over your heads, when he gave movement and life to so many different beings, he used the arm of Hercules or the lyre of Apollo or the flute of Pan?" "That is not likely," they said. "But if it is not likely that he employed the help of others to construct what we see, then it is not plausible that he conserves it by beings other than himself. If Neptune were the absolute master of the sea, Juno of the air, Aeolus of the winds, Ceres of the crops, and one of them wanted a lull while another wanted wind and rain, you must see that the order of nature would not exist as it now does. You assign four white horses to the sun and two black horses to the moon; but is it not better for day and night to be the effect of movements imposed upon the stars by the master of the stars, than to have them produced by six horses?" The two citizens looked at each other and answered nothing. Finally Socrates proved to them that one could have crops without giving money to the priests of Ceres, go hunting without offering small silver statues at the chapel of Diana; that Pomona gave no fruit, that Neptune gave no horses, and that one ought to thank the Sovereign Being who had made everything.

His discourse was in the strictest logic. Xenophon, his disciple, a man who knew the world and who later sacrificed to the wind on the retreat of the Ten Thousand, took Socrates by the sleeve and told him, "Your discourse is admirable; you have spoken much better than an oracle; but you are lost:

[4] Mme. Dacier (1631–1720), a distinguished classicist and translator.

butcher who sells sheep and geese for the sacrifices, and the other a goldsmith who makes a lot of money out of fabricating little silver and leather gods for the women; they will accuse you of being an impious person who wants to diminish their trade; they will testify against you with Meletus and one of these honest gentlemen to whom you are talking is a Anytus, your enemies, who have sworn your destruction. Look out for the hemlock; your familiar voice would have done well to warn you not to tell a butcher and a goldsmith what you ought to tell only to Plato and Xenophon."

Some time later the enemies of Socrates had him condemned by the council of the Five Hundred. Two hundred and twenty votes were for him. That makes one suspect that there were two hundred and twenty philosophers in that tribunal; but it makes one see that in every group the philosophers are always in the minority.

Thus Socrates drank the hemlock because he had spoken in favor of the oneness of God; and subsequently the Athenians dedicated a chapel to Socrates, to the man who had protested against the chapels dedicated to inferior beings. —— "Socrate," in *Dictionnaire philosophique,* in *Oeuvres,* XX, 428-30.

Was there not something of the quack in Socrates, with his 4 familiar daemon and the precise declaration of Apollo that pronounced him the wisest of all men? . . . Why didn't he let youth know that this was pure quackery? Socrates understood his time badly. Perhaps a hundred years earlier he would have ruled Athens. ——"Charlatan," in *Oeuvres,* XXVIII, 146.

What was Jesus in the eyes of the people, who certainly 5 could not suspect his divinity? He was a man of goodness who, born in poverty, talked to the poor against the superstition of the rich pharisees and the impertinent priests; he was the Socrates of Galilee. ——"Homélie sur l'interprétation du Nouveau Testament," in *Oeuvres,* XXX, 353.

6   Socrates, who was not one of their sect [the Stoics], showed
that one could push virtue as far as they did without belong-
ing to any party; and the death of this martyr of the Deity
is the eternal disgrace of Athens, regardless of the fact that the
city repented of it. ——"Des Stoiciens," in *Le philosophe ignorant* (1766) in *Oeuvres*, XXVI, 90.

7   The Greeks had so much *esprit* that they abused it; but
what does them much honor is the fact that none of their governments interfered with people's thinking. There is only Socrates of whom we are assured that his opinions cost him his
life; and he was even less the victim of his opinions than of a
violent faction which had risen against him. ——"Des sectes
des Grecs," in *Essai sur les moeurs et l'esprit des nations*
(1767), chap. 26, in *Oeuvres*, XI, 77.

8   Then why were the Epicureans never persecuted and Socrates condemned to drink the hemlock? There absolutely must
have been a reason, other than fanaticism, for the condemnation of Socrates. The Epicureans were the most companionable
people in the world, and Socrates seems to have been the most
uncompanionable. He himself admits in his *Apology* that he
went from door to door in Athens in order to prove to people
that they were blockheads. He made himself so many enemies
that finally they went to the extreme of condemning him to
death. ——"Des Grecs, de Socrate et de la double doctrine,"
in *Dieu et les hommes* (1769), chap. 12, in *Oeuvres*, XXVIII,
153.

9   The criminal proceedings against Socrates were, after all,
the mildest of all barbarities. There was no ordinary or extraordinary inquisition; no cartwheel on which the limbs of a
citizen were folded back after they had been methodically
crushed by the blows of an iron bar; no burning stake upon
which the dislocated still living body was hurled; nothing that
resembled the inventions of the learned savages of the twelfth
century. There was an old man of seventy, who, overcome by

the intrigues of two hypocrites, died an easy death in the arms of his friends, blessing God and proving the immortality of the soul. And hardly was that beautiful soul on its flight to the God who had shaped it when the Athenians, ashamed of their judicially committed crime, even more judicially condemned the accusers of Socrates and erected a temple for him. Thus the death of this martyr was actually the apotheosis of philosophy. ——"Prix de la justice et de l'humanité" (1777), article 11 in *Oeuvres*, XXX, 557.

JEAN JACQUES ROUSSEAU (1712–1778)

It is true that some sages have resisted the general torrent and have safeguarded themselves against vice by sojourning with the muses. But listen to the verdict which the first and the most unfortunate among them passed on to the scholars and the artists of his time: "I have examined," Socrates said, "the poets, and I look upon them as people whose talents impress themselves and others, who pose as sages, whom one takes to be such, and who are nothing of the kind."

"From the poets," he continued, "I have moved on to the artists. Nobody knew less about the arts than I did; nobody was more convinced that the artists possessed some pretty fine secrets. However, I perceived that their condition is no better than that of the poets and that these as well as the others live in the same prejudice. Because the most skilled among them excel in their specialty, they consider themselves the wisest of beings. In my eyes, this presumption has tarnished their knowledge completely; so much so that when I put myself in the place of the oracle and ask myself whether I would prefer to be what I am or what they are, what they have learned or what I don't know, I have answered to myself and to the God: I want to remain what I am.

"We do not know—neither the sophists, nor the poets, nor the orators, nor the artists, nor I myself—what the true, the good, and the beautiful is. But there is this difference between us, that although these people do not know anything, they all believe they know something; whereas I, if I know nothing, at least am not in doubt about it; so that all the superiority of wisdom which is conceded to me by the oracle is reduced merely to being thoroughly convinced that I do not know what I do not know."

So this is the way in which the wisest of men, according to the judgment of the gods, and the wisest of the Athenians, according to the sentiment of all Greece, Socrates, eulogizes ignorance. Can one believe that, if he rose again among us, our scholars and our artists would make him change his opinion? No, gentlemen: this just man would continue despising our vain sciences; he would give no aid whatever to that mass of books with which people inundate us from all sides, and would leave nothing as his whole precept to his disciples and to posterity but the example and the memory of his virtue, as he actually did. This is the way in which one ought to teach people. Socrates had commenced in Athens; Cato the Elder continued in Rome, freeing himself from the chains of those artificial and subtle Greeks who seduced virtue and softened the courage of their fellow citizens. . . . *——Discours sur les sciences et les arts* (1750), Pt. I, in *Oeuvres complètes* (Paris, 1872), I, 468.

2   In a word, it is in natural feeling rather than in subtle arguments that one must look for the cause of the repugnance that all men, even without the maxims of education, felt for the doing of evil. Although it might be proper for Socrates and the spirits of his mettle to acquire virtue by reason, the human species would not long have existed if its preservation had depended upon the reasonings of those who compose it. *——Discours sur l'origine et le fondement de l'inégalité parmi les hommes,* in *Oeuvres,* I, 548.

3   The love of country, a hundred times more vital and more delightful than that of a mistress, cannot be conceived without being felt; but it is easy to observe in all the hearts which

it warms, in all the actions which it inspires, that boiling and sublime ardor without which the purest virtue does not shine. Let us even dare to put Socrates against [a man like] Cato: the one was more a philosopher, and the other more a citizen. Athens was already doomed, and Socrates no longer had a country, but the entire world. Cato always carried his at the bottom of his heart; he could only live for it and he could not survive it. The virtue of Socrates is that of the wisest of men; but by the side of Caesar and Pompey Cato seems to be a god among mortals. The one instructs some individuals, fights the Sophists, and dies for truth; the other defends the state, liberty, and the laws against the conquerors of the world, and finally leaves the earth when he no longer sees on it a country he can serve. A worthy follower of Socrates would be the most virtuous of his contemporaries; a worthy imitator of Cato would be the greatest of them. The virtue of the first would make his own happiness; the virtue of the second would seek his happiness in that of all. We would be instructed by the one and guided by the other, and that alone would decide which is the superior: for no one has ever made a nation of wise people, but it is not impossible to make a people happy. ——"De l'économie politique," in *La Grande Encyclopédie* (1751–65), V, 337-49, sec. 2, in *Oeuvres*, I, 592-93.

. . . What prejudices, what blindness it takes to compare 4 the son of Sophroniscus with the son of Mary! What distance between the two! Socrates, dying without pain, without disgrace, maintained his character easily to the end; and if this easy death had not honored his life, one would doubt whether Socrates with all his genius was anything but a sophist. They say that he invented morality; others before him had put it into practice, and all he did was to put into words what they had done, or to turn their examples into lessons. . . . But where had Jesus picked up among his people that exalted and pure morality of which he alone provided the lessons and the example? From the bosom of the most furious fanaticism the highest wisdom emerged, and the simplicity of the most heroic virtues honored the vilest of all peoples. The death of Socrates, philosophizing quietly with his friends, is the sweetest that one could desire; that of Jesus expiring under tortures, injured, ridiculed, cursed by his entire people, is the most horrible that one might dread. Socrates taking the poisoned cup blesses the one who weeps and presents it with tears; Jesus in the midst of a frightful ordeal prays for his hardened executioners. Indeed, if the life and death of Socrates are those of a sage, the life and death of Jesus are those of a god.[5] —— "Profession de foi du vicaire Savoyard," in *Émile,* Bk. IV in *Oeuvres,* IV, 771.

5   I cannot deny myself a remark on the parallel between the Hebrew sage and the Greek sage. As an admirer of the one and the other, I cannot by any means be suspected of prejudice in speaking about them. I do not believe you are in the same position. I am not greatly surprised that you give all the advantage to the second; you have not had enough acquaintance with the other, and you have not taken sufficient care to separate what truly belongs to him and what is alien to him and disfigures him in your eyes as well as in those of many others who, in my opinion, have not looked any closer than you have. If Jesus had been born in Athens and Socrates in Jerusalem, so that Plato and Xenophon had written the life of the former and Luke and Matthew that of the other, you would change your language considerably; and what lowers him in your mind is exactly what makes his spiritual elevation

---

[5] Voltaire, who wrote some furious comments like "false," "pitiful" in the margin of the whole paragraph (see "Notes inédites sur la profession de foi du Vicaire Savoyard," in *Annales de la société de Jean-Jacques Rousseau* [Geneva: *Jullien,* 1905], pp. 272-84) also commented on the part given above in a letter of 1767 to the Abbé d'Olivet, in the following manner: "A quack . . ., speaking of the anxiety and the Passion of Jesus Christ, went even so far as to say that if Socrates died as a hero, Jesus Christ died as a god: as if there were gods used to dying; as if one knew how they die; as if perspiring blood were the characteristic feature of the death of God; finally as if it were God who had died" (*Oeuvres,* XLV, 13).

more astonishing and more admirable, namely his birth in
Judea among perhaps the vilest people that existed at the
time; whereas Socrates, born among the most instructed and
most amiable of peoples, found it easy to adopt the high tone
which he assumed. He rose up against the Sophists like Jesus
against the priests; but with this difference, that Socrates often
imitated his antagonists, and that, if his fine and sweet death
had not done honor to his life, he would have passed for as
much of a Sophist as they. . . . ——Letter to A. M. de ***
(Bourgoin, Jan. 15, 1767), in *Oeuvres,* IV, 771.

DENIS DIDEROT (1713–1784)

Socrates, born with a great soul, great judgment, and a mind   1
directed toward things of importance and of general and
prime utility, saw that it was necessary to work toward making men good before beginning to make them wise; that, as
long as you had your eyes attached to the stars, you overlooked what was happening at your feet; that, as a result of
living in the sky, we had become strangers in our own home;
that thus perhaps the understanding was perfected but the
will was abandoned to itself; that time was lost in frivolous
speculations; that man grew old without having asked himself about true happiness in life; and so he brought back to
earth a philosophy lost in the regions of the sun. He spoke of
the soul, of the passions, of the vices, of the virtues, of moral
beauty and ugliness, of society, and of the other topics which
have an immediate connection with our actions and our felicity. He showed extreme freedom in his manner of thinking.
He had no interests or fears which kept him from speaking
the truth. He listened to nothing but experience, reflective
thought, and the law of what is decent; and he deserves, compared to those who had preceded him, the title of the philosopher *par excellence,* a title of which those who succeeded him
did not deprive him. He withdrew our ancestors from the
shadow and the dust and made of them citizens, even states-

men. This project, in the midst of bandits interested in per-
petuating vice, ignorance, and prejudices, could not be carried out without danger. Socrates knew that; but who could
have intimidated the man who had placed his hopes beyond
this world and for whom life was nothing but an uncomfort-
able place in which he was detained in a prison, far from
his true fatherland?

 . . . After the death of his father, Socrates was obliged to
forego his own tastes, because of indigence, and to practice a
profession to which he felt no call whatever; but, when he
was engaged in meditation, he would often let the chisel fall
from his hand and would spend days leaning against the
marble. . . . Nor did he believe by any means that his profession of philosopher freed him from the dangerous duties of a
citizen. He left his friends, his solitude, and his books in
order to take up arms, and served in the cruel war between
Athens and Sparta.

 . . . The Tyrants did not awe him at all; he never stopped
reproaching them for their exploitations and their crimes; he
braved their power. When [they said] it was necessary to sign
the condemnation of some innocent person whom they had
condemned, he said that he could not write. . . . One found
him always ready to serve. He was never satisfied with the
good: he proposed to himself to seek the better in all things.
 . . . During all his life he was the model of a well-accomplished
and very happy person. If we knew more about his use of
time, it would perhaps show more clearly than any reasoning
that we have nothing better to do for our happiness in this
world than to practice virtue—an important thesis which com-
prises all of ethics and which has not yet been proved at all.
 . . . What a man! What a citizen! What a magistrate! What
a husband! What a father! The less Xanthippe deserved his
defense of her, the more we must admire Socrates. Oh Socrates, I resemble you little; but at least you make me shed
tears in my admiration and joy! Socrates did not believe that
he was on this earth merely for himself and for his family;
he wanted to be useful to everybody, but specifically to the

young men, in whom he hoped to find less obstacles to the
Good. He took away their prejudices; he made them love
truth. He inspired them with the taste of virtue. . . . This man
of consummate prudence and experience, who had heard so
much, read so much, meditated so much, had readily perceived that truth is like a thread which comes at one end
from the dark and loses itself at the other end in darkness,
and that in regard to every question the light [of truth] in-
creases gradually up to a certain point on the length of the
unraveled thread, beyond which it gradually becomes fainter
and is extinguished. The philosopher is the one who knows
the proper point at which to stop; the foolish sophist marches
on and confuses himself and others. . . .

Socrates was accused of impiety, and one must admit that
his religion was not that of his country. He despised the gods
and the superstitions of Greece. He pitied their mysteries. He
had lifted himself up by the sole force of his genius to the
knowledge of the oneness of the divinity, and he had the
courage to reveal that dangerous truth to his disciples. . . . He
had not the least desire to save himself from going to prison.
He listened to his death sentence smiling. . . . He disregarded
insults. The disregard and the pardon of insults, which are
acts of Christian virtue, are the philosopher's vengeance. . . .
This charity, like that of the Supreme Being, made no exceptions. What should we think of the glibness and the com-
placency with which some people, both ancient and modern,
have accepted and repeated charges against the purity of his
morals? A slander which we blush to mention: actually they
themselves were envious and corrupt. ——"Socrate," in *La
Grande Encyclopédie* (1751–65), XV, 261-65; also in *Oeuvres
complètes* (Paris, 1876), XVII, 151-6.

The existence of intermediate spirits between man and God   2
is so well established as to deny the assumption that the interval is empty, and that in the great chain it is man who
presents himself next to the universal creator; and at the top
of the human species stands a Socrates or a Titus or a Marcus

Aurelius or a Pascal or a Trajan or a Confucius or a Bayle or
a Descartes or a Newton or a Leibniz. ——"Leibnitzianisme,"
in *La Grande Encyclopédie* (1751–65), IX, 369-70.

BARON D'HOLBACH (1723–1789)

1   Socrates, who is considered to be the Father of Morals,
made it [i.e., philosophy], as they say, descend from Heaven
in order to enlighten man. But his principles, as they have
been presented to us by his disciples Xenophon and Plato,
although adorned with the charm of poetic eloquence, offer to
the mind nothing but confused concepts and poorly stabi-
lized ideas, presented with the *élan* of an imagination brilliant
but hardly able to provide us with real instruction. ——*La
morale universelle ou les devoirs de l'homme fondés sur la
nature* (Amsterdam, 1776), I, ii.

2   Socrates, who carried submission to the laws of an ungrate-
ful and frivolous people to the point of fanaticism, and who
wanted to be a martyr to it, was unjust to himself: had he
left his prison, he would have saved the Athenians a crime
which has covered them with eternal infamy. ——*Ibid.,* II, 60.

MARQUIS DE CONDORCET (1743–1794)

1   Socrates, fighting the Sophists, and covering their vain subtleties with ridicule, appealed to the Greeks to call back to
earth that philosophy which had lost itself in the sky. Not
that he despised astronomy or geometry or the observation of
natural phenomena; not that he had the childish and false
idea of reducing the human spirit to the exclusive study of
ethics; on the contrary, it is precisely to his school and his
disciples that the mathematical and physical sciences owed
their progress. Among the ridiculous things which they try to
hang on him in the comedies, the reproach which brings

about the greatest ridicule is the one of cultivating geometry, of studying meteors (*météores*), of drawing geographical maps, of making observations on burning glasses of which, by a remarkable coincidence, the earliest phase has been transmitted to us only by the buffoonery of Aristophanes.

Socrates merely wanted to urge people to confine themselves to such objects as nature had put within their reach, to make sure of every step before trying new ones, to study the space which surrounded them before reaching out haphazardly into unknown space.

The death of Socrates is an event of importance in human history; it was the first crime to mark the warfare between philosophy and superstition, a warfare which still continues among us, as does that of philosophy against the oppressors of humanity. ——*Esquisse d'un tableau historique des progrès de l'esprit humain* (1793), Quatrième époque (Paris, 1933), pp. 50-51.

Socrates could not escape their [the priests'] blows. . . . 2 There was no longer a Pericles in Athens watching over the defense of genius and virtue. Besides, Socrates was guilty of much more [than the impiety of believing in the simplest physical truths]. His hatred of the Sophists, his zeal to lead a philosophy gone astray back to more useful subjects, announced to the priests that truth and only truth was the aim of his investigations; that he did not want men to adopt a new system and subject their imagination to his, but to make use of their reason. Of all crimes this is the one which priestly arrogance can least forgive. ——*Ibid.*, p. 52.

LOUIS VICOMTE DE BONALD (1754–1840)

Socrates found in his meditations, or perhaps in the books of the Hebrews, which were already widely distributed in the Orient, intimations of those important verities for the proofs of which philosophy has so long been seeking: the oneness of God as creator, conserver, and rewarder, and the immortality of the soul. He was the first of the Greek philosophers to make morality descend from heaven; and without a doubt he would have established it on earth if the genius of one man, whoever he might be, could be an authority for man and a guarantee for society. —*Recherches philosophiques* (1818), in *Oeuvres complètes* (Paris, 1817–1830), VIII, 11.

NAPOLEON BONAPARTE (1769–1821)

1   There are many paths to Paradise, and decent men have always been able to find theirs, from Socrates to the Quakers. This is my profession of faith.   —*Napoléon sténographié au Conseil d'État (1804–5)*, ed. Alfred Marquiset (Paris, 1913-), quoted in J. Christopher Herold, *The Mind of Napoleon* (New York, 1955), p. 32.

2   I would believe as firmly in Christ as does Pope Pius VII— if Christianity dated back to the beginning of the world, if it were the universal religion. . . . And then, Socrates and Plato would have to be damned: that's what I always used to ask the bishop of Évreux.   —Conversation of 1817. Gaspar Gourgaud, *Sainte Hélène. Journal inédit de 1815 à 1818* (Paris, 1847), I, 546-47, as quoted in *Mind of Napoleon*, p. 33.

3   [The Christian religion] was born in the schools of Greece. It was the triumph of men such as Socrates, Plato, Aristides, over the Flaminiuses, the Scipios, the Pauluses. The Romans conquered Greece by the strength of their arms, but they were insensibly subjugated by the irresistible influence of the spirit, the arts, and the sciences of the vanquished.   —Dictation of about 1817. *Campagnes d'Égypte et de Syrie (Correspondance de Napoleon Ier)*, XXIX, 475, as quoted in *Mind of Napoleon*, p. 54.

ALPHONSE DE LAMARTINE (1790–1869)

During all his life Socrates had fought that empire of the 1
senses which Christ came to overthrow. His philosophy was
completely religious; it was humble, for he felt it to be inspired; it was sweet; it was tolerant; it was resigned; it had
divined the unity of God, the immortality of the soul, and
even more than that, if the commentators of Plato are to be
believed and some strange words that came from those two
sublime mouths, i.e., Socrates and Plato. Man had already
gone as far as he could go; it needed a revelation to make him
take one more immense step further. Socrates himself felt the
need of it; he indicated it; he made preparations for it by his
discourses, by his life and his death. He was worthy to see it
briefly in his last moments; in a word, he was inspired. He
tells us so, he repeats it, and why should we refuse to believe
the word of a man who gave his life for the truth? Are there
many testimonies that are equal to the words of the dying
Socrates? Yes, without doubt he was inspired; he was a forerunner of that definitive revelation which God has prepared
from time to time by partial revelations. For truth and wisdom are not ours; they descend from heaven into the chosen
hearts that are stirred by God according to the need of the
times. He sowed them here and there; He spread them drop
by drop, giving to men only the awareness and the desire until
the moment when He was to fill us with abundance.

Apart from the sublimity of the doctrines Socrates announced, his death was a picture worthy of being watched by
men and angels; he died without hate for his persecutors, a
victim of his virtues, offering himself as a sacrifice for truth.
He could have defended himself; he could have recanted. He
did not want that, for it would have meant lying to the God
who spoke in him; and there is nothing to show that a sentiment of pride had altered the purity and beauty of this sub-

lime devotion. His words reported by Plato are as simple at the end of his last day as during the middle of his life; the solemnity of that great moment of death does not give his expressions any tension or any weakness. Obeying the will of the gods which he likes to see at work in everything, his last day does not differ in anything from his other days except that there will be no other day! He continues with his friends the subject of the conversation begun the night before; he drinks the hemlock like an ordinary drink; he retires to die as he would have retired to sleep: so sure is he that the gods are present, before, after, everywhere, and that he will awake in their bosom.   ——"La Mort de Socrate" (1823), Avertissement, in *Oeuvres de Lamartine, Poésies* (Paris, 1849), pp. 286-88.

2   SOCRATES: the whole world knows that name, synonymous with wisdom; a small number know his doctrine; nobody knows anything of his life, except his conversations and his death.

He is not a prophet, he offers no revelations, he is not a founder of a religion or a sect; he does not speak to men in the name of God; he does not impose any faith upon them, he does not surround himself with mystery, he does not promulgate any oracles, he performs no miracles; he is a man, he undergoes everything human, even human weaknesses and doubts; but he lives well, and he dies well, that is to say, he performs simply, in all its humbleness and in all its grandeur, the role which Providence has assigned to every man here below: to think justly, to live decently, to die hopefully!

Such is Socrates, the purest incarnation of good sense and practical philosophy that Greece, his country, displayed to Antiquity.   ——*Vie des grands hommes* (Paris, 1851–6), I, 67.

3   As to ourselves, while we admire with Xenophon the wisdom of the philosopher of Greece, we cannot keep ourselves from preferring a thousand times the more divine wisdom of India, of China, and, chiefly, of the Christian revelation. The

wisdom of Socrates is merely intelligence, it is not sufficiently love. It thinks well, but it does not dedicate itself sufficiently. He lacks sacrifice, that fulfillment of all virtue and that price of all truth, in spite of his martyrdom, which was completely political and not at all religious.

He is wise, but he is not a martyr; he accommodates himself to the customs, the beliefs, and even the decent vices of his period and his country. He gives highly spiritual and highly practical counsel of virtue to those who reject it—but he also gives counsels of vice to the young men and the courtesans. He believes in one unique god, the intelligence and providence of the universe, and he worships in public carnal and multiple divinities formed in the image of man. He dies well, but he dies for himself as well as for truth. Even his death is a piece of good fortune for his fate, which he seizes upon as a man of superior intelligence. "I am old," he tells Xenophon, "nothing would be left to me but to fail in my senses and my intellect: this is the hour to die deliberately."

Socrates evidences little tenderness for the human race, not even for his wife and his children, being always more the man of intellect (*homme d'esprit*) than the man of devotion to his fellows. His conversations, however sublime they may be at times, attest this lack of divine charity in his nature and his wisdom. He is at times abusive, often mocking, and always amused. Irony, which makes even truth offensive, is the constant form of his dialogues; he proceeds by tricky questions, as if to force his partner to cut his own throat; he leads him from detour to detour, artfully concealing the goal toward which he wants to take him. In the end he catches his antagonist by the latter's admissions, as one might catch a truth in a trap. He is constantly the epilogue, almost never the lyricist. Plato, his divine disciple, gave him wings; without them, he would often be a low creeper on the earth.

From all this we conclude that Socrates was neither the wisest nor the most virtuous nor the most religious among the philosophers, especially of antiquity, but that he was the

most spiritual and the most lovable among the decent people
of Athens; that he knew how to think well, and that, in one
word, there was, for our feeling, too much prudence in his
wisdom, and too much skill in his virtue.

Charity had not yet been born into the world.   ——*Ibid.*,
pp. 105-07.

AUGUSTE COMTE (1798–1857)

1   If we should make a thorough examination of the series of
metaphysical speculations on the supreme good in morals and
politics, we should discover a certain vague tendency to conceive of social economy in complete independence of all theological philosophy. But such a premature hope, which actually
could lead to nothing but the chimerical rule of an impotent
metaphysics, could in effect have nothing but a merely critical
influence, as has been directly, to say the truth, all the influence of a similar philosophy, which was then [i.e., in ancient Greece] the active tool of an intellectual and moral anarchy very similar to our own in many important regards.
The radical incapacity of metaphysics as a basis of organiza-
tion, even simply intellectual and, even more, social, becomes
undeniable during this period of its chief spiritual activity, of
which nothing could change the outcome very much, if one
sees the progress of universal and systematic doubt which leads
with frightening rapidity from school to school, beginning
with Socrates, to Pyrrho and Epicurus, to deny finally all external existence. This strange outcome, directly incompatible
with any idea of true natural law, reveals already the fundamental antipathy which is to develop further between the
metaphysical spirit and the positive spirit from the time of the
separation between philosophy and science, a separation
whose approaching necessity had been well anticipated by the
good sense of Socrates, who however had no suspicion of its
limits or of its dangers.   ——*Cours de philosophie positive*
(1841), 53rd lesson, V, 261-62.

We can understand the civic motives of the sentence which 2 ultimately consolidated the revolutionary influence of Socrates, whose old age would have ended peacefully had the magistrates been wiser. Notwithstanding his good sense and honesty, that estimable debater undeniably shared in the various aberrations peculiar to the unsound school of thought [of pseudo-philosophers disturbing the public order] I have been describing. The institution of this school was indeed chiefly due to his narrow genius, which blindly rejected the scientific movement on the vague plea of exclusive devotion to morals. But the reprobation ultimately in store for such a phase of thought must chiefly fall on his brilliant successor, who, for all the glorification temporarily conferred upon him by the monotheistic tradition, has down to our day exercised an intellectual and social influence of a disastrous kind. ——*Système de politique positive, ou Traité de sociologie* (Paris, 1852–4), tr. J. H. Bridges *et al.* (London, 1875–77), p. 288.

VICTOR HUGO (1802–1885)

Mystical naturalism was the ancient genius of Greece. Its name was poetry and philosophy. It included the group of seven sages, one of whom, Periander, was a tyrant. Then, with Socrates, a certain bourgeois and middle-class spirit entered the scene. It meant sagacity dragging wisdom out into the open. This operation proceeded by reducing Thales and Pythagoras to the level of what was truly immediate: a kind of filtering down, of cleansing and diluting, from which the ancient wisdom seeped drop by drop as something human. Simplifications displease the fanatics; dogmas do not like to be sifted. To improve a religion means to attack it. Progress offering its services to faith insults it. Faith is the kind of ignorance which thinks it knows it all, and which, in certain cases perhaps, knows more than science. In the presence of the haughty assertions of the faithful, Socrates had an embarrassing half-smile. There is some of Voltaire in Socrates.

Socrates declared the whole Eleusinian philosophy to be unintelligible and incomprehensible, and he told Euripides that, in order to understand Heraclitus and the old philosophers, "one had to be a swimmer from Delos," i.e., a swimmer able to reach an island which is constantly receding. This seemed irreligious and sacrilegious to ancient Hellenic naturalism. There is no other reason for Aristophanes' antipathy toward Socrates. ——*William Shakespeare* (Paris, 1864), Bk. IV, p. 205.

HENRI–FRÉDÉRIC AMIEL (1821–1881)

Christianity brings and preaches salvation by the conversion of the will, humanism by the emancipation of the mind. One attacks the heart, the other the brain. Both wish that man should reach his ideal. But the ideal differs, if not by its content, at least by the disposition of its content, by the predominance and sovereignty given to this or that inner power. For one, the mind is the organ of the soul; for the other, the soul is an inferior state of the mind; the one wishes to enlighten by making better, the other to make better by enlightening. It is the difference between Socrates and Jesus. —— *Journal intime,* tr. Mrs. Humphry Ward (New York, 1896), I, 23.

ERNEST RENAN (1823–1892)

1   Jesus founded religion among men, as Socrates founded philosophy and Aristotle science. There was philosophy before Socrates, science before Aristotle. Since Socrates and since Aristotle philosophy and science have made immense progress. But all has been built on the foundation which they laid. ——*La vie de Jésus* (Paris, 1870), p. 462.

2   Philosophy does not suffice for the multitude. They must have sanctity. An Apollonius of Thyana with his miraculous legend is of necessity more successful than a Socrates with his

cold reason. "Socrates," it was said, "leaves men on the earth, Apollonius takes them to heaven; Socrates is but a sage, Apollonius is a god." ——*Ibid., p.* 468.

ALFRED FOUILLÉE (1838–1912)

Must we not credit him [Socrates] with the original achieve- 1
ment of having understood the relation, far too often misconceived, of these two terms: law and sanction? The majority of positive religions tend to make ethics rest on religious sanction. By confusing consequences and principle they adopt this trivial axiom: no law is law that is not sanctioned. . . . Paganism did not understand at all this independence of law in its relation to sanction: fear of the Furies and divine vengeance were the chief movers of pagan piety. Socrates protested against this egoistic virtue, which is not true virtue at all; he revindicates for the good the force of law and the rank of principle, whatever the sanction and the future consequences. "I do not know what happens after this life, but what I do know is that to be unjust is contrary to duty and honor." Thus Socrates appears to be the true father of what is called in our day independent ethics (*la morale indépendente*), at least by virtue of what is true and acceptable in his doctrine. ——*La philosophie de Socrate* (Paris, 1874), II, 153.

Often strange at first sight, mingled with errors and soph- 2
isms, liking to conceal enthusiasm under the guise of irony, the philosophy of Socrates resembles those statues of Silenus of which the *Symposium* speaks, which, on being opened, allow the image of a Divinity to be seen beneath the bizarreness of their form. ——*Ibid.,* p. 555.

The idea of freedom is missing in Socrates as in almost all 3
Greek antiquity. Socrates was too prone to conceive the good as a neutral and impersonal object, exterior and superior to us, to be contemplated by our intelligence and not produced by our will; he failed to see it as a personal and free attribute

which does not depend on objects and external goals, but, since it is its own goal, imposes this goal on everything else.

. . . .

Socrates by trying to found metaphysics on ethics indicated to philosophy its true method. For morality is not morality unless it is not a consequence but a [primary] principle; it must therefore not be deduced from a metaphysical or theological system; but on the contrary, metaphysical creeds must be deduced from the moral act. Nevertheless, Socrates still believes with the whole of antiquity that morality consists in following nature, whereas the true morality consists in surpassing nature and having oneself be followed by her. The moral principle which Socrates put at the head of his doctrine was therefore only half moral. In other words, it was rather an intellectual and rational principle than one of action and will; it was an object of necessary science rather than of spontaneous love. Socrates' philosophy aspires to surpass the sphere of abstract intelligence without successfully reaching the sphere of the living will. So we see him stop halfway in the intermediary zone between the useful and the beautiful. Socrates seems often to be excessively preoccupied with utility, although he understands this word in a higher sense. When forced to ask himself afterwards what is the intimate nature of that supreme good in view of which everything else is useful, he does not succeed in grasping the good except under the form of order and beauty; for him as for Plato the supreme good is more aesthetic than moral. . . .

. . . .

If the doctrine of Socrates, considered in its entirety, was incomplete and perishable, it nevertheless offered, so to speak, truths which always live. Contemporary philosophy can borrow from him chiefly . . . two principles of the highest value; to subordinate, in the philosophical order, metaphysical science to moral science; to subordinate, in the political order, social science to moral science—for the ultimate source of all things lies in the good. . . .

. . . .

The indomitable faith of Socrates in the omnipotence of

the good is what is imperishable in its doctrine and what should inspire us. No one has shown more confidence in the final triumph of justice and in the final friendship of all men in the embrace of the universal good. Just as much as he hesitates and is in doubt about those questions which seem to him to transcend our understanding, he affirms and believes, when it is a matter of what ought to be, the law of our will, *Justice*. Here was his true genius and his divine inspiration; enthusiasm for the good, which made him despise the apparent triumphs of force, seemed to propel him forward into that superior sphere where the only force is that of truth.

The Athenians believed that by condemning him they had fortified their national religion and their political system. As a matter of fact, at first sight one could believe that they had succeeded; for, whatever the regrets and the grief of a small number of faithful friends, public opinion had soon acquitted his judges. Was it then really Anytus and Meletus who had triumphed? Yes, without a doubt, in the eyes of their contemporaries and the short-range politicians; no, in the eyes of that justice, worshiped by Socrates, which submits all things to the inexorable laws of its dialectics. The good must triumph sooner or later, truth cannot be wrong. All the great ideas of Socrates lived again after him, and they will eventually rule the world. Socrates knew it and died with a smile. ——*Ibid.*, pp. 557-62.

GEORGES SOREL (1847–1922)

Why is it that the trial of Socrates still excites the philosophers to such a degree? Even today it is taught that the death of the great dialectician was the inexpiable crime of Athenian democracy. There is no lack of free-thinkers inclined to compare his execution to the passion of Christ. For centuries the philosophers have been fighting authority. They have had to undergo many minor persecutions. By taking the side of Socrates they are defending their own cause. ——*Le procès de Socrate* (Paris, 1889), p. 5.

2   We admire Socrates greatly; his dialectics did philosophy an
inestimable service. Unfortunately, he dealt with morality and
politics.

Some would turn him into one of the apostles and one of
the martyrs of liberty. It is not possible to be more completely
deceived.

Socrates did much to break the chains which confined the
citizens to the ancient city. These chains were those of military discipline. The citizen was a soldier very closely kept
and watched; he was expected to submit to a system of education designed to drill him and to give him good preparation
for war.[6]

In the ideal city of the Socratics the mind would have been
supervised, regulated, oppressed. . . . The Socratic State is
ecclesiastic. . . . The citizen could aspire to one solitary freedom, the freedom to be good.   —*Ibid.,* pp. 6-7.

3   Socrates confused ethics, law, and science, thus leading men
to take a position in which nothing is left but probabilism in
ethics and arbitrariness in politics.[7] . . .

We cannot hold Socrates responsible for works like the
Symposium and the *Republic,* two books which disgrace the
Greek genius. . . . Without a doubt Socrates was not the only
guilty one: prior to his teaching, the Sophists had worked
with much ardor to ruin Greek society. But since he had discovered the viciousness of their arguments and wrecked their

----

[6] "Was Aristophanes [in the *Frogs*] wrong to regret the relaxing of war-
like discipline a few years before the fall of Athens? Let an Englishman
reproach him for that, that is easy to understand, for these people are
hostile to the military spirit on principle. We Frenchmen, we know unfortunately where the fine sentimental theories against pretorian guard
rule and against militarism [*caporalisme*] lead us" (*Le Procès de Socrate,*
p. 44, note).

[7] "Socrates borrows his arguments from utilitarian considerations. . . .
Therefore he has no ethics in the proper sense. All the rules are of a
legal nature; they do not carry their certainty in themselves; they only
demonstrate themselves by their consequences and especially by the existence of a sanction revealed by observation" (*ibid.,* pp. 301-02).

schools for good, why did he not arrive at establishing ethics on solid foundations? Was the problem solvable? With what was it possible to replace the religious morality (*droit sacré privé*) which was in decay and which Socrates too [had] worked to destroy? . . . —*Ibid.*, pp. 9-10.

The social question was a very burning one in antiquity; Socrates was apparently in no doubt about that. We have no definite theories of the Master on this subject. We can, however, conclude from the whole of his system that he did not understand the labor question; he had not grasped its ethical importance. This is one of the most regrettable gaps of his doctrine; consequently, he could not say anything just and reasonable with regard to politics.

It was as impossible for the Athenians as for us to recognize all the errors of Socrates' philosophy; they could not accurately appraise all the evils which were to flow from his theses. But the clear-sighted ones did quite easily distinguish the dangers which threatened the city.

Anytus and his friends believed that by striking Socrates they were striking all the philosophical schools, discouraging the innovators, and reviving the ideals of the heroes of Marathon. They failed; but we must judge them with all the more impartiality, as we see more clearly than they the disastrous consequences of the new doctrines. . . . [We will show] that the accusers were not wrong when they reproached Socrates with being a threat to society. . . .

It is of little interest to know what the Sophists and the predecessors of Socrates thought; their theses disappeared a long time ago and can be of interest only to the antiquarian. But that is not so in the case of the ideas of Socrates and his school.

No thinker has stirred up so many ideas and posed such a large number of problems. All contemporary questions have their origin in his teaching. The methods which he inaugurated are still those which the scholar has to use today. His errors have had a singularly lasting influence on philosophy.

Since the time of Socrates the idea of the State has been unable to establish itself. . . . Criminal law has made no progress since his day; the confusion of ethics and law still vitiates all decisions in criminal matters. . . . On the other hand, philosophy has not known how to make use of the advances which Socrates brought about in human thinking. Because science has failed to understand his dialectics, science is still encumbered with the heavy baggage of materialism. Scientists don't concern themselves with studying the principles of their methods, and in most cases philosophers are strangers to scientific training. Socrates' ethics was detestable, but included the principle of all future research. Since his time men have tried to conceal the difficulties of the problem, and an incalculable number of spurious solutions have been proposed. Socrates' ethics encompasses inescapable contradictions; it therefore cannot lead to anything solid; but, on the other hand, it furnishes the dialectician with an inexhaustible arsenal for the purpose of wrecking false ethical systems.   —*Ibid.*, pp. 12-17.

5   Socrates was curious like all the Greeks, but we believe that he satisfied his curiosity with a pretty futile kind of science. He had not much taste for physical research; the great schools of ancient philosophy followed his example. People wrote fat volumes about nature, but they did not make experiments. Science is not made by piling up grandiose arguments and by picking up observations without continuity and without a goal.   —*Ibid.*, p. 71.

6   We have established . . . that ancient society was founded on military discipline, on preparation for war, on the equality of the Pnyx among the demobilized (*désarmés*) soldiers. The philosophers, with Socrates at their head, claimed that the legitimate government belonged to the scholars. We have tried to bring to light the principal consequences which this sophism fomented. The Athenians had no need of many arguments to make them realize the value of the philosophers' theory; they had undergone a hard and humiliating experi-

ence. . . . Tyranny had not been the work of Socrates but of all the philosophers. During the periods of calm and prosperity people had found the utopian ideas of the Sophists admirable; they had perhaps wished that a lucky accident would permit them to put these theories into practice. What a good fortune it would have been if the assembly, instead of being formed by old sailors, had been composed of dialecticians! Then it would really have been possible to discover the natural laws and to make infallible decisions.

They had been watched at their work, those famous dialecticians (or at least the students of that novel philosophy); they had ruined the city, oppressed all the citizens, and united all the men of honor in one single sentiment of reprobation for oligarchy.

For the people, Socrates summed up the whole new education; and the people needed a symbol to serve as a focus for their ideas. —*Ibid.*, pp. 237-39.

Socrates did not want to rush into death, but it would have 7 cost him too much to escape dishonorably. He knew how to leave life as a hero. —*Ibid.*, p. 261.

The question is in order why no new religion arose from 8 Socrates' teaching. This problem has great importance in the system which we have expounded; it should be examined with care.

Socrates was perfectly equipped to found a religion: he was an enthusiast, he was eloquent, and he was evidently far superior to Mohammed, to the Bab, and to so many other personalities who have intensely stirred the people of Asia. It is certain that the environment was not favorable. —*Ibid.*, pp. 273-4.

We have seen that Socrates looked upon all the cults as 9 equivalent, since he made it a rule to observe the national rituals. A man of indifference cannot carry out transformations in the religious system of a nation. Finally, Socrates was not the man to create symbols; everybody admits that he had nothing to do with the myths which Plato inserted into his dialogues. ——*Ibid.*, p. 278.

10   When the wars of the cities had exhausted all the political energy of the Hellenes, when the new customs had gained the upper hand, people were no longer concerned with the quarrels of the old parties; that whole phase of ancient life no longer interested anyone but the erudite. Greece became the meeting place of studious youth who had come to listen to orators and philosophers. The memory of the Sophists faded gradually, while the glory of Socrates grew to such a point that it seemed he could find only prattle and puerile chicanery in his predecessors. The world greeted in him the creator of philosophy. Never has homage paid to a man been more legitimate. The ancient theories and the argumentations of the Sophists no longer interested anybody; the Greek world seemed to date from Socrates. ——*Ibid.*, p. 280.

HENRI BERGSON (1859–1941)

The philosopher who is so enamored of this noble doctrine [that all men are brothers, having come from the same God] as to become wrapped up in it doubtless vitalizes it by translating it into practice. . . . But it is a far cry from that to the enthusiasm which spreads from soul to soul, unceasingly, like a conflagration. . . . To find something of the kind in classical antiquity, we must go not to the Stoics, but rather to the man who inspired all the great philosophers of Greece without contributing any system, without having written anything, Socrates. Socrates indeed exalts the exercise of reason, and particularly the logical function of the mind, above everything else. The irony he parades is meant to dispose of opinions which have not undergone the test of reflection, to put them to shame, so to speak, by setting them in contradiction with themselves. Dialogue, as he understands it, has given birth to the Platonic dialectics and consequently to the philosophical method, essentially rational, which we still practice. The object of such a dialogue is to arrive at concepts that may be circumscribed by definitions; these concepts will become Platonic Ideas; and the theory of Ideas, in its turn, will serve as a model for the systems, all essentially rational, of traditional metaphysics. Socrates goes further still; virtue itself he holds to be a science, he identifies the practice of good with our knowledge of it; he thus paves the way for the doctrine which will absorb all moral life in the rational function of thought. Reason has never been set so high. At least that is what strikes us at first. But let us look closer. Socrates teaches because the oracle of Delphi has spoken. He has received a mission. He is poor, and poor he must remain. He must mix with the common folk, he must become one of them, his speech must get back to their speech. He will write nothing, so that his thought shall be communicated, a living thing, to minds who shall convey it to other minds. He is indifferent to cold and hunger, though in no way an ascetic; he is merely delivered from material needs, and emancipated from his body. A "daemon" accompanies him, which makes its voice heard when a warning is necessary. He so thoroughly believes in this "daemonic voice" that he dies rather than not follow it; if he refuses to defend himself before the popular tribunal, if he goes to meet his condemnation, it is because the "daemon" has said nothing to dissuade him. In a word, his mission is of a religious and mystic order, in the present-day meaning of the words; his teaching, so perfectly rational, hinges on something that seems to transcend pure reason. But do we not detect this in his teaching itself? If the inspired, or at all events lyrical, sayings which occur throughout the dialogues of Plato were not those of Socrates but those of Plato himself, if the Master's language had always been such as Xenophon attributes to him, would we understand the enthusiasm which fired his disciples, and which has come down the ages? Stoics, Epicureans, Cynics, all the Greek moralists spring from Socrates—not only, as has always been said, because they develop the teaching of the Master in its various directions, but also, and, above all, because they borrow from him the attitude which is so little in keeping with the Greek spirit and which he created, the attitude of the Sage. Whenever the philosopher, closeted with his wisdom, stands apart from the common rule of mankind—be it to teach them, to serve as a model, or simply to go about his work of perfecting his inner self—Socrates is there, Socrates alive, working through the incomparable prestige of his person. Let us go further. It has been said that he brought philosophy down from heaven to earth. But could we understand his life, and above all his death, if the conception of the soul which Plato attributes to him in the *Phaedo* had not been his? More generally speaking, do the myths we find in the dialogues of Plato, touching the soul, its origin, its entrance into the body, do anything more than set down in Platonic terms a creative emotion, the emotion present in the moral teaching of Socrates? The myths, and the Socratic conception of the soul to which they stand in the same relationships as the explanatory program to a symphony, have been preserved along with the Platonic dialectics. They pursue their subterranean way through Greek metaphysics, and rise to the open air again with the Alexandrine philosophers, with Ammonius perhaps, in any case with Plotinus, who claims to be the successor of Socrates. They have provided the Socratic soul with a body of doctrine similar to that into which was to be breathed the spirit of the Gospels. The two metaphysics, in spite, perhaps because, of their resemblance, gave battle to each other, before the one absorbed the best that was in the other; for a while the world may well have wondered whether it was to become Christian or Neo-Platonic. It was Socrates against Jesus. To confine ourselves to Socrates, the question is: what would this very practical genius have done in another society and in other circumstances; if he had not been struck, above all, by the danger of the moral empiricism of his time, and the mental anarchy of Athenian democracy; if he had not had to deal with the most crying need first, by establishing the rights of reason; if he had not therefore thrust intuition and inspiration into the background, and if the Greek he was had not mastered in him the Oriental who sought to come into being? We have made the distinction between the closed and the open: would anyone place Socrates among the closed souls? There was irony running through Socratic teaching, and outbursts of lyricism were probably rare; but in the measure in which these outbursts cleared the road for a new spirit, they have been decisive for the future of humanity. ——*Les deux sources de la morale et de la religion* (1932), tr. R. Ashley Audra and Cloudesley Brereton (New York, 1935), pp. 52-55.

JULIEN BENDA (1867–1956)

I could find no better way to give a feeling of the novelty of the attitude of the intellectual [*le clerc*] than by recalling the famous answer of Socrates to the realist in the *Gorgias:* "You exalt then the men [like Themistocles or Cimon or Pericles] who catered to the citizens and satisfied their desires. People say that they have made the city great, but they fail to see that this is all the result of an abscess to be attributed to these elder statesmen; for they stuffed the city with ports and arsenals and walls and tributes and similar foolishness without concern for temperance and justice" (518e).

It is safe to say that until our days, at least in theory (but we are talking here about theories), the supremacy of the spiritual proclaimed in these lines has been accepted by all those who, explicitly or not, have proposed to the world a scale of values: by the Renaissance, by the eighteenth century. Today one can guess the outbursts of laughter of a Barrès or of some Italian moralist (to speak only of Latin writers) in the face of this contempt of force in favor of justice, and their merciless contempt for the way in which that child of Athens passes judgment on those who had made his city temporarily powerful. To Socrates, in this respect the perfect model of the intellectual faithful to his nature, the ports, the arsenals, the walls are trifles [*niaiseries*]; it is justice and temperance that are the serious matters. To those who hold his position today, it is justice which is a trifle, a "cloud," and it is the arsenals and the walls which are the serious things; in our day the intellectual has made himself the servant of war. It caps the climax that a modern moralist,[8] one of the most respected, has plainly approved of the judges who, as good guardians of the earthly interests, condemned Socrates, a thing which has never occurred among the educators of the human soul since the evening when Crito closed the eyes of his master. ——*La trahison des clercs* (Paris, 1927), p. 129.

ANDRÉ GIDE (1869–1951)

1   I do not know that there can be found a single one among those who have offered humanity new evaluations in whom these Messrs. Binet-Sanglés cannot discover, and quite rightly, what they would perhaps call a blemish—what I should like to call simply: a provocation. Socrates, Mahomet, St. Paul, Rousseau, Dostoyevsky, Luther—M. Binet-Sanglé has only to enumerate them to suggest still others; there is not one of them that I should not recognize as abnormal.—And of course it is possible *after these men* to think as they do without being unbalanced oneself; but it is an unbalanced state that in the beginning brought these thoughts to our rescue, which the reformer needed to re-establish in him the broken equilibrium. It was necessary, in fact, that in the beginning, one should be ill to permit, later on, the health of many. ——*The Journals of André Gide*, tr. Justin O'Brien (New York, 1949), II, 242.

2   Had Socrates and Plato not loved young men, what a pity for Greece, what a pity for the whole world!

8 Georges Sorel.

Had Socrates and Plato not loved young men and aimed to please them, each one of us would be a little less sensible. ——*Ibid.*, p. 246.

LÉON BRUNSCHVICG (1869–1944)

Pythagoreanism and Neo-Pythagoreanism remain on the threshold, as it were, of occidental consciousness. Not until we encounter Socrates, or rather the portrait of him left us by the Socratics, is it possible to define this consciousness. From then on, as we know, man becomes aware of the fact that he is charged with the assignment of forming his own constitution by building on the practical power of reflection, which links up the reformation of his individual conduct and of public life with the reformation of man's interior being. ——*Le progrès de la conscience dans la philosophie occidentale* (Paris, 1927), p. xvii. 1

The connection between what Heinrich Maier calls the Socratic gospel and the personality of Socrates, taken by itself, is not what decided the course of Hellenic thought. . . . The refraction which incessantly, throughout the centuries, diverts the rays of moral and religious conscience will be just as important, at times even more important, to consider than its original direction. ——*Ibid.*, p. xxi. 2

Conscience in the occidental world has an authentic birth certificate: the *Memorabilia* of Socrates. Surely, considering the miserable state of our information, we should be at a loss to justify the historical objectivity of Xenophon. At the start of almost all intellectual movements, we are struck by the same paradox: we know enough to assert that they are due to the initiative and the rise of a personality, but yet not enough to separate this personality from obscurities, from contradictions, from legend. . . . The only thing which we know surely about Socrates is that we know nothing. . . . The *Memorabilia* 3

are sufficient to inform us that in the fifth century before
Christ a certain thing took place, prepared for by a marvelous
flowering of poets and "physiologists," of technicians and
sophists: *an appeal to the consciousness of oneself, which was
to mark the course of our civilization with an indelible im-
print.* —*Ibid.*, p. 4.

4   With Socrates, a living reason has joined the reason of his
contemporaries, compelling them to focus their attention on
themselves. Taking account (to use a significant expression of
Alcibiades in Plato's *Symposium*) of the fact that his contemporaries are defenseless against him, they have either to
flee from him or else, if they stop to listen to the voice which
in them answers the voice of the master, they find themselves
in a new world which reveals to them the true vocation of
human intelligence. . . .

We are by nature egoists. But reflection detaches us from
the merely individual center of our desire to make us realize,
in the function of son, friend, and citizen a relationship of
which our own individuality is only one of the poles, thus
introducing at the root of our will a condition of reciprocity
which is the law of justice and the foundation of love. It is in
this way that reason reveals what constitutes its specific character and its effectiveness. It is fair to say that the teaching
of Socrates is summed up in the discovery of practical reason. . . .

The difficulties of Socratism show themselves during Socrates' lifetime in what remains obscure and enigmatic in him
according to the views of his contemporaries. Certain traits,
indicated by Xenophon and Plato and amplified in the apocryphal dialogue *Theages*, cast something like a suggestion of
daemonic inspiration around the Hellenic sage who sets himself
off in his zone of light, around the hero of rational humanism.
And even in the daily programs which he is reported as
making, a kind of fundamental indecision shines through
incessantly, a disconcerting mixture of effrontery and timidity;

the *élan* of intellectual self-confidence slows up abruptly and seems to lose itself under the action of irony. Thus the historian is led to ask himself whether these peculiarities are not linked to an inadequacy of his teaching, to a gap, perhaps impossible to fill, between the program Socrates outlined to his listeners and the means which he put at their disposal.

Socrates' goal is not in doubt: to make man adequate to his destiny by providing him with the satisfaction of depending on himself alone, to be himself the builder of his own philosophy (*autourgos tes philosophias*), according to the expression of the *Symposium*. The tool on which he relies is the examination of conscience; from actions performed spontaneously we ascend to the maxim from which they proceed, and we submit this maxim to the control of reason. But how far does this tool, as Socrates forged it, render the services which he expected of it? Concerning this point we would find ourselves rather at a loss to give a firm and precise answer. —*Ibid.*, pp. 11-12.

JACQUES MARITAIN (1882—)

It was Socrates who saved Greek thought from the mortal 1 danger into which Sophists had brought it. . . . The Sophists claimed to know everything and did not believe in truth; Socrates professed ignorance and taught his hearers to seek nothing but the truth. Thus his entire work was a work of conversion. He reformed philosophic reasoning and directed it to the truth, which is its proper goal. This work was of such importance for the future of the human intellect that it is not strange that Socrates accomplished it as a mission divinely inspired. . . .

He compared himself to a gadfly sent to sting the Athenians awake and force upon their reason a constant examination of conscience, a service which they repaid with hemlock, thus affording the aged Socrates, already on the verge of the grave,

opportunity for the most sublime death to which merely human wisdom can lead.   ——*An Introduction to Philosophy*, tr.
E. I. Watkin (New York, 1932), pp. 68-69.

2   . . . This unwearied disputer, for all his superficial skepticism, possessed an invincible confidence in the intellect and
in science—but of an intellect disciplined, humble in its attitude towards reality, and a science aware of its limitations, ad-
vancing successfully and securely in the apprehension of truth
only so far as it respected the sovereignty of the real and was
conscious of its ignorance in every direction. In this we recognize Socrates as a teacher of the scientific spirit, as also of the
philosophy which we shall learn to know as *moderate intellectualism*. By his logical and critical work he forged the
instrument indispensable for the progress of the mind and
turned the crisis created by sophistry to the profit and salvation of reason. By his work as a teacher of morality, he not
only founded the science of ethics, but liberated thought from
the fascination of the sensible, and unintentionally perhaps
set philosophic speculation on the road to metaphysics, wisdom in the strict sense. This he did simply by raising philosophy (this was the true significance of the Socratic demand
for self-knowledge) from exclusive occupation with the physical universe to the study of human nature and human ac-
tivities, which contain a spiritual element of a higher order
altogether than the stars or the entire universe of matter.

But Socrates was no more than a pioneer genius. He gave
the impulse, but never reached the goal. When he died everything was still in the air. For method is not enough, a systematic body of doctrine is necessary; and Socrates, though his
teaching was fertile in fruitful hints, possessed, apart from the
elements of ethics, no doctrine in the strict sense. The doc-
trinal completion of his work and the construction of the true
philosophy were reserved for Plato and Aristotle.   ——*Ibid.*,
pp. 72-73.

JEAN-PAUL SARTRE (1905——)

When Socrates stopped to talk with a slave about geometric patterns, it was as if he had said, "This slave is as capable as I of being a member of the Council." ——"Légende de la vérité," *Bifur* VIII (Paris, 1931), p. 86.

ALBERT CAMUS (1913–1960)

I fear that . . . after an interval of two millennia we are running the risk of witnessing again the oft repeated sacrifice of Socrates. The program for tomorrow is either the city of free discussion (*dialogue*) or the putting the witnesses of discussion to a solemn and symbolic death. After having presented my answer, the question which I, on my part, want to put before Christians is this: Will Socrates still stand alone? Is there nothing in him, nothing in your doctrine that impels you to join us at his side? ——"L'Incroyant et les Chrétiens," address to the Dominicans of Latour-Maubourg (1948), in *Actuelles* I (Paris, 1950), p. 218.

GERMAN AND RELATED

GOTTFRIED WILHELM LEIBNIZ (1646–1716)

The term "enthusiasm" had at first a good connotation. . . .
Socrates maintained that a god or a daemon gave him internal
warning; hence enthusiastic seems to mean a divine instinct.[1]
——*Nouveaux essais sur l'entendement humain* (completed
1704, published Amsterdam & Leipzig, 1765), Bk. IV, chap.
19, § 16.

FREDERICK THE GREAT (1712–1786)

1   . . . Let us attack the sun of paganism . . . Socrates, that
great philosopher, that goodly man [*homme de bien*], that
oracle of his time, the one of whom Plato said that he counted
it for one of the three favors he had received from the gods
to have been born at the time of Socrates, this same Socrates
who seems to us so virtuous from one side appears to me as
very wicked [*vicieux*] from the other, when I consider him
with regard to the inclination he had for the young Alcibiades.
Doesn't this mean to be branded [*marqué*] very conspicuously
as debasing humanity [*d'une manière très-évidente au coin de
l'humanité*], and did not this vice also blacken many of his
virtues? After that I am no longer astonished to see Xanthippe's outbursts [*emportements*] and Socrates' patience in supporting them. He had the feeling of having offended her.

[1] John Locke, in the chapter of his *Essay on Human Understanding*
(Bk. IV, chap. 19, sec. 3) on which Leibniz is commenting, had described
"enthusiasm" as that ground of assent "which, laying by reason, would
set up revelation without it. Whereby in effect enthusiasm takes away
both reason and revelation, and substitutes in the room of them the
undergrounded fancies of a man's own brain, and assumes them for a
foundation both of opinion and conduct."

Hence his reason obliged him to suffer the bad tempers of his wife as a light punishment for the insults which he had done her. ——Letter to Manteuffel (March 18, 1736), in *Oeuvres de Frédéric le Grand* (Berlin, 1853), XXV, 419.

Socrates preferred the hemlock to the inconvenience of hold- 2
ing his tongue [*la gêne de contenir sa langue*]. But I do not know whether it is a pleasure to be the martyr of other people's error. What is more real for us in this world is life. It seems to me that every reasonable person should try to conserve it. ——Letter to Voltaire (July 6, 1737), in *Oeuvres,* XXI, 71.

. . . Socrates was the wisest and the most temperate of mor- 3
tals, and Alexander the Great the most dissolute and the most uncontrolled. . . . It is certain that so intemperate a character could in no manner be compared with Socrates. But it is also true that, had Socrates found himself at the head of the campaign against the Persians, he would perhaps not have matched the activity or the daring decisions by which Alexander subjected so many nations. ——Letter to Voltaire (February 16, 1774), in *Oeuvres,* XXIII, 274.

IMMANUEL KANT (1724–1804)

It would be easy to show how common sense reason, in 1
every case that comes up, is quite able to tell what is good, what bad, and what is in accordance with or contrary to duty, provided only that it makes itself pay attention, as Socrates did, to the principle it employs. ——*Grundlegung zur Metaphysik der Sitten* (1785), erstes Hauptstück, in *Sämtliche Werke,* ed. Hartenstein (Leipzig, 1867–68), IV, 251-52.

A system of metaphysics composed in conformance with a 2
critique of pure reason . . . would be no negligible gift . . . especially if one considers the inestimable gain of ending for

good all the objections raised against morality and religion, after the fashion employed by Socrates, namely by presenting the clearest possible proof of the opponent's ignorance. ——Preface to 2nd edn., *Critique of Pure Reason* (1787), in *Werke,* III, 25.

3   It is true, the so-called moral sense, a kind of special sense (*sensus moralis*) is frequently misused sentimentally [*schwärmerisch*] as if—like the genius of Socrates—it took precedence over reason, or even as if it could dispense with reason, yet it means a moral perfection to make one's own each specific end that is likewise a duty. ——*Metaphysik der Sitten,* zweiter Teil (1797), in *Werke,* VII, 190-91.

4   Milder than "megalomania" (*Wurm,* literally "worm") is "crotchet" (*Grille,* literally "cricket") which a person feeds within himself, a supposedly popular maxim which however finds no approval among the intelligent, referring to a gift of having premonitions, i.e., certain influences similar to those of Socrates, although unexplainable, such as those of sympathy, antipathy, or idiosyncrasy (all occult qualities)—a thing which chirps in his head, as it were, like a cricket on the hearth, yet which no other can hear. ——*Anthropologie in pragmatischer Hinsicht* (1798), in *Werke,* VII, 520.

FRIEDRICH GOTTLIEB KLOPSTOCK (1724–1803)

Socrates—it is true that you do not know him, but I quiver with joy when I name him: the noblest life that ever was lived he crowned with a death which exalted even that life— I have always admired that sage and have incessantly studied his image. I saw him in a dream, and he named his immortal name: "I, Socrates, whom you admire, am come over to you from the regions beyond the graves. Unlearn your admiration of me! For the Deity is not what we took it to be, I in the

shadow of a sterner wisdom, you (worshiping) at altars." [2]
——Portia reporting her dream to her husband, Pilate, in *Der
Messias* (1751–1773), Canto VII, ll. 399-407.

GOTTHOLD EPHRAIM LESSING (1729–1781)

The wisest of men, according to a pronouncement of the
oracle in which it was least like itself, endeavored to fetch
curiosity back from that foolhardy flight [into the heaven of
the Pythagoreans]. Foolish mortals, what is above you is not
for you! Turn your eyes inward! In you are the unexplored
depths in which you may lose yourselves to advantage. Investigate here the most secret nooks. Here learn to know the
weakness and strength, the concealed corridors and the manifest outlets of your passions. Here construct the empire in
which you are both subject and king. *Here* comprehend and
rule the only thing that you are expected to comprehend and
rule: yourselves!

Thus Socrates admonished [men], or rather God through
Socrates.

"What?" cried the Sophist. "Blasphemer of our gods!"

. . . .

And yet, what can malice do against a sage? Can it compel
him . . . to disclaim the truth? Unhappy sage, if malice were
so strong. Ridiculous malice which, as its supreme achievement, can take from him nothing but his life. Even his enemies were to testify that Socrates was a preacher of the truth;
and how else could they have testified to it but by killing him?

2 "Sokrates,—zwar du kennest ihn nicht, doch ich schaure vor Freuden,
  Wenn ich ihn nenne: das edelste Leben, das jemals gelebt ward,
  Krönt' er mit einem Tode, der selbst dies Leben erhöhte—
  Sokrates, immer hab' ich den Weisen bewundert, sein Bildnis
  Unaufhörlich betrachtet, ihn sah ich im Traum. Da nannt' er
  Seinen unsterblichen Namen: 'Ich, Sokrates, den du bewunderst,
  Komm' aus den Gegenden über den Gräbern herüber. Verlerne,
  Mich zu bewundern! Die Gottheit ist nicht, wofür wie sie hielten,
  Ich in der strengeren Weisheit Schatten; ihr an Altären.' "

Few of his disciples took the road he had pointed out. Plato began to dream dreams and Aristotle to draw conclusions. ——"Gedanken über die Herrnhuter" (1750), in *Sämtliche Schriften,* ed. K. Lachmann (Leipzig, 1898), XIII, 155.

2   Socrates was the teacher and friend of Euripides; and how many a person might think that the poet owed to the friendship of the philosopher nothing more than the wealth of beautiful moral maxims with which he is so lavish in all his plays. I think his debt was much greater: he might have been just as sententious without it, but perhaps, in that case, he would not have become as tragic. Beautiful sentiments and moral maxims are in fact precisely what we hear least from a philosopher like Socrates: his way of life is the only morality he preaches! But to know man and ourselves; to pay heed to our feeling; to explore and love in everything the plainest and straightest paths of nature; to judge everything according to its intention; this is what we learn in his company; this is what Euripides learned from Socrates and what made him foremost in his art. Fortunate the poet who has such a friend —and can consult him every day, every hour. ——*Hamburgische Dramaturgie,* 49. Stück (October 16, 1767), in *Werke,* ed. G. Witkowski (Leipzig, 1911), VI, 126.

MOSES MENDELSSOHN (1729–1786)

1   [When Socrates, the wisest and most virtuous among the Greeks, took the great decision to spread virtue and wisdom among his fellow men] he had, on the one hand, to overcome the prejudices of his own education; to expose the ignorance of others; to fight sophistry; to put up with malice, envy, slander, and insult from his opponents; to bear poverty; to combat established authority; and, what was his most difficult task, to counteract the dark terrors of superstition. On the other hand, he had to spare the weak souls of his fellow

citizens, to avoid scandal, and to keep from losing the good influence which even the silliest religion has upon the morality of the simple-minded. He overcame all these difficulties with the wisdom of a true philosopher, with the patience of a saint, with the unselfish virtue of a philanthropist, with the determination of a hero, at the expense and with the loss of all earthly possessions and enjoyments. He gave up in the most loving fashion health, power, comfort, reputation, peace, and, in the end, life itself for the well-being of his fellow humans. So powerful was the effect on him of the love of virtue and righteousness, and the inviolability of the duties toward the creator and supporter of all things whom he recognized as such in an active way by means of the unclouded light of reason. But the higher aspects of his world citizenship did not keep him from fulfilling the common duties he owed to his own country. ——"Leben und Charakter des Sokrates," in *Phädon oder über die Unsterblichkeit der Seele* (4th edn., Berlin, 1776), pp. 8-9.

Concerning the spirit which Socrates claimed to possess and which, as he said, always stopped him when he wanted to undertake something harmful, the opinions of scholars are divided. . . . Is it necessary that an excellent man should be free from all weaknesses and prejudices? . . . Perhaps in the time of Socrates that required an effort of genius which he put to more profitable use. Anyhow, he was inclined to tolerate any superstition which could not lead directly to immorality. ——*Ibid.*, pp. 27-28.

2

JOHANN KASPAR LAVATER (1741–1801)

. . . There is absolutely no room for doubt of the ugliness of Socrates. And yet, from all we know about him, Socrates was the wisest, best, and most incomparable of men. ——*Physiognomik* (Wien, 1829), I, 148.

1

2   Anyone who is only accustomed to give heed to fleeting expressions, to the movement of fluid features, and who, as is
commonly wont to happen, has not devoted very particular
study to the more fixed forms of the face and to the features
of it when at rest, will, like Zopyrus [3] viewing the face of
Socrates, observe neither the peculiarity and excellence of its
basic plan nor the improvement of those parts of the plan
which might seem bad, and he will therefore arrive at an
erroneous judgment. I consider it very important to make
this idea quite clear. Assuming that the great character traits
of Socrates were also and even pre-eminently expressed in the
form of his face, although it was crude and unpleasing, that
this facial form and those fixed features were not studied, and
that only the gross, raw, and massive facial traits met the eyes
of the Greek, who sought only beauty, and prejudiced the
Greeks against him; assuming further, as every observer will
note, that betterments of those elements of his facial plan
which men are wont to call bad hardly caught men's eye save
in moments when the face was in action—then nothing is
more likely than a false physiognomical conclusion. ——*Ibid.*,
p. 150.

3   If Zopyrus, or rather a true physiognomist, had been wont
to direct his observations to the fixed parts of the human face,
he could never have said, "a natural blockhead!" Anyone who
regards that frontal structure as the abode of stupidity has
never in all his life studied human foreheads. . . . However
great may be the effects of good or bad training, of a fortunate
or disastrous situation, no matter how much better or worse a
man may have been made by the one or the other: a forehead
like this remains the same in its main form and its main char-

---

[3] About Zopyrus, apparently a contemporary of Socrates, see Cicero, *De
fato* V.10: "Do we not read how Zopyrus, the physiognomist, who professes he could recognize people's morals and characters from their bodies,
eyes, faces, and foreheads, berated Socrates? He said, 'Socrates was stupid
and obtuse, since he had no hollows in his neck above the collar bone—
these parts of his physique,' he used to say, 'were blocked and stopped
up; he also was amorous. . . .'" See also *Tusculan Disputations* IV.80.

acter, and should never deceive the true physiognomist. Verily, in that high and spacious arch dwells a spirit which knows how to find its way through the mist of prejudices and how to disarm hosts of hindrances. Moreover, the sharpness of the eyebones, the eyebrows, the flexing of the muscles between the brows, the broad bridge of the nose, the depth of the eyes, and that lifting of the pupil under the eyelid—how eloquent all this is, each detail in itself, and all details collectively, all agreeing as to the great natural endowments of the mind, indeed as to the truly developed and matured powers of the intellect! ——*Ibid.*, p. 153.

We are so bold as to say that in this face ineradicable traits of extraordinary greatness are still evident, and a steadfastness not easily shaken; and the whole, however bad single features may be, has the character of incorruptibility. Over and beyond what we previously said in favor of the face now before us, we will add this: in the upper part of the chin there is vigorous good sense, in the lower part, force and courage which borders on fearlessness. The stocky, plump, short neck —according to the universal judgment of all nations—expresses an inflexible will—a stiff-necked obstinacy.

Now if we do not forget that the absence of the finer and more living features, together with even the slightest coarsening of the coarser ones, does to be sure leave the identity of a face of this type unimpaired, but takes away its soul, we shall not be at all surprised to see in this countenance, at one and the same time, so much of the great and the small, so much that is promising with so much that is repellent.

We could certainly convince ourselves of this, as soon as we should see the living nature before us. Those eyes, now so rigidly set, how differently they would speak to us, if we saw them alive and in motion; yes, if they looked into our soul at the moment when their noble owner was teaching reverence toward the Deity, hope of immortality, or simplicity and modesty. Can any knower of men doubt it?

This vexatious mouth, which can be shown to have been in-

correctly drawn, since very much is lacking to it which no
natural mouth fails to have; consider this vexatious mouth
in such a moment as the one we have just characterized: is it
possible for you not to feel, O you observers and lovers of
mankind, that it must assume an entirely different shape? [4]
—*Ibid.*, p. 156.

JOHANN GOTTFRIED HERDER (1784–1803)

It is an often repeated but, it seems to me, exaggerated
praise of the philanthropic Socrates that it was he who first
and foremost called philosophy from heaven down to earth
and made it friendly to the moral life of man. At least, this
praise applies only to Socrates' own personality and to the
narrow circle of his life. Long before him there had been philosophers who had philosophized both morally and actively
for the benefit of mankind, since, beginning with the legendary
Orpheus, precisely this was the hallmark of Greek culture.
Pythagoras, too, by means of his school had laid a much
broader foundation for the development of human morality
than Socrates could ever have done through all his friends.
That Socrates did not like abstractions of a higher order was
due to his station, to the range of his knowledge, but chiefly
to his time and way of life. The systems of speculative imagination unaided by further experience of nature were exhausted, and Greek wisdom had become a playful chatter of

[4] Goethe on Lavater: "What caused him the greatest distress was the
existence of persons whose external ugliness irrevocably made them determined enemies of his doctrine of the significance of the human shape.
They usually employed common sense, and even other gifts and talents,
with passionate ill-will and petty doubt to an extent sufficient to invali-
date a doctrine which seemed insulting to their personality; for it is not
easy to find a man as great-minded as Socrates, who interpreted his faunlike shell as particularly favorable to the acquisition of virtue. The hardness, the obstinacy of such opponents was dreadful to him, his opposition
not without passion" (*Dichtung und Wahrheit*, Pt. III, Bk. XIV, in
Werke, XXV, 199).

Sophists, so that no great step was needed in order to despise or push aside what could not be outdone.

Socrates' daemon, his natural honesty, and the common humdrum course of his life protected him from the glittering spirit of the Sophists. This also set up before his philosophy the proper goal of mankind, which had such fine consequences for almost all with whom he had contacts. To be sure, the time, the place, and the circle of men with whom Socrates lived were part of that influence. In a different place the civic sage would have been just an enlightened, virtuous man, and perhaps we would not even know his name; for it was no invention, no new doctrine which he recorded in the book of the ages as his own. What made him a model for the world was merely his method and his mode of life, the moral training which he gave himself and tried to give to others, and—most especially—the manner of his death. It took much to be a Socrates, above all the admirable ability to forego anything, and the fine taste for moral beauty which he seems to have heightened in himself to a kind of instinct; however, we should not lift this modest, noble man out of the sphere into which Providence itself put him. He trained few disciples quite worthy of himself, precisely because his wisdom was only part of his own life-equipment, as it were, and because his excellent method in the mouths of his best students could only too easily degenerate into mockeries and sophisms whenever the ironical questioner lacked Socrates' mind and heart. . . . His life coincided with the point of highest culture in Athens, but at the same time with that of the supreme exertion of the Greek states against one another; these two conditions could not fail to usher in unhappy times and manners, which not very much later brought about the ruin of Greek freedom. No Socratic wisdom could protect it against that ruin; it was too pure and refined to decide the destiny of the nations. . . . In short, Socrates' philosophy has been more serviceable to mankind than it was to Greece, and this is without doubt its greater glory. ——*Ideen zur Philosophie der Geschichte der Menschheit* (Stuttgart, 1784–91), Bk. XIII, sec. 5.

JOHANN WOLFGANG GOETHE (1749–1832)

1   I esteemed Socrates as an excellent and wise man, who in life
and death might well be compared with Christ.——Goethe describing himself as of 1764 in *Dichtung und Wahrheit*, Pt.
II, Bk. VI (written in 1811), in *Sämtliche Werke* (Jubiläums-
Ausgabe, 1902 ff.), XXIII, 8.

2   Now I am studying the life and death of another hero and
dialoguing it (*dialogisiere's*) in my mind. It is still merely a
vague idea (*Ahndung*). Socrates, the philosophical hero-spirit
with his "mania for conquering all lies and vices, especially
those which do not wish to appear so," or rather: the divine
calling to be the teacher of men, the power of repentance
(*exousia* of *metanoeite*), the crowd of gapers, the few who have
ears to hear, the Pharisaic Philistinism of the Meletuses and
Anytuses, [these men] not the cause, only the conditions for
the gravitation and final preponderance of villainy (*Nichts-
würdigkeit*). I need time to develop the feeling for all this.
Then too, I'm not really sure about my relationship to Aesop
and La Fontaine, insofar as they, according to Hamann, are in
sympathy with the genius (*daimon*) of Socrates; or whether
I can soar from the worship of the idol which Plato paints and
gilds, to which Xenophon offers incense, to that true religion
which sees instead of the saint a great man, one whom I only
press to my breast with love and enthusiasm, crying, "My
friend and my brother!" And to be privileged to say that con-
fidently to a *great* man! Were I Alcibiades for a day and a
night, then I'd be willing to die! ——Letter to Johann Gottfried Herder (written from Frankfurt early in 1772), in *Briefe
und Tagebücher* (Leipzig, n.d.), I, 104-05.

3   Since I last heard from you [Herder] the Greeks have been
my only study. At first I confined myself to Homer; then I
investigated Socrates by way of Xenophon and Plato. This has

opened my eyes to my own unworthiness. ——Letter to Herder (written from Wetzlar, about July 10, 1772), in *Briefe,* I, 106.

. . . For it was not easy to find a thinker as great-minded as 4 Socrates, who would have interpreted his own faunlike body as favoring the acquisition of virtue. (Cf. p. 226, note 4.) ——*Dichtung and Wahrheit,* Pt. III, Bk. XIV (written between 1811 and 1813), in *Sämtliche Werke,* XXIV, 199.

In all epochs it is only individuals—not the age of itself— 5 who have wrought for science; it was the age which executed Socrates by means of poison; it was the age which burned Huss; the ages have always remained persistent. ——*Maximen und Reflexionen* (1826), in *ibid.,* IV, 219.

Just as Socrates invited the moral human being to talk to 6 him with a view to enlightening him somewhat about himself, so Plato and Aristotle confronted Nature in like manner as those having authority. And therefore every possible approach to these three, as a whole or in detail, is an event which we experience with the greatest joy and which always proves effective in promoting our education. ——*Ibid.,* XXXIX, 85.

We should note how great the ancients were, especially the 7 Socratic school, in presenting to view the source and guideline of all living and doing, and summoning us not to empty speculation but to life and action. ——*Ibid.,* IV, 237.

FRIEDRICH SCHILLER (1759–1805)

Socrates perished because of the Sophists. . . . ——"Rous- 1 seau" (1781), in *Werke,* ed. Bellermann (Leipzig, 1895), I, 22.

All it takes to feel greatly moved by the heroic self-sacrifice 2 of a Leonidas, by the quiet resignation of an Aristides, by the

voluntary death of a Socrates, is to be a human being.
—"On Tragic Art" (1792), in *Werke*, VIII, 45.

3   Pythia's mouth declared you to be the wisest Greek. True,
the wisest may often be the most difficult.[5] —"Xenien," No.
616 (1724), published posthumously, in *Werke*, IX, 194.

4   A teaching method is good when it proceeds from the
known to the unknown: it is still better if it is Socratic, i.e.,
if by questioning it elicits the same truths from the head and
heart of the listener. In the first, convictions are formally *demanded* of the mind, in the second they are *enticed* from it.
Letter to Gottfried Körner (February 23, 1793), in *Schillers
Briefe*, ed. Jonas (1892–6), III, 23.

JOHANN GOTTLIEB FICHTE (1762–1814)

1   By bringing the principle of understanding under observation, and by expressing and shaping this faith, and directing
it toward moral and religious truth, Socrates attacked the very
roots of antiquity's basic principle, and was on the way to
founding a new age. —*Die Staatslehre* (1813), in *Sämtliche
Werke*, ed. I. H. Fichte (Berlin, 1835–64), IV, 505.

2   Now this spirit emanating from the Father had become ob-
jectified even before the coming of Christ, without His knowing it or having to know it, and had actually burst into objective form in Socrates of Athens. It was in him that the understanding had seized upon itself, and had discovered itself
as a peculiar and strictly aprioristic source of cognitions, and
thus been put to use by aiding the development of truth. And
this was just as great a miracle with respect to the *form* of
truth, and as tremendous an advancement of mankind, as was
the miracle in Jesus with respect to the *content* of truth.
—*Ibid.*, pp. 569-70.

    [5] Dich erklärte der Pythia Mund für den weisesten Griechen,
       Wohl, der weiseste mag oft der beschwerlichste sein.

FRIEDRICH SCHLEIERMACHER (1768–1834)

The awakening of the idea of knowledge, with its first mani- 1
festation: this must have been the content of Socrates' philosophy; and this is the reason why he is always rightly considered to have been the author of that later Hellenic philosophy
whose whole essence, along with all its detailed variations, is
determined by this very idea. It was impossible for him to
know only that he did not know; behind this was of necessity
the claim that he knew what knowing was, that in all true
thoughts the knowing was the same, that all knowing was one
and indivisible. ——"Über den Wert des Sokrates als Philosophen" (Abhandlungen der Berliner Akademie, philosophische
Klasse, 1818), pp. 50 ff., in *Sämtliche Werke*, III, 2, 300.

Socrates was the true originator of dialectic, which remained 2
the soul of all later great edifices of Hellenic philosophy. . . .
Hence we can but approve of the historical instinct which
has always assigned such a high rank to this man. ——*Ibid.*,
p. 303.

Socrates did not range far beyond this center, but devoted 3
his whole life to the dissemination and activation of his main
idea; it was his sole desire that—no matter what shape man's
peculiar nature may give to his historical wishes and hopes—
before men should begin to range widely, this foundation
should first achieve real solidity. ——*Ibid.*, pp. 305-06.

FRIEDRICH HÖLDERLIN (1770–1843)
Socrates and Alcibiades

"Why, holy Socrates, do you always pay homage to this 1
youth? Do you know nothing greater? Why does your eye
dwell upon him as upon gods?"

He who has thought what is deepest loves what is most living; he who has looked out upon the world understands noble youth, and in the end the wise often bow their heads to that which is fair.[6] ——*Sämtliche Werke,* ed. Fr. Beissner (Stuttgart, 1943), I, 1, 260.

2   Only, each has his measure. For misfortune is hard to bear, fortune even harder. But one sage was able, from noon to midnight, and till the (next) morning was bright, to remain clear-headed at the banquet.[7] ——From "Der Rhein" (1801), ll. 202-09, in *Sämtliche Werke* (Berlin), IV, 179.

GEORG WILHELM FRIEDRICH HEGEL (1770-1831)

1   Dialectic is nothing new in philosophy. Among the ancients Plato is called the inventor of dialectic, and rightly so, inasmuch as it is in Platonic philosophy that dialectic occurs in purely scientific and thus at the same time objective form. In Socrates the dialectical element, in accordance with the general character of his philosophizing, has still a predominantly

----

6   Warum huldigest du, heiliger Sokrates,
            Diesem Jünglinge stets? Kennest du Grösseres nicht?
                Warum siehet mit Liebe,
                    Wie auf Götter, dein Aug' auf ihn?

        Wer das Tiefste gedacht, liebt das Lebendigste,
            Hohe Jugend versteht, wer in die Welt geblickt,
                Und es neigen die Weisen
                    Oft am Ende zu Schönem sich.

   (For the new reading "Jugend" for the older "Tugend," see *Kommentarband* (1943), I, 2, 574-75.

7   Nur hat ein jeder sein Mass.
                        Denn schwer ist zu tragen
                        Das Unglück, aber schwerer das Glück.
                        Ein Weiser aber vermocht es
                        Vom Mittag bis in die Mitternacht
                        Und bis der Morgen erglänzte
                        Beim Gastmahl helle zu bleiben.

subjective form, namely that of irony. For one thing, Socrates pits his dialectic against the ordinary consciousness and then especially against the Sophists. Then, in his conversations he would pretend that he wished to inform himself about the matter under discussion. In this connection he would raise all kinds of questions and thus he would lead those with whom he was talking to take a view opposite to that which they had originally thought was correct. ——*Enzyklopädie der philosophischen Wissenschaften* (1817), Pt. I, 82, in *Werke* (1832–45), VI, 153-54.

[In the teaching of Socrates, reason (*nous*) is shown as determining on its own authority what is right and good. Socrates makes knowledge embrace virtue, since only knowledge can distinguish the good (from the bad).] Thus his starting point is inwardness, moral consciousness. The moral man is not the one who merely wants to do what is right and does it, nor the man without guilt, but he who is conscious of what he is doing.

By making man's actions subject to his rational conviction, Socrates gives the individual who thus sets himself up as an oracle, in the Greek sense, authority as over against country and customs. Socrates claimed that he had a daemon in himself which advised him what to do and revealed to him actions which would be useful to his friends. For this reason and because this made him an opponent of Greek morality, the Athenians condemned him. Socrates' pupil Plato [even] banished Homer and Hesiod, the authors of the Greek world of religious ideas, from his state, and thus subjective freedom and moral subjectivity took the place of their plastic (i.e., sensuous) culture. The principle which guided Socrates proves to be revolutionary in its effect upon the Athenian state; when he wants to make his friends think, his remarks are always negative, i.e., he makes them aware that they do not know what the right is. But then, when he is condemned to death for enunciating the principle which is destined to predominate from now on, his fate involves this tragedy: the Athenians had to find out that what they had condemned in Socrates had already taken firm root among them, and that therefore they themselves were equally guilty or equally innocent. Feeling this, the Athenians [later] condemned the accusers of Socrates and declared him innocent. ——*Vorlesungen über die Philosophie der Geschichte,* in *Werke,* IX, 279-80.

3   Consciousness had advanced to this point in Greece when Socrates entered—the great figure of Socrates. The subjectivity of thought was made conscious in Socrates in a more definite, more penetrating way. However, he did not spring up from the soil like a mushroom; he has his position in the continuity of his time. He is not only an extremely important figure in the history of philosophy—the most interesting in ancient philosophy—but he is a key personality in world history. He himself constitutes the main turning point of the World Spirit in himself; this turn expressed itself in Socrates in the form of thought. ——*Vorlesungen über die Geschichte der Philosophie,* in *Werke,* XIV, 39.

4   Socrates fulfilled the command of the Delphic Apollo, "Know thyself," and made it the motto of the Greeks. He is the hero who in place of the Delphic god established the principle: man himself knows what the truth is; he should look into himself. . . . This is Socrates' revolution; he puts the self-awareness of each individual, the general consciousness of thought in each individual, in place of the oracle. This inner certitude is indeed a new and different god, not the one whom the Athenians had previously worshiped, and therefore the charge made against Socrates is quite valid. ——*Ibid.,* pp. 91-92.

5   The people of Athens upheld the right of their laws and customs against Socrates' attack upon and violation of them. Socrates did violence to the spirit and the moral life of his people, and this violation brought on punishment. But Soc-

rates was at the same time the hero who had the right on his side, the absolute right of the self-confident spirit, of the consciousness that is its own authority. Now, as this new principle collided with the existing mentality, with the spirit of his people, the latter had to react against it. But only the individual was annihilated by the penalty, not the principle; the spirit of the Athenian people did not recover from its violation, from its *Aufhebung* (i.e., dialectical negation). The wrong form of individuality is wiped out, even violently, by the execution of the penalty. (But) the principle (itself) will rise later in its true form. . . . It was not possible for Socrates' own world to see him in this light, but posterity can do so, since it stands above both of them. ——*Ibid.*, pp. 100-1.

Thus the fate of Socrates is a genuine tragedy. In general, the nature of a morally tragic fate is just this, that one right challenges another: not as if only one were right and the other wrong, but in such a way that each is right as opposed to the other and shatters itself on the other. So both are losers and both are also mutually justified. The Athenian people had entered that period of their development when the consciousness of the individual detached itself from that of the social whole and became independent. The Athenians were aware of this in Socrates (they were right, so was he), but at the same time they felt that this meant disaster; and so it was a force within themselves that they were punishing. In establishing this new principle, Socrates did not commit a crime as an individual, for all the Athenians were involved in it; it was a crime that the spirit of the people committed against itself. This insight "negates" the condemnation of Socrates. Socrates did not seem to himself to have committed a crime. . . . For the spirit of the people is now the individual consciousness, which returns from the general consciousness into itself. It is the disintegration of this people, whose spirit will therefore soon disappear from the world, but in such a conflagration, as it were, that from its ashes a higher spirit will arise. For the

World Spirit has risen to a higher consciousness. Socrates is
the hero, inasmuch as he has consciously recognized and enunciated the higher principle of the spirit. The higher principle has absolute validity. . . . The principle of the Greeks
could not yet tolerate the principle of subjective reflection,
which therefore entered the scene as something hostile and
destructive. Consequently the Athenian people, in accordance
with their laws, were not only entitled but bound to react
against it; and therefore they regarded this (Socratic) principle as a crime. This is the general position of heroes in
world history; they cause new worlds to rise. Such a new principle is in conflict with the preceding one, seems to be a disintegrating influence; the heroes appear as destroyers, as vio-
lators of the laws. As individuals they are doomed; but the
principle they represent, although [it may be] in different
form, breaks through and undermines the existing world.
The Socratic principle was one which in a different form put
an end to the Greek way of life; [for] Alcibiades and Critias
were the greatest favorites of Socrates: Critias, the most efficient of the Thirty Tyrants, and Alcibiades, a genius of irre-
sponsibility, who had made a plaything of the Athenian
people. This was another thing which put Socrates in a bad
light. The principle of relying on one's individual judgment
took a practical form in them; they lived their lives according
to this principle.

The Athenian State continued to exist for a long time, but
the blossom of its originality soon wilted. The originality of
Socrates consists in the fact that he had conceived this principle in thought and in knowledge, and applied it to the latter
only. This is the higher method (than that of Critias and Alcibiades). Knowledge has brought the Fall (*Sündenfall*), but
it has also brought the principle of salvation. Thus that which
in others was only disaster, in Socrates (being a principle of
knowledge) was also the principle which included both the
disaster and the cure. The development of this principle
makes up the whole of subsequent history. —*Ibid.*, p. 102 ff.

NOVALIS (1772–1801)

Illustrations of the difference between acquired greatness and high (inborn) harmony: Themistocles and Socrates. In the latter, happiness seems not to be the result of favorable circumstances, but a true emanation of his being. Misfortune itself is turned into fortune by his touch. ——*Schriften,* ed. J. Minor (Jena, 1923), III, 169.

FRIEDRICH SCHLEGEL (1772–1829)

Socratic irony interweaves the most sacred with the gay and the frivolous. ——*Geschichte der Poesie der Griechen und Römer* (1798), in *Prosaische Jugendschriften,* ed. J. Minor (Vienna, 1882), I, p. 239. 1

Not only the cities and the mores of the Greek city-states, but also the arts of oratory, all the knowledge which makes use of speech for action and communication, and the general mode of thinking, had been poisoned, corrupted, and thoroughly ruined until Socrates moved to resist the stream of corruption and hemmed it, as far as this was still possible. In so doing, this eager friend and investigator of truth, a mere citizen of Athens living in the plainest and most modest circumstances, and acting upon only a small circle of picked disciples and like-minded friends, exerted an influence on the cultural training and literature of the Greeks, and achieved an epoch in it, hardly equaled by the legislator Solon before him and the conqueror Alexander after him. ——*Geschichte der alten und neuen Literatur* (1812), in *Kritische Friedrich-Schlegel-Ausgabe,* ed. Ernst Behler (Munich, 1961), VI, 43. 2

In the midst of this general atheism [of the Sophists] Socrates arose and taught God once again in a completely prac- 3

tical manner, first by fighting the Sophists and revealing their
vacuousness, and then by putting before people's eyes, and
bringing close to their hearts, the good and the beautiful, the
noble and the perfect, justice and virtue, and in all their
forms, in short, whatever leads to God and comes from him.
Thus he became the second founder and restorer of all the
better and higher education of the Greek spirit, but became
himself a victim of his eagerness and of the truth. His death
is too noteworthy an event in the history of mankind for us
not to dwell on it for some time.   —*Ibid.*, pp. 52-53.

FRIEDRICH WILHELM SCHELLING (1775–1854)

1   Zeno of Elea might be called the Chronos of philosophy, because he tried to keep everything immovable and fought
against plurality. The destroyer of this unity, the man whose
appearance marks a no less important period in the history of
the philosophizing spirit than the appearance of Dionysus
does in the movement of mythology, the true Dionysus of philosophy, is that daemonic man—Socrates, who first dissolved
that immovable unit of the Eleatics by a *real*, destructive dialectics, not a merely seeming one, which leads back again to
such unity; who made room for free life, for free distinctive
variety; Socrates, of whom one of the ancients said that jok-
ingly and playfully he had blown away like smoke the bom-
bast of the Eleatics, and of the Sophists who had descended
from them; who is celebrated for having led philosophy at
last from heaven to earth, surely in no other sense than the
one that religion, by the agency of the god whom he resembled, had descended from the regions of heaven, the infinite
and uniformly One, to earth, the scene of variegated and
changing life; who had led philosophy from the narrowness of
merely substance-bound (*substantiell*) and unfree knowledge
into the breadth and freedom of intelligent, discriminating,
explaining knowledge, which alone made Aristotle possible.
But even the mythological method of presentation of Socrates

might permit a different evaluation from that superficial and cheap one which sees in all this nothing but lack of science. The great thing in Socrates is the consciousness that certain questions do not admit of rational, but only of historical answers. He might well have liked to substitute real history for myths, had he not lacked great and necessary data which are now in our possession. ——*Philosophie der Mythologie* (1842 and 1845–6), 13th Lecture, in *Sämtliche Werke* (Stuttgart, 1856 ff.), II, Abteilung II, 283–84.

There are human deeds and actions which not everybody 2 understands. How many are there who would have been able to die like Socrates? One may assume with near certainty that to the majority of his contemporaries his accusers were by far more reasonable people than he, just as one might assume that in a similar case of life and death they would have behaved before the judges quite differently from Socrates. —— *Philosophie der Offenbarung* (1841), 24th Lecture, in *Werke*, II, Abteilung IV, 26-27.

Socrates was sufficiently great to fill the whole distance be- 3 tween the accounts of Xenophon and Plato. True greatness consists in condescension, in the ability to step down to the lowliest positions without losing one's height. The secret of this condescension in Socrates, which we notice is Xenophon's *Memorabilia,* lies in the persistently moral significance even of his highest and most speculative concepts, which resulted in the fact, celebrated by Alcibiades, that none of his students left him without feeling at the same time morally better and uplifted. ——*Ibid.,* p. 325.

ARTHUR SCHOPENHAUER (1788–1860)

The wisdom of Socrates is an article of philosophical faith. 1 That the Platonic Socrates is an ideal, hence a poetical personality expressing Platonic ideas, is patent. In Xenophon's

Socrates there is not very much wisdom to be found. According to Lucian, Socrates had a potbelly, which after all is not one of the trademarks of genius. Equally in doubt are the high intellectual capacities of all those who did no writing, hence also of Pythagoras. ——"Fragmente zur Geschichte der Philosophie," sec. 3, in *Parerga und Paralipomena* (1851).

2   One can find quite a few similarities between Socrates and Kant. Both reject dogmatism. Both confess their ignorance in matters of metaphysics and regard as peculiar to themselves their definite consciousness of this ignorance. Both however assert that the practical, that which man is to do and not to do, is completely certain. It was the fate of both that their immediate successors and declared disciples, for all their loyalty, diverged from their masters just in the matter of these fundamental concepts and, by dint of working in metaphysics, erected completely dogmatic systems; furthermore, that these systems turned out to be extremely different from each other, though all the thinkers agreed in claiming to have started from their teachers Socrates and Kant. ——*Ibid.*

3   The advantage of the Socratic method, as we know it from Plato, consists in having one's partner as opponent admit one by one the reasons for the propositions which one intends to prove, before he has realized the implications [of his several admissions]. . . . Meanwhile, one of the things of which Plato tries to convince us is this: that by the use of this method Socrates had the privilege of proving to the Sophists and other fools that that was what they were. Such a claim is out of the question. ——*Ibid.*

HEINRICH HEINE (1797–1856)

That Xanthippe's husband became such a great philosopher is remarkable. That he was able to think during all that nagging! But write he could not, for that was impossible; Soc-

rates did not leave one single book. ——"Gedanken und Ein-
fälle," in *Sämtliche Werke,* ed. Ernst Elster (Leipzig, 1890),
VII, 443.

MAX STIRNER (1806–1856)

Socrates says: you must be "of pure heart" if you want your
shrewdness to be respected. With him the second period of the
Greek liberation of the spirit begins, the period of the pure
heart. . . . The intellect of the Sophists had mastered the previously prevailing powers to such an extent that they had
only to be chased from the heart, where they lived unmolested,
to lose in the end their share of man completely. This war,
begun by Socrates, did not attain to its peace treaty until the
death day of the ancient world. With Socrates the examination of the heart begins, and all the content of the heart is
sifted. In their last and extreme efforts the ancients removed
all content out of the heart and no longer allowed it to beat
for anything; this was the feat of the skeptics. The sophist
education had the effect that nothing any longer gives pause
to the intellect, and the effect of the skeptic education was
that the heart was no longer moved by anything. . . . The
gigantic work of the ancients had this result: man knows himself as a being without ties and without a world, simply as a
spirit. ——*Der Einzige und sein Eigentum* (1847), (Leipzig,
1892) 1. Abteilung I, 27-28.

KARL MARX (1818–1883)

The character of the sage . . . is embodied in the center of   1
Greek philosophy, as it were, in Socrates, its demiurge. ——
"Die Philosophie des Epikurus," in Marx and Engels, *Ge-
samtausgabe* (Frankfurt, 1937), I, 14.

If there is an analogy at all between Socrates and Christ, it   2
would be that Socrates is philosophy personified, Christ religion personified. ——*Ibid.,* p. 135.

JACOB BURCKHARDT (1818–1897)

1   Socrates was the gravedigger of the Attic city. The son of
Sophroniscus, with his disconcerting dialectic, educated the
sons of the city, but not for the republic. Alcibiades is half
charlatan, half genius, but a baroque one; he is useless to a
free state. . . . Such a seminar testifies to the teacher. The
democrats were quite right, from their standpoint, when they
condemned him. With his arrogant *Apology* and his stub-
bornness he ruined his own case completely. His greatness remains all the same; but it is not right if we utterly disregard
the motives of the Athenian democrats, those (in part) wholly
honest and sincerely pious men, or reject them with a super-
ciliousness equal to our lack of understanding. Furthermore,
gentlemen, I can very well understand that so proud, ironical,
and negativistic a man as Socrates was highly unpopular in a
democracy. His cross-questioning made people utterly per-
plexed. The young gentlemen, his pupils [*die Herren Schüler*],
would stand by and smile. Hence the animosities which
brought death upon him. He wanted to "make the Athenians
better," he said. But he only made them confused and left
them to themselves. . . . He must have been odious to many
people. He himself says so in his *Apology*. This is only too
understandable. Just imagine that someone should appear in
the market place or walk into the city hall and ask the first
member of a trades union who went by, "Tell me, brother,
your trade is one of a certain kind, isn't it?" The more the
latter makes concession on concession, answering with the
habitual courtesy and urbanity of the Athenians by "that is
understood," "it seems so," "strikingly correct," "you speak
the truth," the more inexorably our philosopher continues his
hounding and his catechizing; mercilessly he cuts off all re-
treats. He drives the poor philosophical test specimen from
position to position, until at last he is struggling helplessly in
the nets of Socrates' analytical method and his dialectical
snares. Imagine then as a chorus the whole overbearing gang

of the *jeunesse dorée* of Athens, with an Alcibiades and a Critias at the head of it; of course they burst out into a salvo of laughter and glee at the dialectical success of their teacher, while the refuted solid citizen sneaks away, shamed and with bitter resentment in his heart. Yes, gentlemen, the appearance and the behavior of Socrates and the Socratics may have had a striking effect by virtue of their novelty, but he decidedly did not make his company popular. ——From a lecture taken down by Heinrich Geltzer and printed in *Ausgewählte Kleine Schriften* (Leipzig, 1907), pp. 312 ff.

Let us begin our consideration of the free personality [in 2 Greece] with the great original figure of Socrates. Next to the mythical Ulysses Socrates is the best known Greek and, even if seen in the fullest light, the first personality in the entire history of the world about whom we are fully and accurately informed—not, to be sure, as to his life (especially in his earlier years) but about his being. The remarkable figure who planted himself in the midst of Athens and exerted from there the greatest influence upon the whole world, was not only a model of piety, self-control, unselfishness, and steadfastness, but also an extremely peculiar individual, whose actions were equally peculiar. ——*Griechische Kulturgeschichte,* III, in *Gesamtausgabe* (Stuttgart, 1931), X, 352.

We should not be in the least surprised at the hostility 3 which he encountered in his day. Improving others is in itself something which people do not always accept with good grace, since everyone thinks that he is certainly good enough for his station, and when Socrates confused people, leaving them afterwards to the effects of their confusion, he necessarily impressed some as a hairsplitter, and encouraged his being confused with the Sophists. But that which still seems highly suspicious is the emphasis he put upon Chaerephon's inquiry at Delphi,[8] the oracle of which had even then become notorious. ——*Ibid.,* p. 354.

[8] See *Apology* 21a.

FRIEDRICH ALBERT LANGE (1828–1875)

1   In the summertime of the new Athenian philosophy . . .
ethical and logical questions came so much to the fore that
everything else was forgotten. Whence came this one-sided
prominence of ethical and logical problems? The answer to
this question must at once show us what was the inmost principle of life through which the new tendency arose, and whose
force gives it a higher and more independent value than that
of a mere reaction against materialism and sensationalism.
Here, however, it is impossible to separate the men from the
doctrines, the purely philosophical doctrines from the whole
intellectual movement, if we wish to understand why certain
philosophical innovations could attain such significance. It
was Socrates who called the new tendency into life. Plato gave
it its idealistic stamp, and Aristotle, by connecting it with
empirical elements, created out of it that ultimate system
which thenceforth dominated the thought of so many centuries. Opposition to materialism culminates in Plato; the
Aristotelian system made the most obstinate stand against ma-
terialistic theories; but the attack was begun by one of the
most remarkable men of whom history tells, a character of
rare greatness and resolution—the Athenian Socrates. —*Geschichte des Materialismus* (1866), tr. E. C. Thomas (Boston,
1877), I, 59-60.

2   The Socratic "irony" . . . with which he professes ignorance
and asks instruction from his opponent, is often only the thin
veil of dogmatism which is ever ready, in the least embarrassment, innocently and to all appearances only tentatively, to
impose a ready-made opinion, and, unobserved, to gain it acceptance. Yet this is a dogmatism which consisted in the constant repetition of few and simple dogmas: virtue is knowledge . . . and so on. . . .

With regard to the special meaning of self-knowledge and the doctrine of virtue, Socrates remains always a seeker only. ... When we reach the point where we should be given something more, we find either a mere attempt or the everlasting Socratic ignorance. He is apparently content with the negation of the negation. . . . This result, however, purely negative as it appears, is as far removed from skepticism as the heavens. . . . He contents himself with making room for genuine knowledge by destroying mere sham knowledge and by the constitution and employment of a method which shall be capable of discerning true from seeming knowledge. Criticism, therefore, as opposed to skepticism, is the function of this method; and in the vindication of criticism as the instrument of science we have at least one achievement of his activity that possesses a permanent value. And yet his chief significance for the history of philosophy does not lie here, but in his belief in knowledge and its object, the universal essence of things, the stationary pole in the flight of phenomena. Although this belief may have overshot the mark, yet the indispensable step, which the flagging energies of Relativism and Materialism were incapable of taking, was taken—the treatment of the universal in its relation to the individual, of conceptions in contrast to mere perception. The tares of Platonic idealism grew up together with the wheat; but the ground was again prepared: when a strong hand took the plough, the field of philosophy again bore fruit a hundredfold, just when it seemed destined to be unproductive. —*Ibid.*, pp. 69-71.

WILHELM DILTHEY (1833–1911)

In the powerful intellectual system of Socrates, a profound 1
and sustained labor of thought was carried out, whereby a new stage in the purposeful framework of knowledge was reached. In the sophistic philosophy he had found the searching, doubt-

ing intellect, which existing metaphysics could not withstand. Amid the immense upheaval of all concepts, he tried to find some solid ground; it was this positive element in his great spirit, thirsting for truth, which differentiated him from the Sophists. He was the first to apply systematically the method of *going back from the actual knowledge and belief of the time to the justifying ground of each proposition*. That is, in place of a procedure which derived from brilliant assertions, he employed a method which traced each theorem back to its logical foundation. Specifically, since with this Greek people even scientific life went on in public, the simplest and most obvious form of search for the justifying ground of current opinions had to be the *question* as to that justifying ground, a question which did not release the one questioned until he had said his last: *the Socratic dialogue*. With it, the history of the intellect witnessed the birth of that analytic procedure which goes back to the final cognitive foundations of our scientific knowledge and ultimately of all scientific conviction. And this is why, once the untiring questioner had been silenced by his judges, the dialogue became the art form of his school of philosophy. By thus examining the existing science and the existing convictions to find their justifying ground, he proved that *science was not yet in existence*, not in any field. Of the entire science of the cosmos nothing withstood his method save the reference of the purposive connections in the cosmos to a world-shaping intelligence. Nor did Socrates meet with any distinct awareness of scientific necessity in the area of moral and social life. He saw that the actions of the statesman and the procedure of the poet were lacking in clarity as to their justifying ground, and hence impotent to justify themselves in the light of reason. But at the same time he discovered that *just* and *unjust, good* and *bad, fair* and *ugly*, possess an unalterable meaning above the conflict of opinions.

Here, in the field of action, the power of introspective reflection, which entered history with Socrates, arrived at posi-

tive results. . . . Did Socrates transcend the limits which we have pointed out as those of Greek man as such? Even on Socrates, with all his introspective reflection, it did not dawn that the external world is a phenomenon of our consciousness, yet that in this very phenomenon a being and a reality are given, whose recognition reveals to us, for the first time, an incontestable reality. True, this introspective reflection represented the deepest level ever reached by Greek man in his retreat to the truly positive, just as the frivolity of Gorgias's Nothingness marked the extreme limit reached by his skeptical behavior. But such reflection is only a retreat to the cognitive basis of knowledge; hence it gives rise to logic as a theory of science, seen by Plato as a possibility and developed by Aristotle. Connected with this is the search for the cognitive basis of moral propositions in our consciousness; and this gives rise to the Platonic-Aristotelian ethics. Hence this introspective reflection is logical and ethical. It formulates rules for relating thought to external being in the knowledge of the external world, and for relating the will to this being by way of action. But it still lacks any anticipation of the fact that consciousness means the rise of a powerful reality, in fact, the only one of which we are immediately aware, and even less of the fact that all reality is given us only in our lived experience. . . .
——*Einleitung in die Geisteswissenschaften* (1883), in *Gesammelte Schriften* (Leipzig, 1913 ff.), I, 177 ff.

The realization of the nature and the value of individuality developed slowly in Europe. Socrates was the first to rise to the consciousness of that moral process in himself which made the full formation of a unified personality possible. This "know thyself" applied at first to what is uniform in human nature. However, against the background of knowledge stood out the potent but unexplorable phenomenon which he dubbed the *daimonion,* and which, without a doubt, belonged to the depth of the subjective. From then on Socrates became for his students, for the Stoics, [later] for Montaigne and others, the model of a mind which turns its thinking inward into the depths of its own nature. —"Ideen über eine beschreibende und zergliedernde Psychologie" (1894), in *Schriften,* V, 225.

3   Even in the pedagogical genius there is something original. He has appeared in history perhaps more rarely than the poet and the artist. Socrates, Plato, Comenius, Pestalozzi, Herbart, Fröbel, are undoubtedly of this type. . . . Where this [un-broken naïveté] is combined with a strong intellectual ability, that uniquely enthralling form of spiritual life appears which Plato depicted in the Socrates of the *Symposium.* On the back-ground of naïve understanding there arises then a reflection upon the spiritual life so vivid, so full of reality, that it does not admit of scientific analysis. —"Über die Möglichkeit einer allgemeingültigen pädagogischen Wissenschaft," in *Schriften,* VI, 4.

4   The idealism of freedom (*Idealismus der Freiheit*) is the creation of the Athenian spirit. The form-giving, creative, sov-ereign energy in it becomes the principle of the understanding of the universe in Anaxagoras, Socrates, Plato, Aristotle. Cicero stated emphatically his agreement with Socrates and everything Socratic in the subsequent Greek period. And eminent Christian apologists and Church Fathers find them-selves in conscious agreement with the Socratic spirit, as well as with Roman philosophy. —"Die Typen der Weltan-schauung und ihre Ausbildung in den metaphysischen Sy-stemen," in *Schriften,* VIII, 107.

5   *The Pedagogical Genius of Socrates and His Pedagogical Principle*

Socrates was a pedagogical genius the like of which an-tiquity never had again. This can be proved by the immediate impression made upon his contemporaries, but it can also be inferred from his effects. With him an entirely new element entered the history of education: penetration into the most intimate life of the young. Here the Platonic *eros*—a pedagogical love—the attempt to assist in the birth of ideas in their minds by means of conversation, the effort to make knowledge and truth the guiding powers in their conduct, were inextricably connected. How great was the spell which he exerted! . . .

It is in keeping with the pedagogical genius of Socrates that the leading principle attributed to him was a pedagogical one: Virtue is knowledge, therefore it is teachable. . . .

If this idea is compared with the pedagogical method prevalent until then, whose only goal it had been to fill the individual with the great moral-political ideas already realized in the nation, the literature, and the state, no more radical change can be imagined. No longer were the traditions of the community to establish for the individual what was the good, the law, and the task of individual education. The individual was to develop out of his own consciousness what was law for him. If, however, one views Socrates in the context of the intellectual movement which had disintegrated all ideas and, through the Sophists, was now also taking hold of education, he appears as the representative of the only mentality which was in a position to stop the decay of the Greek states for some time to come.

Socrates had the idea of reforming the moral-political condition of Athens, by establishing scientifically the highest moral and political concepts and by developing pedagogically the scientific consciousness in young and old. It was a moment when the highest tasks of education and of scientific inquiry seemed to coincide. He was no more in a position to solve this task than his great pupil Plato, but they founded a scientific school and made scientific progress in the development of mankind which, across the ruins of the Greek states, has influenced the spiritual life of all nations. ——"Geschichte der Pädagogik," in *Schriften,* IX, 38.

FRANZ BRENTANO (1838–1917)

1   We simply cannot admit that only a miracle can make corrupt human nature accept and follow a doctrine as noble
and fair as the Christian religion, as Pascal argues. Even without any connection with Christianity noble moral ideas have
been enunciated, and those who pleaded them not only translated them into their own lives but also influenced others to
adopt them as their guides in action: Socrates in his poverty,
Aristotle in his wealth, Epictetus in his slave's attire, and
Marcus Aurelius on his throne.   ——*Die Lehre Jesu und ihre
bleibende Bedeutung* (Leipzig, 1922), p. 51.

2   Jesus calls himself meek, but one cannot say with sincerity
that in his meekness he equaled Socrates.   ——*Ibid.*, pp. 73-74.

3   Is adjustment to others something good in itself? . . . Had
Socrates been adjusted in this manner, he would not have
emptied the cup of hemlock. . . . It is the nonadjusted Socrates in whom we revere the morally superior person and
whose ethical feeling and judgment we revere as the nobler
and the better. . . . We recognize in him a man who has overtaken his time in the direction which it has begun to take, and
this is why we pay him reverence.   ——*Grundlegung und
Aufbau der Ethik* (Bern, 1952), pp. 71-72.

4   Socrates was so convinced of the idea [that natural law demanded obedience to a conflicting positive law] that he, while
believing himself to be condemned unjustly, refrained from
escaping. . . . It is open to question whether Socrates did not
go too far in this matter.   ——*Ibid.*, pp. 351-52.

FRIEDRICH NIETZSCHE (1844–1900)

1   Socrates, to confess it frankly, is so close to me that almost
always I fight against him.   ——Fragment from "Wissenschaft

und Weisheit im Kampfe" (1875), in *Nietzsches Gesammelte Werke* (Leipzig, Stuttgart, 1920–29), VI, 101.

In a certain sense, Euripides was only a mask; the deity 2 which spoke through him was not Dionysus and not Apollo either, but a completely newborn daemon named Socrates. This is the new antithesis: the Dionysian and the Socratic, and the art of Greek tragedy died of it. ——*Die Geburt der Tragödie* (1873), in *Nietzsches Werke* (Stuttgart, 1921), I, 118.

. . . Socratism condemns equally the existing art and the 3 existing ethics; wherever it directs its testing glance, it sees nothing but lack of insight and threat of illusion and infers from this lack the inner pervertedness and unworthiness of the existing. Under this one aspect Socrates believes he is to straighten out life: as the forerunner of a totally different culture, art, and morality he, the single individual, enters with an air of disrespect and superiority a world such that we would count it supreme happiness to touch the hem of it.

This is the immense hesitation which restrains us every time we encounter Socrates, and which stirs us again and again to find out the meaning and purpose of this most questionable phenomenon of antiquity. Who is this man who, a single individual, dares deny the Greek essence which, as Homer, Pindar, and Aeschylus, as Phidias, as Pericles, as Pythia and Dionysus, as the deepest abyss and highest peak, is certain of our admiring adoration? What daemonic power is this which has the audacity to pour his magic draft into the dust? What demigod is this to whom the spirit-choir conceived by the noblest of mankind must exclaim:

Woe! Woe! You have destroyed the lovely world with mighty fist; it tumbles and falls apart! [9]

We are offered a key to the essence of Socrates by that strange phenomenon which goes by the name of the *daimonion*

[9] Goethe, *Faust* I, 1607-08.

of Socrates. In special situations in which his enormous intellect lost its balance he gained a firm support by a divine
voice expressing itself in such moments. This voice when it
comes always *dissuades*. In this utterly abnormal being instinctive wisdom manifests itself only in order to obstruct conscious knowledge occasionally. Whereas in all productive people instinct is precisely the creative, affirmative power, and
consciousness acts critically and warningly, in Socrates instinct
becomes the critic, consciousness the creator—a veritable mon-
strosity by way of defect! To be more specific, we observe here
a monstrous lack of every mystic endowment, so that Socrates
should be named the distinctive *nonmystic* in whom the logical element has been just as excessively developed by over-
growth as that instinctive wisdom has developed in the mystic.
On the other hand that logical drive which appeared in Socrates was denied completely the power to turn against itself;
in this uncontrolled torrential stream it shows an elemental
power such as we encounter with shuddering surprise only in
the most immense instinctive forces. Anyone who has gained
from the writings of Plato as much as a whiff of the divine
naïveté and assurance which marks the Socratic orientation
of life will also feel how the huge driving-wheel of logical
Socratism is in motion, as it were, behind Socrates, and how
this must be looked at through Socrates as through a shadow.
However, the fact that he himself had an inkling of this relation is expressed in the dignified seriousness with which, everywhere and even before his judges, he asserts his divine mission.
To refute him on this point was fundamentally just as impossible as to approve of his influence in promoting the disintegration of the instincts. In view of this hopeless conflict,
only *one* form of condemnation was indicated, once the matter
had been brought before the tribunal of the Greek state, and
that was banishment; he could have been expelled and taken
across the border as somebody who was thoroughly enigmatic,
unclassifiable, unexplainable, thus giving posterity no right
to accuse the Athenians of a shameful deed. However, that
death rather than banishment was the sentence was the result

which Socrates himself brought about with clear determination and without the natural abhorrence of death; he went to his death with the calmness with which, according to Plato's account, he left the symposium as the last of the guests at early dawn, to begin a new day; while behind him on the benches and on the ground the sleepy companions stayed to dream of Socrates, the true exponent of Platonic love. The dying Socrates became the new ideal, never before envisaged, of the noble youths of Greece; in advance of all the others that typical Hellenic youth, Plato, prostrated himself before this image with all his ardent devotion. . . .

Let us now imagine the one great Cyclops eye of Socrates turned on tragedy, that eye in which the sweet madness of artistic enthusiasm never glowed; let us think how this eye was forbidden to look with approval into the Dionysian abysses—what was it really bound to see in the "sublime and much praised" tragic art, as Plato called it? Something quite irrational, with causes that seemed to be without effects and effects without causes; moreover, the whole so motley and variegated that it could not but antagonize a balanced mind and constitute dangerous fuel for emotional and sensitive souls. We know what was the only type of poetry that Socrates understood: Aesop's fables. . . . But now, in Socrates' eyes, tragic art did not even "tell the truth," not to mention the fact that it appealed to him who "has not much brains," consequently not to the philosopher: two reasons for keeping away from it. Like Plato, he counted it as one of the blandishing arts, which present only the pleasant and the useful, and therefore he required of his disciples abstinence and rigid separation from such unphilosophical enticements—with such success that the youthful tragedy writer Plato burned his own poems at the outset, to become a student of Socrates. —*Ibid.*, pp. 126-29.

If even before Socrates we have to assume a trend working 4 against the Dionysian (principle) which, not new, merely finds incredibly magnificent expression in him: then we must not shrink from asking the question where a phenomenon such as Socrates points, since in view of the Platonic dialogues we are not in a position to interpret him only as a negative force promoting disintegration. And although the immediate effect of the Socratic drive was directed toward the disintegration of tragedy in the Dionysian vein, an experience of deep significance in Socrates' own life forces us to raise the question whether the only possible relation between Socratism and art is antagonism, and whether the birth of an "artistic Socrates" is in itself a contradiction in terms.

For that despotic logician had the feeling, now and then, of a gap in his relation to art, of an emptiness, of half a reproach of a possible neglect of duty. . . . That saying of the Socratic dream apparition in prison ["Socrates, make music"] is the only indication of a doubt about the limits of the logical: perhaps—so he had to ask himself—that which is unintelligible to me is not necessarily unreasonable? Perhaps there is one domain of wisdom from which the logician is banned? Perhaps art is even a necessary correlate and supplement of science?   ——*Ibid.*, pp. 133-34.

5   In order to claim for Socrates such a leading role, it is not enough to recognize in him a form of existence without precedent before him, the type of the theoretical man. . . . A profound delusion entered the world in the personality of Socrates—an unshakable faith that thought, conducted by the guiding thread of causality, can reach down to the depths of being, and that thought is not only able to know being but even to correct it. . . . Let us now look at Socrates with the torch of this idea: he appears to us as the first man who, guided by that instinct of science, was able not only to live, but, what is far more, also to die; and for that reason the picture of the *dying Socrates* as that of the man raised above the fear of death by knowledge and reason is the escutcheon which, above the entrance gate of science, reminds everyone of its mission: to make existence appear as intelligible and hence as justified; this purpose, however, if reasons do not

suffice, must be achieved by a myth which I have already designated as even a necessary implication, indeed as an objective, of science.

Anyone who calls to mind how after Socrates, the mystagogue of science, one philosophical school followed another like wave upon wave, how a never-suspected universal craving for knowledge, spread through the widest range of the educated and conceived as the proper task for every superior intelligence, took science out onto the high seas, from which since then it could never be completely chased back again, how this universality at last suspended a common network of thought over the whole globe, indeed with perspectives toward the order of the whole solar system—whoever brings to his inner presence all this, together with the amazingly high pyramid of our present knowledge, cannot refrain from seeing in Socrates the one turning point and vortex of so-called world history. For should we conceive of the whole incalculable sum of energy which was consumed by that development of the world as applied, not to the service of knowledge, but to the practical, that is, selfish, ends of individuals and nations, then [this would follow:] as the result of universal battles of annihilation and continuing migrations of nations, the instinctive zest of living would probably have been weakened to such an extent that, in view of man's tendency to commit suicide, the individual would perhaps have to show his last remaining sense of duty by emulating the inhabitants of the Fiji Islands in strangling, as a son, his parents, or, as a friend, his friend: a practical pessimism which could produce in turn a horrifying ethics of mass murder out of a sense of pity. . . .

In view of this practical pessimism, Socrates is the model of the theoretical optimist, who, in his aforementioned belief in the accessibility of the reasons of things, assigns to knowledge and cognition the power of a panacea and conceives of error as the absolute evil. To penetrate into these reasons and to segregate true knowledge from illusion and error appeared to the Socratic man as the most noble, even as the only truly human vocation: just as ever since Socrates the mechanism of concepts, judgments, and conclusions was prized as the highest occupation and most admirable gift of nature, far above all other faculties. Even the most sublime moral feats, the emotions of sympathy, of self-sacrifice, of heroism, and that not easily attainable tranquility of the soul, like that of a calm sea, called *sophrosyne* by the Apollonian Greek, was derived from the dialectics of knowledge and hence termed teachable by Socrates and his like-minded successors. Anyone who has experienced the pleasure of a Socratic insight, and senses in himself how it attempts to embrace the whole world of phenomena in wider and wider circles, will thereafter feel no incentive which could urge on to existence more violently than the desire to complete that conquest and to weave the net impenetrably tight. To a person thus attuned, the Platonic Socrates appears to be the teacher of a completely new form of "Greek serenity" and bliss of being, which seeks its discharge in action and will find suitable discharge chiefly in exerting maieutic and educational influences upon noble youths in whom it is hoped that genius may be produced. —*Ibid.*, pp. 136-40.

6   . . . Some time there had to be a break when the great form of Greek life could no longer be filled; immediately all was over, just as in the case of tragedy. One single influential crank [*Querkopf*] like Socrates—and the break had become incurable. With him the self-destruction of the Greeks became complete. I think it was because he was the son of a sculptor. If these devotees of the plastic arts ever talked, they would seem superficial to us; in Socrates, the sculptor's son, their superficiality came into the open. . . .

Earlier Greek philosophy is the philosophy of real statesmen. . . . In this teaching we do not find "that hideous demand for happiness," as we do after the time of Socrates. . . . Besides, they did not gossip and malign, and they did not write. . . .

. . . The Greeks had little sense of humor; that is why there has been so much ado about the irony of Socrates. . . . While Greeks, guided by Empedocles and Democritus, had been well on the way to a correct appraisal of human existence, its unreason and its suffering, *they never achieved it,* thanks to Socrates. All the Socratics lack an unprejudiced observation of men; in their heads are those horrid abstract entities, "the Good" and "the Just." Read Schopenhauer and ask yourself why the ancients should have lacked such a deep and free perspective. I don't see it. On the contrary. It was Socrates who caused them to lose their ingenuousness. ——Drafts (end of 1875), in *Gesamtausgabe* (1905 ff.), X, 155-56.

SOCRATES: "Nothing is left to me but I myself"; anxiety for 7 one's self becomes the soul of philosophy. . . .

· ·

Socrates' influence:
1. He destroyed the ingenuousness of ethical judgment;
2. He annihilated science;
3. He had no feeling for art;
4. He tore the individual out of his historical context;
5. He promoted dialectical prattle and talkativeness.
——*Ibid.,* p. 157.

Socrates objected with all his might to men's haughty neg- 8 lect of what is human in favor of the abstract man, and was fond of using a phrase from Homer to remind people of what he took to be the true sphere and summation of all our concerns and reflections. "This and only this," he would say, "is what happens to me at home, in the way of both goodness and badness." ——*Menschliches, Allzumenschliches,* II (1879), No. 6, in *Werke,* IV, 193.

Divine missionaries: Socrates too felt himself to be a mis- 9 sionary. But I don't know what touch of Attic irony and love of joking it was that can be sensed tempering even here his odious [*fatal*] and arrogant concept. He talks of it without unction: his metaphors, about the gadfly and the horse, are plain and unpriestly, and the genuinely religious assignment which he feels has been given him, namely, *to put the god to the test* in a hundred ways as to *whether* he has spoken the truth, allows one to infer a bold and frank attitude by which the missionary meets his God as an equal. This putting God to the test is one of the most subtle compromises ever conceived between piety and freedom. ——*Ibid.*, No. 72, p. 240.

10   SOCRATES: If all goes well, the time will come when, in order to improve oneself morally and intellectually, one will rather open the *memorabilia* of Socrates than the Bible, and when Montaigne and Horace will be used as preparers and road-markers leading to an understanding of the simplest and most imperishable mediator-sage, Socrates. He is the one to whom all the roads of the most diverse philosophical ways of life return, which are at bottom the ways of life of the different temperaments, established by reason and habit and altogether pointing toward joy of life and of one's own self; from which fact one might like to infer that what made Socrates most peculiar was the fact that he shared in all temperaments. Socrates even excels the founder of Christianity by his gay type of earnestness and that prankish wisdom which constitutes the best inner condition of man. Besides, he had the greater intellect. ——*Ibid.*, No. 86, p. 248.

11   The dying Socrates—I admire the fortitude of Socrates in everything he did and did not say. This ironic and amorous monster [*Unhold*] and Pied Piper of Athens, who made the most frivolous youths tremble and sob, was not only the wisest prater that ever was; he was equally great in his silence. I wish he had also remained silent during the last moment of his life—perhaps he would then belong in a still higher order of spirits. Whether it was death or the poison or piety or malice—something released his tongue at that moment and he said, "O Crito, I owe Asclepius a cock." This ridiculous and terrible last word means for him who has ears to hear: "O Crito, life is an illness!" Is it possible! A man like Socrates,

who had lived cheerfully and like a soldier in the sight of all men—was a pessimist! He had only put on a bold front toward life, and had concealed his ultimate judgment, his innermost feeling during all his life! Socrates, yes, Socrates *suffered from life!* And he finally took his revenge for it—with that unconcealed, terrifying utterance, pious and blasphemous at once. Must such a man as Socrates *take vengeance,* too? Was there one grain of magnanimity missing in his abundant virtue? ——*Die fröhliche Wissenschaft* (1882), No. 340, in *Werke,* VI, 290-91.

Plato was really too noble for Socratism. . . . Its [Socratism's]   12
way of reasoning smacks of the populace, which considers only the unpleasant consequences of bad conduct and actually judges, "it is stupid to do wrong," while simply identifying "good" with "useful and pleasant." . . . Plato did everything in his power to read something refined and noble into his teacher's thesis that the bad was bad only as the result of error, but chiefly to read himself into it—he, the most daring of all the interpreters, who took the whole of Socrates merely as the musician takes a popular theme or song from the street, in order to add variations even to an infinite and impossible degree, that is to say, even to the addition of all his own masks and multiplicities. Speaking facetiously and even Homerically: what else is the Platonic Socrates but Plato in front and Plato in back, a goat in the middle. ——*Jenseits von Gut und Böse* (1885), No. 190, in *Werke,* VIII, 120.

To be sure, Socrates himself had at first taken the side of   13
reason in accordance with the taste of his talent—the talent of a superior dialectician. And, truthfully, what did he do during all his life but laugh at the awkward incapacity of his noble Athenians, who were men of instinct like all noble men and were never able to give an account of the reasons for their actions? But ultimately, in silence and secrecy, he laughed even at himself: he discovered in himself, by virtue of his subtler conscience and self-examination, the same difficulty

and incapacity. . . . This was the real deceitfulness of that great mysterious ironist: he persuaded his conscience to put up with a kind of self-deception, for at bottom he had seen through the irrationality of moral judgment. Plato, in such matters more guileless and without the cleverness of the plebeian, wanted to prove with all his might—the greatest might that any philosopher had thus far had at his disposal— that reason and instinct spontaneously move toward one goal, toward the good, toward "God."   ——*Ibid.*, No. 191, p. 121.

14   In his origin Socrates was a member of the lowest class: Socrates was rabble. We know and can even see how ugly he was. But ugliness, in itself everywhere an objection, is among Greeks almost a disproof. Was Socrates a Greek at all? Frequently enough ugliness is the expression of hybridization interfering with evolution. Otherwise it appears as evolution downward. The anthropologists among the criminologists tell us that the typical criminal is ugly: a monster's face, a monster's mind. But the criminal is a decadent. Was Socrates a typical criminal? . . .

. . . .

Decadence in Socrates is indicated not only by the admitted nastiness and anarchy in his instincts: the overdevelopment of the logical and the characteristic malice of the rickety point to the same thing. Let us also not forget those acoustic hallucinations which, under the name of the *daimonion* of Socrates, have been interpreted as something religious. Everything is exaggerated, burlesqued, caricatured in him, everything is at the same time concealed, double talk, underground. I am trying to understand what is the origin of that Socratic identification of reason with virtue and happiness—that most bizarre of all identifications and one particularly opposed to all the instincts of the more ancient Greeks.

. . . .

In the figure of Socrates, the Greek taste reverses itself in favor of dialectics. What really happens? Primarily, a sense of nobility is conquered; with the use of dialectics the rabble comes to the top. Before Socrates, good society rejected dialectical manners; they passed as bad manners, they discredited their user. . . . Wherever authority is still a part of good tradition, where one does not "reason" but commands, the dialectician is a kind of clown [*Hanswurst*]; he is laughed at, he is not taken seriously. Socrates was the clown who made himself taken seriously. What was happening?

Dialectics are chosen only if no other means are available. . . . That is why the Jews are dialecticians. So was Reynard the Fox. How then? Could it be that it was the same with Socrates?

Is Socrates' irony an expression of revolt? of the rabble's resentment? Does he, as one of the suppressed, indulge his own ferocity in the knife-thrusts of the syllogism? Does he take revenge on the noble by fascinating him? . . . What? Is dialectics in Socrates nothing but a form of revenge? . . .

. . . .

How did Socrates gain control of himself? . . . His fascination was that of an extreme case, his frightening ugliness spelled him out for every eye; he fascinated even more—that goes without saying—as an answer, as a solution, as the semblance of a cure of the case.

. . . .

If it is necessary to make reason a tyrant, as Socrates did, there must be no small danger that something else makes the tyrant. Reasonableness was then hit upon as the savior; neither Socrates nor his "patients" were free to be reasonable —it was *de rigeur*, it was their last resort.

. . . .

I have intimated how Socrates fascinated; he seemed to be a physician, a savior. Is it still necessary to show the error which his faith in "reasonableness at any price" implied? It is a self-deception on the part of philosophers and moralists that they step out of decadence by making war on it . . . ; they change the expression, they do not abolish decadence itself. Socrates was a misunderstanding; the whole morality of improvement, including the Christian, was a misunderstanding.

. . . To have to fight the instincts, that is the formula for decadence; as long as life is in its ascent, happiness is the same as instinct.

Did he himself reach an awareness of this misunderstanding, that cleverest of all self-deceivers? Did he tell himself about this in the wisdom of his courage to die? It was Socrates, not Athens, that wanted his death: he gave himself the poison cup, he forced Athens to give him the poison cup. "Socrates is not a physician," he said to himself softly. "Death alone is the physician here. . . . It is only that Socrates himself has been ill for a long time. . . ." —"Das Problem des Sokrates," *Götzendämmerung* (1888), in *Werke,* X, 245-51.

EDMUND HUSSERL (1859–1938)

If today, in the perspective of convictions that have been maturing in me for decades, I am to tell who are the philosophers who, as I look back upon the entire history of occidental philosophy, stand out with particular brightness, I would single out two or three: they are the names of the greatest initiators, the trailblazers of philosophy. For first place I nominate Plato, or rather the incomparable double star Socrates-Plato. The creation of the idea of genuine science, or, what for a long time meant exactly the same thing, the idea of philosophy and the discovery of the problem of method, goes back to these thinkers—as a finished creation back to Plato. . . . Socrates was the first to recognize that the problems lightheartedly thrust aside in the Sophists' paradoxes were problems of the destiny of mankind on its way toward genuine humanity. He opposed the Sophists only as a practical reformer. . . . His ethical reform of life consists in his interpretation of the truly satisfying life as one growing out of pure reason. This means: one in which man practices a critique—in the sense of an ultimate evaluation—of his life's goals, and thus, of course, and by means of it, of his ways of life and his changing means. Such an accounting and critique takes place as a process of getting to know, and in particular as a going back to the original source of all justification and its recognition; or, to put it in our terminology, as a going back to "perfect clarity," "insight," "self-evidence," . . . The Socratic method is a method of perfect elucidation. In it, the beautiful and the good themselves, as they emerge in perfect clarification, are contrasted as norms with that which is merely supposed to be beautiful and good, and thus true knowledge of them is attained. Now Socrates teaches that only this knowledge, produced originally by perfect self-evidence, makes man truly virtuous; or, what amounts to the same, that this alone is what can give him true happiness and the greatest possible amount of pure satisfaction. Genuine knowledge is the necessary and, according to Socrates, even the sufficient prerequisite of a reasonable and ethical life. Only unreason, blind vegetating in vagueness, which does not care for genuine knowledge of the truly good, makes men wretched and seekers after foolish goals. The true and the false, the genuine and the spurious, separate in the reflective clarification of what one is really after and what, in so doing, one had vaguely assumed by way of a supposed beauty and ugliness, usefulness, and harmfulness. It separates, precisely because in completed clarity the essential content of the things themselves attains intuitive realization and simultaneously positive and negative value. Each such clarification attains at once exemplary significance. What in a concrete case of history or myth presents itself to intuitive realization as the true and genuine, and to mere vague opinion as a norm, automatically presents itself as an example of the universal. It is intuitively grasped (*erschaut*) as the essentially genuine in general in the pure intuition of essences (*Wesensintuition*), which appears here naturally, and in this pure or a priori universality it functions as a valid norm for all conceivable instances of such essences in general. . . .

Let us sum up: Socrates, the ethical practitioner, reacting against the Sophists, who deny to life any reasonable meaning, put the fundamental contrast of all waking personal life, that between unclear opinion and self-evident fact, into the focus of the (ethico-practical) interest. He was the first to recognize the necessity for a universal method of reasoning, and he recognized the fundamental meaning of this method, to put it in modern terms, as an intuitive and a priori critique of reason. Or, stated more precisely, he recognized its fundamental meaning as the method of clarifying reflections, culminating in apodictic self-evidence, as the original source of all final validity. He was the first to intuit the independent being of pure and general essences as absolute authentic presentations of a general and pure intuition. Related to this discovery, the radical accounting demanded by Socrates for the ethical life in general acquires simultaneously the significant form of establishing normative principles or of a justification of active life in accord with the general ideas of reason to be worked out by pure intuition of essences.

True, in view of the well-known lack of theoretical and scientific purposes in Socrates, all this may be without proper scientific formulation and systematic development into a scientific theory of the method of a true practice of life. Nevertheless it may be considered certain that in Socrates there exist indeed the germinal forms (*Keimformen*) for the fundamental ideas of critical reason, whose theoretical and technical expression and supremely fertile development are the imperishable glory of Plato. ——*Erste Philosophie* (1923–24), in *Husserliana* VII (The Hague, 1956), pp. 7-11.

MAX WEBER (1864–1920)

Socrates discovered the true function of the logical concept. He was not the only man in the world to discover it. In India there are the beginnings of a logic that is quite similar to that of Aristotle. But nowhere else do we find such a realization of the significance of the concept. Greece was the first country to produce a handy means by which one could put the logical screws upon somebody, so that he could not escape without admitting either that he knew nothing or that this and nothing else was truth, the *eternal* truth that never could vanish as the doings of the blind vanish. This was the tremendous experience to which the disciples of Socrates awoke. ——"Science as a Vocation" (1918), in *Essays in Sociology,* tr. H. H. Gerth and C. W. Mills (New York, 1946), p. 141.

MAX SCHELER (1874–1928)

Mere knowledge of moral norms does not determine the   1
will. What was wrong in Socrates' formulation was his rationalism, according to which the mere concept of what was good had the power to determine the will; but nothing was wrong in his knowledge of the good, whose power over the will was demonstrated brilliantly by his death. ——*Der Formalismus in der Ethik und die materiale Wertethik* (Halle, 1916), p. 65, note.

It is no accident, but essential, understandable, and indeed   2
necessary, that the saint as a type does not leave behind him any authentic work in which his personal spirit would become accessible to later history and be presented immediately to the world. One contributing condition for Socrates' unlimited influence was precisely this omission. In the Greek world, which puts the sage above the saint, Socrates approaches saintliness most of all. He too wrote nothing and is known to us only from the reports which Xenophon and Plato gave. ——"Vorbilder und Führer," in *Schriften aus dem Nachlass* (Berlin, 1933), I, 179.

ALBERT SCHWEITZER (1875——)

What did Socrates accomplish in his attempt to stem this   1
tendency of the Sophists? In place of simple hedonism he substitutes a rational hedonism. He maintains that a standard of conduct can be based on rational reflection, a standard in

which the happiness of the individual, rightly comprehended, coincides with the interests of the community. Virtue is true knowledge. . . .

That Socrates used to speak of a secret inner voice, as the highest moral authority in a man, is certain; it is mentioned in the contemporary indictment drawn up against him. His utilitarian rationalism thus expands into a sort of mysticism. An empirical ethic—that is growing out of and developed in accordance with experience—and an intuitive ethic dwell side by side in his mind, undistinguished from one another, but destined to be separated and developed by his disciples as opposing schools. . . . Was Socrates conscious that in making the moral rest on a rational-hedonist basis he only went part of the way and halted at the point where the real difficulty resides, namely, the demonstration of the existence of a universal moral content, inherent in every reasoning mind? Or was he so simple as to take his general formal result for the solution of the problem? From the confidence with which he enters on the stage we may presume the latter. His ingenuousness is his strength. At the dangerous moment when Western thought finds itself in the situation of being obliged to philosophize about morality in order to check the disruption of Greek society introduced by a reckless and litigious school of thought, the sage of Athens destroys skepticism by the mighty earnestness of his conviction that it is possible to determine the nature of the moral by reflection. He does not advance beyond this general position. He is responsible for the earnest spirit in which the ancient world tackled the problem after his time. What, we may well ask, would that world have become without him? ——*Civilization and Ethics*, tr. John Naish (London, 1923), p. 35.

2   Lao Tzu, Confucius, the Indians, Zoroaster, the Hebrew prophets, and Jesus seem to comprehend ethics in some way or other as either derived from, or involved in, a view of the universe. Socrates founds ethics on itself. Against a similar

scenic background, devoid of any thorough perspective, the utilitarians of all the centuries have played their parts as his successors. . . . With Socrates the ethical mysticism of resignation to the inward voice takes the place of a complete theory of the universe, which is necessary to afford a ground for the determination of man's ethical actions. —*Ibid.,* pp. 36-37.

OSWALD SPENGLER (1880–1936)

Socrates—who was the spiritual father of the Stoa and in whom the first signs of inward impoverishment and city-intellectualism become visible. . . . Each of the three [Socrates, Buddha, and Rousseau, standing as representative spokesmen of a great civilization] buried a millennium of spiritual depth. Each proclaimed his gospel to mankind, but it was to the mankind of the city intelligentsia, which was tired of the town and the late culture, and whose "pure" (i.e., soulless) reason longed to be free from them and their authoritative form and their hardness, from the symbolism with which it was no longer in living communion and which therefore it detested. The culture was annihilated by discussion. If we pass in review the great nineteenth-century names—Schopenhauer, Hebbel, Wagner, Nietzsche, Ibsen, Strindberg—we comprehend in a glance that which Nietzsche, in a fragmentary preface to his incomplete masterwork, deliberately and correctly called the *Coming of Nihilism.* Every one of the great cultures knows it, for it is of deep necessity inherent in the finale of these mighty organisms. Socrates was a nihilist, and Buddha. —*The Decline of the West,* tr. Charles F. Atkinson (New York, 1927), I, 352.

. . . Socrates and Rousseau were intelligent and not "wise" men. There is something root-less in the word. It is only from the standpoint of the Stoic and of the Socialist, of the typically irreligious man, that want of intelligence is a matter of contempt. —*Ibid.,* p. 409.

3   Socrates is alike the heir of the Sophists and the ancestor
of the Cynic itinerants and of Pyrrhonian scepsis. All are
manifestations of the superiority of the megalopolitan intellect
that has done with the irrational for good and all and despises any waking-consciousness that still knows or acknowl-
edges mysteries. ——*Ibid.*, II, 309.

HERMANN KEYSERLING (1880–1946)

1   Only the earliest sages in Greece, and again the latest among
them, were promoters of life. Hence it did not mean a complete misunderstanding that Socrates was condemned by the
Athenians as a corrupter of youth. . . . The intellect has disintegrated all that could be disintegrated; Socrates' work
can be considered completed. ——*Schöpferische Erkenntnis*
(Darmstadt, 1922), p. 139.

2   With Socrates a new type becomes effective in intellectual
history, one which had never existed in the East and which
neither before nor after him appeared in such typical form,
which is the reason why the later conception of the Greek
philosopher was involuntarily oriented toward him: the sage
as the consciously ignorant, not as the knowing one. Of course,
even the Oriental sage did not know most things, but this
was not what he stressed the most; for him the realization of
valuable truth, once acquired and possessed, was the goal.
Socrates, however, wanted to win ever new insights. By thus
shifting the accent of meaningfulness, he also changed the
goal; in his way of questioning, knowledge, not Being, had to
be what mattered ultimately, and, to be precise, knowledge
in the sense of theory. Thus Socrates became the inventor of
the concept, the discoverer of method and the importance of
putting the right questions, and lastly the father of exact science. Hence all scientific research since his day has taken its
start with a good conscience from him rather than from Plato,
although not even Socrates but only Aristotle can pass as the

first scholar in the modern sense. However, Socrates is by no means only the father of theory for its own sake, hence of western unwisdom, as men have begun to judge since Nietzsche in a characteristic new reversal of the accent of meaningfulness; he was at the same time a genuine sage, an embodiment of life based on knowledge. He came to the positive evaluation of theory in the sense of exact science not out of curiosity or a spontaneous urge for knowledge, but because the naïve totality of life from the time of the forefathers had disintegrated, and hence he was moved by wisdom. The old gods were dying, mortally wounded by the emancipated intellect. This intellect acted now in a totally irresponsible fashion. The Sophists would prove anything desired, and refute whatever occurred to them, and did not believe in truth as an obligation. Socrates, as a powerful realistic politician (*Realpolitiker*) of the spirit, saw only one reliable means to put an end to this destructive business: to make the intellect responsible.

He was hoping to found anew the totality of life upon a raised level of knowledge by means of the new ties thus formed. Nothing proves better that this was his real intention than his conviction that virtue must be teachable by way of intellectual insight. However, his age was not ripe for the achievement of the task he had assigned himself. Since its intellectual level was not nearly enough developed to build by itself alone, all Socrates could do was to accelerate the process of disintegration, whereas what he wanted was to transform its forces into reconstructive ones. Thus in the end he was condemned to death as a convicted disintegrator, and during the first centuries after his death he continued to act as a disintegrator or at least as a divider of the totality of life. It is highly remarkable and appropriate for the instruction particularly of those who believe in rapid progress: the center of gravity of his life was not in being, but in a world of ideas put forward (*herausgestellte Vorstellungswelt*); even he lacked the unquestioned knowledge, the instinctive certainty, of the balanced man; even he had no immediate connection with the inner world of the spirit; even he sought the way to it from the outside. Thus Socrates' problem was already literally our own. But since, as we can judge better today, he had posed it, with respect to the possibility of its being solved, too early, not by decades or centuries but by millennia, it was necessarily his fate to become tragically guilty. This is why Socrates' image has fascinated western thinkers as no other has done. In the history of the West it means something similar to what Prometheus' image means in the evolution of mankind: it is a primal symbol (*Ursymbol*) which has made conscious the corresponding problem in each European since then as his own. Most things which distinguish our intellectual history from that of other civilizations go back to him. By hypostatizing conceptual definitions, against which metaphysical soberness has always protected the people of India, he became the father of the peculiar occidental faith in the absolute reality of the external, a materialism which reached its climax only in the *Weltanschauung* of the dying nineteenth century. He is the father of all abstract idealism, the historical model of the mentality in which logically unobjectionable proof creates acknowledged reality, and hence indirect knowledge takes precedence over direct knowledge. He is the model precisely of the most recent Europeans. But his western and as such most model-like character shows up best perhaps in the type of his immortality. The immortality of all the great knowers of the West, in contrast with those of the East, is not one of being but of becoming; it is less their form (*Gestalt*) as such than the movement embodied in it for the first time, which continues acting. The great Indians and Chinese struck eternal chords (*Grundtöne*) to which all of humanity can be tuned; the formation of melody as such did not interest them, nor did it interest them from the level of consciousness they had achieved; their truth, insofar as it exists, is timeless, eternal. The truth of all the great ones of the West since Socrates is inserted inseparably into the body of time and hence is at first perishable. Its eternal character follows in this case from the fact that it continues acting in time. Perhaps in no other Westerner has immortality shown such an extremely occidental character as in Socrates. Even in his own pupil, Socrates survived only as an image; he did not survive as a doctrine but only produced new doctrines. Thus it has gone on ever since to this day. Even as a sage Socrates has been more an incentive than a model. Since he presented himself as inserted in time, and the perfection of this type of wisdom was impossible, he could not be a model in the sense of Buddha and Confucius. He was the sage of the Occident as a draft (*Skizze*). —*Ibid.,* pp. 244 ff.

The immense and never interrupted influence of Socrates is 3 based on the fact that on the one hand he never committed himself inwardly, whereby his attitude remained decisive even historically, and that on the other hand he died prematurely for a conviction whose content nobody has ever quite understood. Thus his example, which was unambiguous only in his approach and in his way of asking questions, has stimulated ever renewed contemporary interpretations. —*Ibid.,* p. 471.

Socrates had pure Russian features, and he argued as un- 4 endurably as a Russian student. —*Europe,* tr. Maurice Samuel (New York, 1928), p. 331.

The immense positive effect of Socrates was based chiefly 5 upon the fact that he emphasized again and again his lack of knowing. The productivity of this approach was not based primarily upon the fact that he committed himself less to falsehood than others, nor that this allowed him a maximum amount of openness for world and God (which anyway never took effect in Socrates since he lacked the proper aptitude), but upon the correct insight into the vocation of the critic. This insight has made him the father of European science. —*Betrachtungen der Stille und Besinnlichkeit* (Jena, 1941), p. 206.

Socrates, to be sure, in his later influences founded the exact 6 sciences, but personally he sacrificed to the gods of the city and never arrived at a clear inner decision; this is why he could survive only as a mythical figure evoked by others. —*Ibid.,* p. 232.

MORITZ SCHLICK (1882-1936)

Socrates, one might say, despised science. He did not believe in all the speculations about astronomy and about the structure of the universe in which the early philosophers indulged. He believed one could never gain any certain knowledge about these matters, and he restricted his investigations to the nature of human character. He was not a man of science, he had no faith in it, and yet we all acknowledge him to be one of the greatest philosophers who ever lived. It is not Socrates, however, who created the antagonism that we find to exist later on between science and philosophy. . . . The important feature which we should observe in Socrates, in order to understand his particular attitude as well as the nature of philosophy, is that this wisdom that dealt with human nature and human behavior consists essentially of a special *method,* different from the method of science and, therefore, not leading to any "scientific" results. . . . Socrates' philosophy consists of what we may call "The Pursuit of Meaning." He tried to clarify thought by analyzing the meaning of our expressions and the real sense of our propositions. . . . Socrates has set the example of the true philosophic method. —"The Future of Philosophy," in *Publications in Philosophy* (Stockton, Calif., 1932), pp. 49-54. Reprinted in Daniel J. Bronstein *et al.* (eds.), *Basic Problems of Philosophy* (New York, 1955), pp. 575-78.

KARL JASPERS (1883——)

1   After a study of the record, everyone retains a picture of Socrates. With all the floating possibilities, despite one's knowledge of the uncertainty, a picture of Socrates establishes itself which we regard as real and not an imaginative fiction.

If Socrates seems to hide from us according to the measure of what is unambiguously real and vivid, yet his human force, his thrilling nature is inescapably before our eyes. It is quite impossible *not* to form a picture of the historic Socrates. More than that: to keep Socrates in view is one of the indispensable presuppositions of our philosophizing. Perhaps one can say: no philosophizing today without Socrates, and even if he were to be sensed as no more than a pale gleam from a remote past. The way in which Socrates is experienced affects a basic feature of one's thinking. ——*Die grossen Philosophen* (Munich, 1957), I, 124.

In the sphere of Socrates' influence what happens is the spontaneous conviction of the individual, but no "confession." Here, friendship can result from concern with truth, but no establishment of sectarian creeds. In the holiness of what is humanly possible Socrates meets any other on the same level. He rejects discipleship. Therefore he even tries to neutralize his overpowering personality by treating himself with irony. ——*Ibid.*, p. 127.

KARL BARTH (1886——)

Jesus would not be the Christ, if figures like Abraham, Jeremiah, Socrates, Grünewald, Luther, Kierkegaard, Dostoevski should remain forever historically remote from him and were not rather understood as immanent in him, in view of their essential identity, their contemporaneity, and their intrinsic connection, and if the positive aspects in them were only annulled in the negation announced in him and not at the same time established. ——*Der Römerbrief* (2nd edn.; Munich, 1923), p. 93.

PAUL TILLICH (1886——)

Socrates, who in the power of his essential self conquered the anxiety of death, has become the symbol for the courage to take death upon oneself. . . . Socrates is certain that the self which the executioners will destroy is not the self which affirms itself in his courage to be. He does not say much about the relation of the two selves, and he could not because they are not numerically two, but one in two aspects. But he makes it clear that the courage to die is the test of the courage to be. . . . It was the courage of Socrates which more than any philosophical reflection revealed to the ancient world that everyone belongs to two orders. ——*The Courage to Be* (New Haven, 1952), pp. 168-69.

MARTIN HEIDEGGER (1889——)

Socrates was the purest thinker of the Occident. It remains the secret of a still unrevealed history that all thinkers since Socrates, their greatness notwithstanding, have to take cover before him. I am asked in horror, "What about Plato, Augustine, Thomas Aquinas, Leibniz, Kant, Nietzsche? May one minimize these thinkers as compared with Socrates?" But the objectors did not listen; what was said was this: all the thinkers of the Occident after Socrates, "their greatness notwithstanding." It could be that a man might remain the purest thinker without being one of the greatest. ——*Was heisst Denken?* (Tübingen, 1954), p. 56. [This text has been reconstructed from the summary, since the original lecture has not been published.]

ALFRED ROSENBERG (1893–1946)

1   No one before Socrates could preach the madness that virtue can be taught, taught to *all* men. The development of such an individualistic, raceless, intellectualist world-view put the ax to the root of Greek life; and at the same time precisely this insubstantial intellectualism set free the Asiatic customs which had been repressed by the Apollonian discipline of Greece. ——*Der Mythus des 20. Jahrhunderts* (Munich, 1930), pp. 78-79.

The "imitation of Jesus," where the devout rolled in the 2
ashes, flogged themselves, walked about covered with fester-
ing wounds, loaded themselves with iron chains, squatted for
thirty years on a pillar like Simon or spent ten years wedged
in a cartwheel like Saint Thalelaeus, in order to spend the
rest of his "life" in a straight cage, such "imitation" was a
parallel to the abstract "goodness" of Socrates and to the later
"Dostoevski man."   —*Ibid.*, p. 213.

Silenus is . . . the concrete representation of the properties 3
of an alien race-soul as the Greeks saw it. The later rapid
growth of the phallic worship, the wild Bacchanalia, and the
whole late Dionysian disintegration, are the result of the
racial proliferation of the subjugated Ostic-Oriental racial
types, which I have already characterized as dull and narrow-
minded. In the elephantine strength of Socrates this racial
regrouping found its characteristic turning point. There can
be no doubt that Plato glorified the hairsplitter out of all
proportion. Yet one personal confession of Socrates is certainly
authentic. He declares that a written paper scroll could lure
him away from the most beautiful scenery. Among Greeks
with their interest in the outside world, this was a profession
of the most platitudinous school pedantry. Socrates is an il-
lustration of the fact that the soul and race-energy of genius
is far from identical with a moral philosophy, however good,
and an esthetics, however "all-human." . . . It was not a new
epoch of Greek history that began with Socrates, but he ush-
ered an entirely *different kind of human being* into Hellenic
life. True, he too was formed by the sacred traditions of
Athens, by Homer, the tragedies, Pericles, and the architects
of the Acropolis; true, he took part as a soldier in the struggle
of power politics; all the same, Socrates is a man without real
genius, though noble and brave, of a different *non-Greek race.*
He lived during a period when Athens pursued will-o'-the-
wisps and when its once aristocratic democracy (which com-
prised only Greeks, no foreigners) slid downhill into a chaotic
abyss. Under the tyrannical rule of demagogues the great Al-

cibiades was exiled, the whole army of Athens perished before Syracuse, and almost all other conquests were lost. The conquering aristocrats then made the democrats drink poison by the hundreds, whereupon the same fate caught up with them. Aristophanes ridiculed the old traditions, and the new teachers, Gorgias, Protagoras, etc., reveled in mere beauty of form. At that moment the alien type, previously described again and again under the name of Silenus, entered. He represents the other race in the greatest development of which it was capable, spiritually shaped by Hellenic culture: sober, ironic, robust; conscious of being confronted by a disintegrated form of life; undaunted, brave. With powerful logic and with razor-like dialectics, the ugly Socrates drives to despair the beautiful Greek teachers, who have no inner supports left them. Besides, he seeks "the good" as such, preaches the "community of good men," and assembles around himself a new, struggling Greek generation.

When master of Athens, Pericles once had humbly to beseech the court for the privilege of having citizenship granted to his son, borne him by a foreign wife. This was granted as an exception. The strict racial law of Athens, once passed on the motion of Pericles himself, broke down, as Athenian blood declined. But it was Socrates, the non-Greek, who during a time of disintegration gave it the death blow. The idea of a "community of good men" resulted in a new human classification based not on races and nations but on the single individual. Thus, after the collapse of the Athenian racial democracy Socrates was the international social democrat (*Sozialdemokrat*) of his time. His personal courage and cleverness furnished his race-destroying doctrine with a propagandistic consecration. It was his disciple Antisthenes (son of a slave woman from Asia Minor) who drew the conclusions from this doctrine and preached a human progress to be sought by tearing down all the barriers between races and nations.

Only thanks to Plato does Socrates live as the hero revered by all the celebrities of our lecture halls (*Kathedergrössen*). The Greek genius used Plato to give thanks to the man who represented sober sense in a time of disintegration; he loved this man and set up a monument to him by putting into Socrates' mouth even the words of his own soul. Thus the true Socrates disappeared from the eyes of the world. Not many passages in Plato point to him. For instance, in the *Phaedo* Plato says about Socrates that he declared he had no aptitude for the investigation of biological processes. . . . Certainly Plato did not make up this passage; it is in keeping with the Socrates who declared that the pursuit of a written paper scroll would lure him away from the loveliest scenery; but in keeping also with the one who turns away from the racial beauty of Greece and proclaims an abstract humanity, a brotherhood of the good. That was like turning away from the sunshine of the ideal to the shade of a compulsory rationalizing doctrine. As the Jewish dogma settled over religion, so Socrates' life-hostile "scientific" method settled over Europe. Aristotle was his schematizing apostle, Hegel his last great disciple. "Logic is the science of God," said this Hegel. That saying is a blow of the clenched fist hurled into the face of any genuine Nordic religion, or of any science that is genuinely Germanic, or indeed genuinely Greek. But that saying is genuinely Socratic, and so it is not for nothing that Hegel along with Socrates is a saint to most of our university professors.

Certainly, soul-image and external appearance do not always coincide. But in the case of Socrates they did. In an environment where love (*Eros*) and Nordic racial beauty are represented by the blond Aphrodite and the blond Jason (whose hair has never been touched by shears); where, from the white-skinned, slender, and blond Dionysius of Euripides to the "lovely little head" in the *Birds* of Aristophanes, the same ideal of beauty prevails, carrying and shaping the genuinely Greek humanity—there the frowzy type of the satyr emerged as the symbol of the alien, as it were.[10] If ever, it was here that turning the eyes away from the world could mean nothing but catastrophe. The truly beautiful disappears; bastard

[10] The German original of this sentence is confused; hence the translation is based on slight emendations.

shapes appear even in art; and what was repulsive, absolutely ugly, and unnatural, now becomes "beautiful."

The sermon preaching what is "reasonable and good" was a phenomenon parallel to the disintegration of the Greek race and soul. The "good" then destroyed the racial ideas of beauty in art, as well as the supporting ideas of political and social life. The highest, since noblest, symbol of the inrushing chaos, disrupting the race and soul of Hellenic civilization, was Socrates.

What this means in the history of evolution is this: Plato pours out the gifts of his genius over the imperturbably prosaic man and bestows immortality upon him. But what Plato himself stood for essentially was not Socratic; he was an Aristocrat, an Olympic fighter, a poet drunk with beauty, a plastic artist, an exuberant thinker, one who, to sum it all up, wanted to save his people on a racial basis by a high-handed constitution, indeed dictatorial down to the last detail. It was the last fine flowering of a spirit-drunk Hellenism. What Praxiteles created at a later time was a protest against all Socratism, was the last paean on Nordic-Greek racial beauty, like the magnificent Nike of Samothrace. But Socrates was a symbol all the same. Hellas died out amid the racial chaos, and instead of proud Athenians it was the universally despised *graeculi* who peopled the provinces of the growing Roman empire, the unprincipled *graeculi* who could make one "educated," who were hired—or fired if they no longer gave satisfaction.

Socrates-Antisthenes won, and Greece fell. "Sound common sense" came upon genius in a weak hour and destroyed it. The ugly became the norm after the beautiful had conceded to it the value of "the good."

When Socrates faced his judges, he said: "Athens has never had greater service than I gave it." It would appear that the "humility" and "modesty" of the "divine messenger"—another tribute which he paid himself—had after all its other side. Socrates felt subconsciously that Greece was going to pieces.
—*Ibid.*, pp. 283-88.

ALBRECHT HAUSHOFER (1903–1945)

In Athens they still point out the spot where Socrates is said to have awaited the completion of the pious festival, then to bow to the death-dealing law. I walked past the dark threshold, my eyes being lifted to the Parthenon, and, spellbound by that bright splendor, overlooked the death-cup. Now I regret that I passed by. It would have been becoming to drop to my knees, and, knowingly, to drink of the hemlock with him. Greatness was his who thus had the courage to keep faith with the blind, murderous powers of his own state.[11] ——"Der Schierlingsbecher," in *Moabiter Sonette* (Zürich, 1948), p. 14.

[11] Man will noch in Athen den Ort bezeugen,
wo Sokrates gewartet haben soll,
bis jene Frist der frommen Feste voll,
um sich dem tödlichen Gesetz zu beugen.

Ich ging vorüber an der dunklen Schwelle,
den Blick zum Parthenon emporgewandt,
und übersah, vom lichten Glanz gebannt,
den Todesbecher in der Tageshelle.

Nun reut mich, dass ich dort vorüberging.
Es hätte sich geziemt, ins Knie zu sinken
und wissend von dem Schierling mitzutrinken.

Es war ein Grosser, der sich unterfing,
des eigenen Staates blinden Mordgewalten
als Opfertier die Treue so zu halten.

ITALIAN

GALILEO GALILEI (1564–1642)

SALVIATI [i.e., Galilei]: [In support of the view that we should first try to understand one thing well] we have the experience of those who understand, or have understood, something, and who, the wiser they were, confessed the more freely that they knew little; indeed the wisest one in all Greece, proclaimed by the oracles to be the wisest, said openly that he knew nothing.

SIMPLICIO [i.e., the Aristotelian]: So it is fair to say that either the oracle or Socrates himself lied, since the former called him most wise and the latter said that he knew he was most ignorant.

SALVIATI: Neither the one nor the other follows, since it so happens that both these pronouncements can be true. The oracle judges Socrates most wise in comparison with the other humans whose wisdom is limited; Socrates knows that he knows nothing in relation to absolute wisdom, which is infinite; and since any part of an infinite amount cannot be called much or little or nothing (for to arrive, for instance, at an infinite number it is all the same whether we add thousands or tens or zeros), therefore Socrates knew well that his limited wisdom was nothing compared with the infinite wisdom which he lacked. But since, nevertheless, some knowledge is found among men, and this knowledge is not equally distributed among all, it is possible that Socrates had a larger share of it than others, and thus the answer of the oracle is borne out. ——*Dialogo sopra i due massimi sistemi del mondo* (1632), Giornata I, in *Opere* (Florence, 1933), VII, 127.

TOMMASO CAMPANELLA (1568–1639)

Every law or doctrine of mankind which forbids its followers to investigate natural things should be suspected of

falsehood. . . . The unbelieving Gentiles established the law
that inquisitive search should not be made concerning the
gods. . . . The Athenians sought the death of Anaxagoras,
Socrates, Aristotle, and other philosophers because they dared
boldly to violate the law which prohibited inquiry concerning
the gods. ——*Apologia pro Galileo,* tr. Grant McColley,
"Smith College Studies in History," Vol. XXII (1937), pp.
28-29.

GIAMBATTISTA VICO (1668–1744)

Socrates (who was called the father of all the schools of philosophy) stands out as symbolizing the spirit of philosophy
which has formed since the primitive epoch. ——*La Scienza
Nuova,* written in 1725 (Bari, 1937), I, 224.

GIACOMO LEOPARDI (1798–1837)

Socrates will always be more admired than lamented, and 1
he is a most unsuitable subject for tragedy. ——*Zibaldone di
pensieri,* ed. Francesco Flora (Milan, 1937), I, 224.

The philosophy of Socrates was and always will be able not 2
only to conform to literature and poetry but also to do them
an infinite service, and it will always help mankind more than
our present philosophy, from which, as I will not deny, mankind may receive some improvement, as an accessory or as a
second flowering, as it were. But the philosophy of Locke, of
Leibniz, and others cannot possibly harmonize with literature
or with true poetry. The philosophy of Socrates shares a good
deal with nature. But the other has no such share and is all
reason. Therefore neither it nor its language is compatible
with literature, in contradistinction to the philosophy of Socrates and its language; which philosophy is of such a nature
that all people with even a little wisdom have always more or
less participated in it at all times and in all nations, even be-

fore Socrates. It is a philosophy little removed from the one which nature herself teaches to man as a social being. —— *Ibid.*, pp. 914-15.

3   And Socrates himself, the friend of truth, the pretty and chaste talker, the enemy of the speechifiers and drones, of all unnecessary ornament and of all affectation: what was he in his thinking if not a sophist, no less than those whom he despised? ——*Pensieri* (Florence, 1898–1900), II, 112.

VILFREDO PARETO (1848–1923)

Not a few writers contrast Socrates with the Sophists. Others say he was a Sophist too. The controversy cannot be settled unless the term "Sophist" is defined. We need not go into the matter here, but of one thing we are certain: that Socrates, and Plato too, are to be classed among our A's [individuals who aimed at undermining group-persistences, at substituting logical for nonlogical conduct, at deifying Reason], since both aim at undermining group-persistences in Athens and replacing them with products of their own thought. They may have differed from Protagoras, Gorgias, Prodicus, and others in the means they used; but their tendencies, whether they were aware of it or not, were the same.

Writers, as a rule, wax indignant that Aristophanes should have named Socrates in the *Clouds*. They may be right from an ethical standpoint, but they are wrong from the logico-experimental standpoint as regards doctrines and social utility. Aristophanes was telling the literal truth when he said that Socrates and, to an even greater extent, Plato aimed at dethroning the Zeus of mythological tradition, to transfer sovereignty to the "clouds" of their metaphysics. The daemon of Socrates is first cousin, at least, to the goddess Reason and own brother to the "conscience" of our Liberal Protestants. . . . From the standpoint of social utility it is evident that working along that line the foundation of nonlogical conduct on which society rests would soon have been demolished. Not, indeed, that the doctrines themselves could have had that effect. Quite the contrary, they are themselves one of the effects of the social disintegration; and that is why the condemnation of Socrates was a useless thing and therefore stupid, wicked, and criminal, just as the condemnation of any man for expressing opinions deemed heretical by the people around him has been and continues to be useless and therefore stupid, wicked, and criminal. ——*Trattato di Sociologia Generale* (1916), tr. as *The Mind and Society* (New York, 1935), IV, No. 2347/8.

BENEDETTO CROCE (1866–1952)

The utilitarian character of Greek ethic has been confirmed 1 on several occasions; but one experiences a certain repugnance in applying so precise a term to the documents of ancient thought that remain to us. Socrates, it is true, posited the useful as the supreme concept of morality, and identified the good life with *eudaemonia;* but for him the useful was nevertheless distinct from the merely pleasing, since it consisted in what is useful to man as man, and his *eudaemonia* bore much resemblance to the tranquil conscience of him who fulfills his proper duties. ——*Philosophy of the Practical* (1908), tr. Douglas Ainslee (London, 1913), pp. 391-92.

Even Napoleon, who had learned the art of administration 2 from Talma, does not appear as great on the rock of St. Helena as Socrates does under sentence of death in his prison or as Dante does in exile. ——*History as the Story of Liberty* (1938), tr. Sylvia Sprigge (New York, 1941), p. 166.

BENITO MUSSOLINI (1883–1945)

Defending his fight against Freemasonry:
Besides, gentlemen, there is a much stronger reason for me

—the sense (*spirito*) of a peasant, and I am proud of it. We must do the maximum of good to our friends and the maximum of evil to our enemies. This maxim is not that of a Fascist partisan (*squadrista*) of the last or the first hour; it is the wisdom of Socrates.[12]   —*Scritti e Discorsi dal 1925 al 1926* (Milan, 1934), V, 69.

[12] Mussolini may be thinking of the *Republic* I. 332a, and confusing the doctrine of Simonides, presented there by Polemarchus, with that of Socrates himself (335d), who tried, both in the *Republic* and in other Platonic dialogues, to refute this maxim.

ORIENTAL

MOHANDAS KARAMCHAND GANDHI (1869–1948)

Jesus Christ, Daniel, and Socrates represented the purest 1
form of Passive Resistance or Soul-Force. All these teachers
counted their bodies as nothing in comparison with their
souls. ——Conversation with the Rev. J. J. Doke, reported in
C. F. Andrews, *Mahatma Gandhi's Ideas* (New York, 1930),
p. 193.

Socrates, we are told, was the most truthful man of his time 2
and yet his features are said to have been the ugliest in Greece.
To my mind he was beautiful, because all his life was a striv-
ing after Truth. ——"A Morning with Gandhiji," by Mahadev
Desai, in *Young India*, November 13, 1924, p. 377.

JAWAHARLAL NEHRU (1889–1964)

I have always hesitated to read books of religion. . . . Some 1
words of the Buddha or of Christ would shine out with deep
meaning and seem to me applicable as much today as when
they were uttered two thousand or more years ago. There was
a compelling reality about them, a permanence which time
and space could not touch. So I felt sometimes when I read
about Socrates or the Chinese philosophers, and also when I
read the Upanishads and the *Bhagavad Gita*. ——*The Discovery of India* (New York, 1946), pp. 66-67.

One of the greatest names of that time [fifth century B.C.] 2
or any time I have not yet mentioned. His name was Socrates.
He was a philosopher, always searching for truth. To him
the only thing worth having was true knowledge, and he often

discussed difficult questions with his friends and acquaintances, so that out of the discussions truth might emerge. . . .
Evidently governments do not like people who are always
trying to find out things; they do not like the search for
truth. The Athenian government—this was just after the time
of Pericles—did not like the methods of Socrates, and they
held a trial and condemned him to death. . . . In life Socrates
served the cause of truth and knowledge well, but better still
he served it in his death. . . .   —*Glimpses of World History,*
. . . Letters to his Daughter . . . (New York, 1942), pp. 44-45.

RUSSIAN

LEO TOLSTOY (1828–1910)

Having read Marcus Aurelius, Epictetus, Xenophon, Socrates . . . I have become more and more surprised and horrified at the ignorance, at the cultured barbarism in which our society is steeped. ——From a letter to an admirer, quoted in Ernest J. Simmons, *Leo Tolstoy* (Boston, 1946), p. 654.

VLADIMIR SOLOVIEV (1859–1900)

In Indian Buddhism the personality finds its absolute significance in the rejection of being that is unworthy of it. In Greek thought, which found its practical embodiment in Socrates, and was put into a theoretical form by his pupil, the absolute value of the personality is justified by the affirmation of being that is worthy of it—of the world of ideas and ideal relations. ——*The Justification of the Good*, tr. Nathalie A. Duddington (New York, 1918), p. 236.   1

Buddha Sakya-muni peacefully dies after a meal with his disciples, while Socrates, condemned and put to prison by his fellow citizens, is sentenced by them to drink a poisoned cup. But in spite of this tragic ending, the attitude of the Greek idealist to the reality unworthy of him is not one of decisive opposition. The highest representative of humanity at this stage— the philosopher—is conscious of his absolute worth in so far as he lives by pure thought in the truly-existent intelligible realm of Ideas or of the all-embracing rationality, and despises the false, the merely phenomenal being of the material and sensuous world. This contempt, when bold and genuine, rouses the anger of the crowd which is wholly engrossed with   2

287

the lower things, and the philosopher may have to pay for his idealism with his life—as was the case with Socrates. But in any case his attitude to the unworthy reality is merely one of contempt. The contempt is certainly different in kind from that characteristic of Buddhism.

. . . The idealist . . . despises and condemns the life that surrounds him, not because it inevitably shares in the illusory character of everything, but because it is abnormal, irrational, opposed to the Idea. Such condemnation is no longer neutral, it has an element of defiance and demand. It is slighting to all who are bound by worldly irrationality and therefore leads to hostility, and sometimes to persecution and the cup of poison. And yet there is something accidental about this conflict. Socrates condemned Athenian customs all his life long, but he was not persecuted for it until he was an old man of seventy; the persecution was obviously due to a change in political circumstances. The irrationality of the Athenian political order was a local peculiarity; the customs of Sparta were better. . . .

The dying Socrates rejoiced at leaving this world of false appearances for the realm of what truly is. Such an attitude obviously excludes in the last resort all practical activity; there can in that case be neither any obligation nor any desire to devote oneself to the changing of this life, to the salvation of this world.   ——*Ibid.,* pp. 238-40.

3   Death is not an Idea, but the rejection of the Idea, the rebellion of blind force against reason. Therefore Socrates' joy at his death was, strictly speaking, simply an excusable and touching weakness of an old man wearied by the troubles of life, and not an expression of the higher consciousness. In a mind occupied with the essence of things and not with personal feeling, this death ought to evoke, instead of joy, a double grief. Grievous was the sentence of death as a social wrong, as the triumph of the wicked and ignorant over the righteous and the wise; grievous was the process of death as a physical wrong, as the triumph of the blind and soulless power

of a poisonous substance over a living and organized body, the abode of a rational spirit. ——*Ibid.,* pp. 243-44.

VLADIMIR ILYICH LENIN (1870–1924)

*While in exile in Switzerland, during World War I, the future leader of Soviet Russia studied thoroughly Hegel's Lec-*tures on the History of Philosophy. *His extensive notes and critical comments deal also with the Socratic philosophy as seen by Hegel, whose dialectical idealism interested the dialectical materialist. Thus he copied without criticism Hegel's characterizations of Socrates as "a personality of world history," as "the most interesting figure in ancient philosophy," as a representative of the "subjectivity of thinking" and of the "freedom of self-consciousness"—the latter two phrases clearly characterizing him as sharing in the idealistic tradition. Hegel's observation that Socrates' objectivity means "universality" he marks heavily in the margin. Then he makes the marginal comment "astute" in connection with the interpretation of Socrates' method as maieutics (midwifery) which helps thought to come into the world, and he continues:*

Meno (in Plato's *Meno*) compared Socrates with the electric eel, which "narcotizes" whoever comes in contact with it; and I too am "narcotized" and *am unable* to answer [*Meno* 80a-b].

After one more paragraph of admiration for Hegel ("very well said") there follows this more general observation:

The discriminating idealism stands much closer to the discriminating materialism than the stupid materialism. [Read] dialectical idealism for discriminating; metaphysical, undeveloped, dead, crude, stationary [materialism] for stupid. —— *Philosophical Notebooks* (Leningrad, 1938) pp. 281-83.

VALENTIN F. ASMUS (b. 1894)

Socrates, an ancient philosopher-idealist. . . . With his oral teaching he soon gathered a large number of students, the

majority of whom were opposed to the socio-political set-up of
Athenian democracy. It seems that Socrates and his followers
arrived at the idea that the democratic form of government
should be replaced by the oligarchical form, while the administration was to consist of those best prepared for the rule of
the country, namely the most educated representatives of the
slave-owning aristocracy. Socrates' propaganda, in its hostility
to the democratic form of government, according to his own
statements and those of his pupils, was not without danger in
the eyes of the democratic rulers of Athens, who, under the
leadership of Anytus, brought Socrates to trial for corrupting
the youth. By verdict of the court, he drank a cup of poison in
399 B.C. . . . The teaching of Socrates served as the basic source
for the development of idealism in ancient philosophy and
was developed by Socrates' student, Plato. ——"Socrat," in
Great Soviet Encyclopedia, LII (1947), 26-27.

SCANDINAVIAN

SØREN KIERKEGAARD (1813–1855)

What Socrates emphasized so much—to stand still, and to 1
reflect, i.e., to be silent—this is what his whole life means in
relation to world history. He has left nothing behind from
which a later period could judge him; in fact even if one
imagined oneself as his contemporary he would still be difficult to comprehend. For he was one of those human beings
whose exterior is not enough. The exterior points constantly
to something different and opposite. His was not the case of a
philosopher who expounds his views, this his exposition being
the representation of the idea itself. What Socrates said meant
something entirely different. The exterior is not at all in harmony with the interior but is rather its opposite, and must
be understood from this angle of refraction. . . . If we now say
that what made up the substance of his existence was irony,
. . . if we furthermore postulate that irony is a negative concept, it is easy to see how difficult it will be to get him into
focus, in fact that it seems impossible or at least just as strenuous as to depict an elf hiding under a cloak of invisibility.
——*On the Concept of Irony with Special Reference to Socrates* (*Über den Begriff der Ironie mit ständiger Rücksicht
auf Sokrates*), pp. 5-6.[1]

We now see how Socrates' position toward the State is 2
entirely negative, how he did not fit into the State at all. But
we see it even more distinctly at the moment when, indicted

[1] This master's thesis, which was written in 1841 and does not express
Kierkegaard's most characteristic position, has not yet been translated into
English; the excerpts given here have been translated from the German
version of Hans Heinrich Schaeder (Munich, 1929). The first half of the
thesis is a detailed study of "Socrates' Standpoint Interpreted as Irony."

for his way of life, he should most easily have become conscious of his odd relationship. Unconcerned about this, he nevertheless develops his position, with the sword above his head. But his speech is not the powerful fire of enthusiasm, his attitude not the absolute self-glorification of the personality, his indifference not a blissful resting in his own abundance. There is nothing like that in him; but instead we have an irony carried through to its limit. The objective power of the State, its demands on the activity of the individual, the laws, the courts—they all lose their absolute validity for him, and he strips off everything like imperfect forms, he rises as if less and less encumbered, sees all those impediments below him in his ironical, bird's-eye perspective, and floats above it in ironical contentment, supported by the absolute consistency of the infinite negativity [Hegel's definition of irony] in himself.   ——*Ibid.*, p. 164.

3   His life is for the observer like a magnificent pause in the pattern of world history. He is not audible at all, and there is a deep silence, until it is interrupted by the many very different schools, by the noisy attempts of his students to derive their origin from this secret and mysterious source. In Socrates the stream of the historical story rushes below the ground for a stretch like the river Guadalquivir, to roar forth again with renewed power. He is like a hyphen in world history, and the lack of knowledge about him, which has its source in the lack of opportunity for immediate observation, does not so much invite us to bypass him quickly as to conjure him up with the help of the idea, to make him visible in his ideal form, in other words, to become conscious of the idea which makes up the meaning of his existence in the world, conscious of the moment in the history of the world spirit which is marked symbolically by the peculiar nature of his existence in history; for as he, in a certain sense, is in world history and then again *is not,* so it is his significance in the development of the world spirit to *be* and yet *not to be;* he is the nothing with which the start has to be made.   ——*Ibid.*, p. 167.

Here, I hope, it will appear [from this study] not only that   4
irony has validity for world history, but also that Socrates is
not minimized by my interpretation but rather becomes a
hero in the proper sense, so that it is possible to see him in
his meaning and so that he who has eyes to see will see him,
he who has ears to hear will hear him. The old Greek civilization had outlived itself, a new principle was about to enter.
But in order that it might enter in its true form, all the luxuri-
ant weeds of pernicious anticipatory misunderstanding had to
be ploughed under, be destroyed down to their deepest roots.
The new principle has to fight for its life, world history needs
a new obstetrician. Socrates fills this position. It was not possible for Socrates himself to establish the new principle in its
full form, it was present in him only in cryptic form, he was
to make its appearance possible. But the intermediate stage,
which is not, and yet is, the new principle (potentially but not
actually) is nothing other than irony. But irony is in turn the
battle sword, the double-edged blade which he wields over
Greece like an angel of death. He himself interprets this correctly in an ironic fashion in the *Apology* by saying that he is
a present of the gods, by defining this further in the sense
that he is a gadfly of which the Greek State is in need, as it
were a great, noble, but lazy horse. . . . Irony is the sting of
subjectivity, and in Socrates, irony is a truly world-historical
passion. In Socrates one development ends, and with him a
new one begins. He is the last classical figure, but he consumes
his excellence and natural abundance in the divinely inspired
service by which he destroys what had been classic. But his
own classic nature makes it possible for him to support his
own irony. In a previous passage I called that the divine
sanity which Socrates must have possessed.   —*Ibid.*, p. 177.

Just as Socrates' students found him, if I may use the ex-   5
pression, indispensable for keeping the inquiry going, so he
has for world history the significance of having set the ship of
speculation afloat. But the very thing which that requires is
an infinite polemical force, strong enough to clear away every

obstacle which would interfere with his course. But he himself does not board the ship, he only steers it out. He himself still is part of an older formation, and yet a new one begins with him. He discovers within himself the new continent, in the same way as Columbus had discovered America before he embarked and really discovered it. His negativity, therefore, prevents a relapse just as much as it promotes the actual discovery. And just as his mental agility and his enthusiasm in daily intercourse were inspiring for his students, so the enthusiasm of his viewpoint was the energy which was the moving force inside the subsequent positive stage. —*Ibid.,* p. 182.

6   History has decided that Socrates was in the right as regards world history. He became a victim. That is certainly a tragic fate. But all the same Socrates' death is not properly tragic; and the Greek State, really, is dilatory about its death sentence and on the other hand does not derive much satisfaction from the execution of the death penalty; for death has no reality for Socrates. . . . For by his ignorance Socrates has prevented all meaningful communication with the idea of death. — *Ibid.,* p. 227.

7   There was once a young man, as fortunately gifted as Alcibiades. He went astray in the world. In his need he looked around him for a Socrates, but among his contemporaries he found none. Then he prayed the gods to change him into one. And behold! He who had been so proud of being an Alcibiades was so shamed and humbled by the grace of the gods that at the very moment of receiving that of which he might have felt proud, he felt himself to be less than all the others. —*The Journals of Søren Kierkegaard,* No. 414 (1842), tr. Alexander Dru (Oxford, 1938), p. 111.

8   . . . When an intellectual tragic hero has his culmination in suffering (in death), then by his last word he becomes im-

mortal before he dies, whereas the ordinary tragic hero on the other hand does not become immortal till after his death. One may take Socrates as an example. He was an intellectual tragic hero. His death sentence was announced to him. That instant he died—for one who does not understand that the whole power of the spirit is required for dying, and that the hero always dies before he dies, that man will not get so very far with his conception of life. So as a hero it is required of Socrates that he repose tranquilly in himself, but as an intellectual tragic hero it is required of him that he have spiritual strength sufficient to carry himself through. So he cannot like the ordinary tragic hero concentrate upon keeping himself face to face with death, but must take this movement so quickly that at the same instant he is consciously well over and beyond this strife and asserts himself. So if Socrates in the crisis of death had remained mute, he would have weakened the impression of his life and awakened a suspicion that the elasticity of irony within him was not a cosmic force but a life-belt which by its buoyancy might serve to hold him up pathetically at the decisive moment. . . . The sentence of death is announced to him; the same instant he overcomes death and carries himself through in the famous reply which expresses surprise that he had been condemned by a majority of three votes. With no vague and idle talk in the market place, with no foolish remark of an idiot, could he have jested more ironically than with the sentence which condemned him to death. —*Fear and Trembling* (1843), tr. Walter Lowrie (Princeton, N.J., 1941), pp. 181-82.

Without these [a new organ, Faith; a new presupposition, the consciousness of sin; a new decision, the Moment; a new Teacher, God] I certainly never would have dared present myself before that master of Irony, admired through the centuries, whom I approach with a palpitating enthusiasm that yields to none. —Under the pseudonym "Johannes Climacus," *Philosophical Fragments or a Fragment of Philosophy* (1844), tr. David P. Swenson (Princeton, N.J., 1944), p. 93.

9

10   Socrates was unpopular, in spite of the fact that he used no technical language, for his ignorance, if it is to be thoroughly grasped and retained, is more strenuous to carry out than all Hegel's philosophy put together.   —*Journals,* No. 511 (1895), p. 138.

11   Socrates . . . was the most unpopular man in Greece, precisely because he said the same thing as the simplest man, but attached infinite thought to it. To hold on persistently to one thought, to hold on to it with ethical passion and intrepidity of spirit, to see the essential duplicity of this one thought without loss of equanimity, and at one and the same time to see in it the deepest seriousness and the highest jest, the deepest tragedy and the highest comedy, that at all times is unpopular for everyone who has not comprehended that the time of immediacy is past.   —*Stages on Life's Way,* tr. Walter Lowrie (Princeton, N.J., 1945), p. 377.

12   *Why did Socrates compare himself to a gad-fly?* Because he only wished to have ethical significance. He did not wish to be admired as a genius standing apart from others, and fundamentally, therefore, make the lives of others easy, because they could then say, "it is all very fine for him, he is a genius." No, he only did what every man can do, he only understood what every man can understand. Therein lies the epigram. He bit hard into the individual man, continually forcing him and irritating him with his "universal" [concept]. He was a gadfly who provoked people by means of the individual's passion, not allowing him to admire indolently and effeminately, but demanding his self of him. If a man has ethical power people like to make him into a genius, simply to be rid of him, because his life expresses a demand.   —*Journals,* No. 577 (1846), pp. 154-55.

13   The Socratic secret, which must be preserved in Christianity unless the latter is to be an infinite backward step, and which in Christianity receives an intensification, by means of more

profound inwardness which makes it infinite, is that the movement of the spirit is inward, that the truth is the subject's
transformation in himself. ——*Concluding Unscientific Postscript* (1846), tr. David P. Swenson, completed by Walter
Lowrie (Princeton, N.J., 1944), pp. 37-38.

One of the most distinguished and significant of all world- 14
historical figures is surely Socrates. How was it with him? Let
the [Hegelian] System, now that it is afterwards, understand
his necessity for him, the necessity of his coming into existence,
of his mother being a midwife. . . . But let us now also look to
see, less systematically and more simply, how he conducted
himself while he lived, when he went about in public places
and mocked the Sophists, when he was a human being. . . .
Did Socrates go about talking of what the age demands, did
he apprehend the ethical as something to be discovered, or
which has been discovered by a prophet with a world-historical outlook, or as something to be determined by an appeal
to the ballot box? No, Socrates was concerned only with himself, and could not even count to five when it was a question
of counting votes (Xenophon); he was unfitted for participa-
tion in any task where several were required, to say nothing
of where it was necessary to have a world-historical mob. He
attended to himself—and then Providence proceeds to add
world-historical significance to his ironical self-contentment.
It is too bad that we have heard nothing from him for the
last two thousand years—God only knows what he thinks
about the [Hegelian] System. ——*Ibid.,* p. 131, note.

I am left entirely to my devices. The only comfort I have 15
is Socrates. He discovered in himself, so it is related, a disposition to all sorts of evil. . . . I willingly admit how little I
otherwise resemble Socrates. . . . ——*Ibid.,* p. 144.

Let us consider Socrates. Nowadays everyone dabbles in a 16
few proofs [for immortality]; some have several such proofs,
others fewer. But Socrates! He puts the question objectively

in a problematic manner: *if* there is an immortality. He must
therefore be accounted a doubter in comparison with one of
our modern thinkers with the three proofs? By no means. On
this "if" he risks his entire life, he has the courage to meet
death, and he has with the passion of the infinite so determined the pattern of his life that it must be found acceptable
—*if* there is an immortality. . . . The bit of uncertainty that
Socrates had helped him because he himself contributed the
passion of the infinite. . . . The Socratic ignorance, which
Socrates held fast with the entire passion of his inwardness,
was thus an expression for the principle that the eternal truth
is related to an existing individual, and that this truth must
therefore be a paradox for him as long as he exists; and yet it
is possible that there was more truth in the Socratic ignorance
as it was in him, than in the entire objective Truth of the
System, which flirts with what the times demand and accommodates itself to *Privatdocents.* —*Ibid.,* pp. 180-81.

17   In the principle that subjectivity, inwardness, is the truth,
there is comprehended the Socratic wisdom, whose everlasting
merit it was to have become aware of the essential significance
of existence, of the fact that the knower is an existing individual. For this reason Socrates was in the truth by virtue of his
ignorance, in the highest sense in which this was possible
within paganism. . . . Socrates' infinite merit is to have been
an *existing* thinker, not a speculative philosopher who forgets
what it means to exist. . . . The infinite merit of the Socratic
position was precisely to accentuate the fact that the knower
is an existing individual, and that the task of existing is his
essential task. . . . To be able to do this [i.e., to speculate], but
to reject the possibility by apprehending the task of life as a
realization of inwardness in existing, is the Socratic position.
—*Ibid.,* pp. 183-85. See also p. 188.

18   Socrates was an ethical teacher, because he took cognizance
of the non-existence of any direct relationship between teacher
and pupil, because the truth is inwardness, and because this

inwardness in each is precisely the road which leads them
away from one another. It was presumably because he understood this that he was so happy about his favorable outward
appearance. What sort of an appearance did he have? Aye,
just venture a guess! . . . He was very ugly, had clumsy feet,
and, above all, a number of growths on the forehead and elsewhere, which would suffice to persuade anyone that he was a
demoralized subject. . . . Why was this old teacher so happy
over his favorable appearance, unless it was because he understood that it must help to keep the learner at a distance, so
that the latter might not stick fast in a direct relationship to
the teacher, perhaps admire him, perhaps have his clothes
cut in the same manner. ——*Ibid.,* pp. 221-22.

. . . I had recourse to paganism, and to Greece as the repre-   19
sentative of the intellectual, and to Socrates as its greatest
hero. After thus having made sure of paganism I sought to
find as decisive a difference as was possible. ——*Ibid.,* p. 329.

When Socrates adopted a negative attitude toward the State,   20
it was partly connected with the fact that his task was precisely
to discover the ethical, partly with his dialectical position as
an exception and *extraordinarius,* and finally with the fact
that he is an ethicist tending toward the limits of the religious.
Just as there is to be found in him an analogy to faith, so there
must also be found an analogy to the hidden inwardness, only
that he outwardly expressed this by means of a negative action, by abstention, and in so far contributed toward help-
ing people to become aware of him. . . . The abstention practiced by Socrates nobody could fail to perceive. ——*Ibid.,* p.
450, note. See also *Journals,* No. 115 (1837), p. 43: "Socrates
represents the individual's emancipation from the State."

Socrates . . . was not a blockhead because he would not be   21
duped into glimpsing this or that, but would be absolutely
ignorant. But on the other hand it never occurred to Socrates,
after he had discredited the common human knowledge, to

want to be admired for a higher understanding, or to want to engage in straightforward conversation with any man, since by his ignorance he had essentially nullified communication with all. ——*Ibid.,* p. 502.

22   Socrates, in my opinion, is and remains the only reformer I know. The others I have read about may have been enthusiastic and well-meaning but they were at the same time decidedly narrow-minded. ——*Journals,* No. 663 (1847), p. 208.

23   It is very true as Socrates said that exile would not have helped him, since things would have gone badly for him in any country. The reason being that Socrates was provocative. ——*Ibid.,* No. 701 (1847), pp. 219-20.

24   The individual: that category has only been used once before and then by Socrates, in a dialectical and decisive way, to disintegrate paganism. ——*Ibid.,* No. 723 (1847), p. 228.

25   There cannot really be the least doubt that what Christianity needs is another Socrates, someone who could existentially express ignorance with the same cunning dialectical simplicity, or as it should be said: I cannot understand the first thing about faith, but I believe. . . . A dialectician is . . . what is necessary, and the eminent dialectician must be a simple man. ——*Ibid.,* No. 733 (1848), p. 232.

26   Socrates did not know with certainty whether he was immortal. (Oh, the rogue, for he knew that immortality was a spiritual qualification and *eo ipso* dialectical, and beyond all immediate certainty. So that even though he did not know to what degree he was immortal—which so many dunces know exactly—he knew what he was saying.) But his life expresses the fact that there is an immortality and that he himself was immortal. The question of immortality, he says, concerns me so infinitely that I stake everything on that "if." ——*Ibid.,* No. 763 (1848), p. 243.

There is a time for silence. That may be learned from the highest example: He was silent. I have learned it from a lesser one, for Socrates had it in his power to save his life— by flattering the people. —*Ibid.*, No. 765 (1848), p. 244. 27

Socrates was certainly an ethical teacher (the Classical age claims him absolutely as the discoverer of ethics); he was the first one, as he is and remains the first in his class; but he begins with ignorance. Intellectually, it is toward ignorance he tends, toward the position of knowing nothing. Ethically, he understands by ignorance quite a different thing, and so he begins with that. 28

But on the other hand, as a matter of course, Socrates is not an essentially religious ethicist, still less a dogmatic one, as the Christian ethicist is. Hence he does not really enter into the whole investigation with which Christianity begins, into the *prius* in which sin presupposes itself, and which is Christianly explained by the doctrine of original sin. . . .

Socrates therefore never really gets to the determinant we know as sin, which is surely a defect in a definition of sin. . . . What determinant is it then that Socrates lacks in determining what sin is? It is will, defiant will. The Greek intellectualism was too happy, too naïve, too esthetic, too ironical, too witty . . . to be able to get it sinfully into its head that a person knowingly could fail to do the good, or knowingly, with knowledge of what was right, do what was wrong. The Greek spirit proposes an intellectual categorical imperative. —"The Socratic Definition of Sin," in *Sickness Unto Death* (1848), tr. Walter Lowrie (Princeton, N.J., 1944), pp. 143-45.

O when one beholds a man who protests that he has entirely understood how Christ went about in the form of a lowly servant, poor, despised, and, as the Scripture says, spat upon—when I see the same man so careful to betake himself thither where in a worldly sense it is good to be, and accommodate himself in the utmost security, when I see him apprehensive of every puff of wind from right or left, as though 29 his life depended upon it, and so blissful, so utterly blissful, so awfully glad—yes, to make the thing complete, so awfully glad that he is able to thank God for it—glad that he is held in honor by all men—then I have often said to myself and by myself, "Socrates, Socrates, Socrates, can it be possible that this man has understood what he says he has understood?" So I have said, and at the same time I have wished that Socrates might be right. For it seemed to me after all as though Christianity were too severe, nor can I bring it into accord with my experience to treat such a man as a hypocrite. No, Socrates, thee I can understand; thou dost treat him as a wag, as a sort of merry Andrew, thou dost treat him as a butt for laughter, thou hast no objection, it has even thine approval, that I prepare and serve him up as a comic dish—provided I do it well.

Socrates, Socrates, Socrates! Yes, one may well call thy name thrice, it would not be too much to call it ten times, if that would do any good. People think that the world needs a republic, and they think that it needs a new social order, and a new religion—but it never occurs to anybody that what the world now needs, confused as it is by much knowing, is a Socrates. But that is perfectly natural, for if anybody had his notion, not to say if many had it, there would be less need of a Socrates.   —*Ibid.,* pp. 148-49.

30   Modern philosophy is neither more nor less than paganism. But this is not the worst, to be akin to Socrates is not the meanest position. But the entirely un-Socratic trait of modern philosophy is that it wants to make itself and us believe that it is Christianity.   —*Ibid.,* p. 151.

31   With respect to the distinction between not being *able* to understand and not being *willing* to understand, even Socrates furnishes no real enlightenment, whereas he is Grand Master above all ironists in operating by means of the distinction between understanding—and understanding. Socrates explains that he who does not do the right thing has not un-

derstood it; but Christianity goes a little further back and says, it is because he will not understand it, and this in turn is because he does not will the right.   —*Ibid.*, p. 154.

I for my part tranquilly adhere to Socrates. It is true, he was   32
not a Christian; that I know, and yet I am thoroughly convinced that he has become one. . . . I can very well call Socrates my teacher—whereas I only believed, and only believe, in One, the Lord Jesus Christ.   —*The Point of View* (1848–49), tr. Walter Lowrie (London and New York, 1939), p. 41.

To take an example which, humanly speaking, stands absolutely alone, and which people are wont to bring into closest   33
relation to Christianity, I have admired that noble simple wise man of ancient times [Socrates]; my heart too has beat violently as did that of the young man [Alcibiades] when he conversed with him, the thought of him has been the enthusiasm of my youth and filled my soul to overflowing. I have longed for conversation with him as I never longed to talk with any man with whom I ever have talked; in the society of those who have comprehended everything and know how to talk about every possible subject, I have many, many times sighed for his ignorance and to hear him who always said the same—about the same things. I have admired his wisdom, that he in wisdom remained simple so that he could catch the shrewd! That he in wisdom remained simple so that without having many thoughts or employing many words he could sacrifice his life in the service of truth—oh, touching simplicity! That he with death before his eyes talked about himself, already condemned to die, just as simply as ever he talked in the market place with a passer-by on the most commonplace topic; that he with the goblet of poison in his hand preserved the fine tone of festivity and talked as simply as ever he did at the banquet—oh, sublime simplicity!—But I have never believed on him, that never occurred to me. I count it also neither wise nor profound to institute a comparison between him, the simple wise man, and Him on whom I believe—that I count

blasphemy. As soon as I reflect upon the matter of my salvation, then is he, the simple wise man, a person highly indifferent to me, an insignificance, a naught. I could not in any way, could not possibly get it into my head, or into my heart, or across my lips, to make answer to the . . . blasphemous question, to which of these two I owe most—the simple wise man or Him, on whom I believe. ——*Christian Discourses*, tr. Walter Lowrie (London and New York, 1940), pp. 245-46.

34   In those days [of Socrates] one sophist after another came forward and showed that the misfortune was the lack of sufficient knowledge, more and more research was necessary, the evil was ignorance—and then along came old father Socrates saying: no, it is precisely ignorance which is our salvation. . . . He was looked upon as representing evil, for, in the eyes of that age, ignorance was evil—and yet Socrates was indeed the doctor. ——*Journals*, No. 1042 (1850), p. 366.

35   Luther is the subject of my entire respect—but a Socrates— no, no, Luther was very far from that. When I talk of men pure and simple, then I say: oh, of all men the greatest is old Socrates, the intellectual hero and martyr; you alone understood what reforming means, and understood yourself as such a reformer, and were one. ——*Ibid.*, No. 1079 (1850), p. 385. See also *Journals*, No. 663. (See above, p. 300, no. 22).

36   Socrates did not possess the true ideal, nor had he any notion of sin, nor that man's salvation required a crucified God. . . . He therefore retained irony, which simply expresses his superiority to the world's folly. ——*Ibid.*, No. 1122 (1850), p. 403.

37   *What I have Desired*
       March 25, 1853   *As I can Now See It*   Good Friday

There is one thought which has been in my soul and occupied it from my earliest years, inexplicably deeply rooted, a thought which has to do with Socrates as a model, the man to whom I have been inexplicably related from my earliest years, long before I really began to read Plato—the thought: How is it that all those who have in truth served the truth have always come out of it badly in this life, *as long as they lived,* and as soon as they are dead, then they are deified?

The explanation is quite simple: the mass of mankind can only relate itself to ideas, the good, the true, through the imagination. But a dead man is at a distance, in the imagination. But on the other hand they cannot endure the living who give them reality, they are scandalized by them, put them to death, tread them down. —*Ibid.,* No. 1291 (1853), pp. 488-89.

Take Socrates! He is not a third person in the sense that 38 he avoids going into danger, avoids staking his life, which one avoids if one is a third person—not an "I." In no sense is that true. But when actually in danger he has an objective attitude to his own personality, and when he is about to be condemned to death speaks of his condemnation like a third person. He is subjectivity raised to the second power, his attitude is as objective as that of a true poet to his poetic works; he is just as objective to his own subjectivity. That is an achievement. —*Ibid.,* No. 1376 (1854), p. 533.

. . . I stand alone. My only analogy is Socrates. My task is a 39 Socratic task—to revise the conception of what it means to be a Christian. . . .

O noble, simple sage of antiquity, the only human being that I acknowledge with admiration as a thinker: there is but little that has been handed down concerning you, true and only martyr of the intellect, equally great as character and thinker; but that little, how infinitely much! How I have longed amidst all these battalions of so-called Christian thinkers . . . for one short hour of conversation with you! . . .

Our so-called Christian civilization is sunk to a depth of

sophistry far, far worse than that which flourished in Greece in the time of the Sophists. These legions of preachers and Christian docents are all sophists, earning their livelihood— here we have, according to the ancients, the characteristic mark of the sophist—by deluding those who understand nothing into thinking that they know something, and then making this mass, this numerical power, this human majority, the test and standard of Truth.

But I do not call myself a Christian. That this is very embarrassing to the sophists, I understand very well; and I understand too that they would much prefer that I should loudly proclaim myself the only true Christian, and I know very well that the attempt has been made, untruthfully, to represent my agitation in this light. But I will not allow myself to be made a fool of . . . I do not call myself a Christian.

O Socrates! If you had only proclaimed yourself the wisest man in Greece, the Sophists would soon have been able to finish you off! No, no, you made yourself ignorant; but at the same time you had the malicious characteristic that you could expose the fact (precisely as being ignorant) that the others had still less knowledge than you, they who did not even know that they were ignorant. ——*The Moment* (1855), No. 10, quoted in David P. Swenson, *Something about Kierkegaard* (Minneapolis, 1941), pp. 38-39.

AUGUST STRINDBERG (1849–1912)

1   Socrates is not a Greek type. His forehead is not that of a thinker; for it is too narrow for its height, and this forehead can be found again today in the Danube region, and it has a special name which does not suggest intelligence; his nose is vulgar and can be seen in satyrs, and his eyes are not placed straight in his head; he is a Silenus. ——"The Conscious Will in World History," in *Moses—Socrates—Jesus: A World Historical Trilogy,* tr. from the German version by Emil Schering (Munich, 1922), p. 162.

PERICLES: Socrates, my friend: this is the farewell of a dying 2
man. You were the wisest of all; but—I hope you won't take it
amiss—don't be too wise; don't strive for the unattainable and
don't confuse men's minds with subtleties; don't make the
single double. You want to see things with both eyes; but anyone who aims a bow must close one eye, otherwise he sees the
target double. You are not a Sophist but you can easily seem
to be one; you are not a libertine but you associate with
libertines; you hate your city and your country, and rightly
so, but you must love it all your life, for that is your duty;
you despise the people, but you must pity them. —*Ibid.,* p.
162.

EURIPIDES: Are you not an Athenian? 3
SOCRATES: I am a world citizen; my thought has no country;
my thought is I; I do not exist, only what I think exists.
—*Ibid.,* p. 192.

SPANISH

JOSÉ ORTEGA Y GASSET (1883-1955)

1   Suddenly in the history of thought there appear persons for whom their contemporaries show great respect, but who have not left any work from which we could today reconstruct definitively their venerable souls. Let Socrates be an example. Yet, what was Socrates? And see what we must answer: Socrates was Plato and Xenophon. Socrates is a little of all of us, who for twenty-five centuries have kept on being born with some Socratic chords within the equivocal harmony of our age. But for us Socrates is an idea which Plato taught, at a time when for that divine philosopher Socrates was an adventure, or, even better, *the* adventure at that very moment of individual life which polarizes, which crystallizes into decisive form, the rest of that individual life. ——"Canto a los muertos" (1906), in *Obras completas* (Madrid, 1950), I, pp. 59-60.

2   . . . We must not forget that culture, or reason, has not always existed on earth. There was a moment, the chronology of which is perfectly well known, at which the objective pole of life, viz., reason, was discovered. It may be said that on that day Europe, as such, came into being. Till then, existence on this continent had been merged with that in Asia or Egypt. But one day, in the market place of Athens, Socrates discovered reason.

I do not think that anyone can speak significantly of the duty of the present-day man without having made himself thoroughly well acquainted with the meaning of the discovery of Socrates. It contains the key to European history, and without it both our past and our present form an unintelligible hieroglyph.

Men had reasoned before Socrates; strictly speaking, two centuries of reasoning had already elapsed, in the Hellenic world. But in order that something may be discovered it is obviously necessary that it should be already in existence. Parmenides and Heraclitus had reasoned, but they did not know it. Socrates was the first to realize that reason is a new universe, more perfect than and superior to that which we find, spontaneously, in our environment. ——*The Modern Theme,* tr. James Cleugh (New York, 1933), pp. 53-54.

Socratism, or rationalism, begets . . . a double life in which **3** our nonspontaneous character, or pure reason, is substituted for our true character, or spontaneity. It is in this sense that Socratic irony is used. For there is irony in every act by which we supplant a primary movement by a secondary, and instead of saying what we think, pretend to think what we say. Rationalism is a gigantic attempt to destroy spontaneous life through irony, regarding it from the point of view of pure reason. . . .

. . . .

We now see that Socrates and the centuries that succeeded him were in error, though their error was proved a fruitful one. Pure reason cannot supplant life. ——*Ibid.,* pp. 56-57.

There is no greater figure in Greece. An ancient writer had **4** already called him the "Hellene of Hellenes," a triple extract of Hellenism. Since for me everything Greek is suspect and ambiguous—not by accident, but by constitution—it does not surprise me that this arch-Greek should be arch-equivocal. There is no way to seize him. . . .

The scene, constantly repeated, disconcertingly dramatic, must have been marvelous: Socrates, with his smile of a nihilist, ferocious à la Lenin, in the middle of the market place, inflicting a knockout on an illustrious general, a famous politician, a shrewd Sophist. Around the harsh limelight of his dialectics, like moths, shaking with delight, the youths of Athens are crowded, stretching their long discus-thrower necks toward that snub-nosed Pan of the bushes. . . . The tricky logic of Socrates made Greece lose forever the feeling of security. Who now will dare to set out with the ingenuity which inevitably feeds audacity on the discovery of cosmic truths, like Heraclitus, like Parmenides, like Democritus, if he feels his own person converted into an unfathomable problem? Socrates places Greek man with his back against the universe and face to face with himself. In one sole generation the Greek spirit veers one hundred and eighty degrees. No other such case is known in history. An intensified anxiety about salvation begins to paralyze the prodigious curiosity of the Greeks. ——"Ethica de los Griegos" (1927), in *Obras,* III, 540-41.

Bibliography

STUDIES DEALING WITH SOCRATES' POSTHUMOUS FAME [1]

ABMA, ERIK. *Sokrates in der deutschen Literatur*. Utrecht: Nymwegen Wachter, 1949.

ALSBERG, MAX. *Der Prozess des Sokrates im Lichte moderner Jurisprudenz und Psychologie*. 3rd edition. Mannheim: Bensheimer, 1933.

BANFI, ANTONIO. *Socrate*. Milan: Garzanti, 1944. —Contains a section, "La Fama di Socrate," with Italian translations from Aristotle, Hamann, Hegel, Kierkegaard, Nietzsche, and Schleiermacher.

BERGMANN, J. "Sokrates in der jüdischen Literatur," *Monatsschrift für die Geschichte und Wissenschaft des Judentums*, XLIV (1936), 1-13.

BÖHM, BENNO. *Sokrates im 18. Jahrhundert*. "Studien zum Werden des modernen Persönlichkeitsbewusstseins." Leipzig: Meyer, 1929.

BRENNING, EMIL. "Die Gestalt des Sokrates in der Literatur des vorigen Jahrhunderts," in *Festschrift der 54. Versammlung der Philologen. . . .* Bremen, 1899.

DEMAN, THOMAS. *Socrate et Jésus*. Paris: L'Artisan des Livres, 1944.

FRIEDLÄNDER, PAUL. "Socrates Enters Rome," *American Journal of Classical Philology*, LXVI (1945), 337-51.

GEFFCKEN, JOHANNES. *Sokrates und das alte Christentum*. Heidelberg: C. Winter, 1908.

[1] Appraisals of Socrates' fame made by a single writer are listed in the Index of Names under ARISTOTLE, BYRON, EPICTETUS, HEGEL, KIERKEGAARD, MILTON, MONTAIGNE, and NIETZSCHE.

GIGON, OLAF. *Sokrates. Sein Bild in Dichtung und Geschichte.* Bern: Francke, 1947. —Deals only with the Socrates myth as it appeared to his immediate disciples.

HERTEL, WOLF. *Sokrates in der deutschen Dichtung der Aufklärung.* Dissertation; Munich, 1921.

KAUFMANN, GEORGE M. A. "Socrates and Christ," *Harvard Studies in Classical Philology.* Cambridge, Mass.: Harvard University Press, 1951. —Contains information about the iconographic tradition in late antiquity and in the Byzantine period.

LEVI, ALBERT W. "The Idea of Socrates: The Philosophic Hero in the Nineteenth Century," *Journal of the History of Ideas,* XVII (1956), 89-108. —Compares the place of Socrates in Hegel, Kierkegaard, J. S. Mill, and Nietzsche.

LEVIN, RICHARD. *The Question of Socrates.* New York: Harcourt, Brace & World, 1961. —Collects all the early Greek source materials.

MARCEL, RAYMOND. " 'Saint Socrate' Patron de l'Humanisme," *Revue internationale de philosophie,* V (1951), 135-43.

MONTGOMERY, JOHN D. (ed.). *The State versus Socrates. A Case Study in Civic Freedom.* Boston: Beacon Press, 1954. —Contains selections from nineteen writers, beginning with J. S. Mill.

PIGLER, ANDREAS. "Sokrates in der Kunst der Neuzeit," *Antike,* XIV (1938), 281-94. —Discusses pictorial representations of Socrates from the third century to the middle of the eighteenth century.

ROLFES, E. "Moderne Anklagen gegen den Charakter und die Lebensanschauungen Sokrates', Platos und Aristoteles'," *Philosophisches Jahrbuch der Görresgesellschaft,* XII (1899), 1-12, 271-91.

ROVILLAIN, EUGÈNE. "Socrates in the French Literature, with a Few Other References," *Michigan Academy of Science, Art, and Letters,* XVIII (1932), 539-50.

SAUVAGE, MICHELINE. *Socrates and the Conscience of Man.* Translated by PATRICK HEPBURNE-SCOTT. New York: Harper & Bros., 1960.—Contains 21 pages of texts on "the 'posthumous life' of Socrates," including brief excerpts from Maurice Merleau-Ponty, C. D. Field, and F. M. Cornford, and many posthumous portraits.

STRADONITZ, KEKULÉ VON. "Die Bildnisse des Sokrates," *Abhandlungen der Berliner Akademie.* Berlin: G. Reimer, 1908. —Collects and compares the ancient portrait busts of Socrates.

Index of Names

WITNESSES TO SOCRATES' FAME WITH RELEVANT BIOGRAPHICAL DATA [1]

ABÉLARD, PETER (1079–1142). One of the founders of the scholastic method; also author of the famous correspondence with Héloïse, including apparently the letters that go by her name. *(50)*

ACTON, JOHN EMERICH EDWARD DALBERG, LORD (1834–1902). Liberal Catholic English historian, whose plan of a *History of Liberty* remained a fragment. See his *Essays on Freedom and Power* (Boston, 1948), pp. 5, 137. *(16)*

ADAMS, HENRY (1838–1918). American historian, grandson of John Quincy Adams. Pessimistic critic of modern civilization. *(127)*

ADAMS, JOHN QUINCY (1767–1848). Sixth president of the United States, ardent supporter of science. *(136)*

ADDISON, JOSEPH (1672–1719). English essayist, poet, and statesman, co-editor of the *Spectator*. *(74)*

AGARD, WALTER R. (1894–––). Professor of Classics, University of Wisconsin. See his *What Democracy Meant to the Greeks* (Chapel Hill, N. C., 1942), p. 282.

ALANUS AB INSULIS (ALAIN DE LILLE, *c.* 1128–1202). One of the leading theologians and encyclopedic minds of early scholasticism. See Migne, *Patrologia Latina*, CCX, 781.

ALBERTUS MAGNUS (*c.* 1193–1280). "Doctor universalis," first of the major scholastic philosophers to incorporate Aristotle's philosophy as a whole into Christian thought. *(50)*

ALCOTT, AMOS BRONSON (1799–1888). American educational reformer; "the Socrates of the Temple School" in Concord, Massachusetts. See his *Journals* (Boston, 1938), p. 63.

ALEXANDROV, GEORGI F. (b. 1908?). Soviet historian of philosophy, head of the Institute of Philosophy in the Academy of Science. His textbook on the *History of Philosophy* was publicly condemned by Zhdanoff as Secretary of the Communist Party, apparently under instructions from Stalin, and subsequently by a conference of 83 Soviet philosophers. See P. E. Cobbett, "The Alexandrov Story," in *World Politics*, I (1949), 161-74. See also his *The Philosophy of the Blossoming of Ancient Slaveholding Democracies*, I (1940), 133, 136 ff.

[1] For texts of testimonies of persons listed in the Index, see the page numbers given in italics and parentheses at the end of each entry.

AMIEL, HENRI-FRÉDÉRIC (1821–1881). Swiss poet and philosopher, famous chiefly for his *Journal intime*. *(200)*

APULEIUS, LUCIUS (b. A.D. 125). Latin writer, in philosophy a Platonist. See his *De Deo Socratis*.

ARCESILAUS (*c.* 315–*c.* 241 B.C.). Greek skeptic philosopher; head of the middle Platonic academy. *(28)*

ARISTIPPUS OF CYRENE (*c.* 448–*c.* 386 B.C.). Founder of Hedonist philosophy, advocating maximum pleasure of any type. *(28)*

ARISTOPHANES (*c.* 448–*c.* 380 B.C.). Attic writer of comedies. *The Clouds*, first produced in 423 B.C., contains the only extant record of Socrates written while he was alive. While making him the scapegoat for all the Sophists and the natural philosophers of the time, this account may have some truth as to his early interest in nature studies. Main appraisals in lines 93-105, 185-206, 217-36, 1506-9.

ARISTOTLE (384–322 B.C.). Plato's emancipated student, first builder of a philosophical system, the "philosophus" to the great scholastics, "the master of those who know" to Dante. For Aristotle's picture of Socrates, see W. D. Ross, Introduction to Aristotle's *Metaphysics* (Oxford, 1924); also Thomas Deman, *Le Témoignage d'Aristote sur Socrate* (Paris, 1942). *(26)*

ARNOBIUS AFER (*c.* 300). Latin apologist of Christianity. See his *Against the Pagans* I. 40. *(44)*

ARNOLD, MATTHEW (1822–1888). English critic, poet, and educator; an apostle of "culture" against aristocratic "Barbarians," middle-class "Philistines," and the "Populace." *(104)*

ARNOLD, THOMAS (1795–1842). Headmaster of Rugby; leading English educator of the time; father of Matthew Arnold. See his short appraisal of Socrates in *The Life and Correspondence of Thomas Arnold* (New York, 1898), I, 188 f.

ASMUS, VALENTIN F. (b. 1894). Soviet philosopher, collaborator in the *History of Philosophy* with G. F. Alexandrov and others, and contributor to the *Great Soviet Encyclopedia*. *(289)*

ATHANASIUS, ST. (*c.* 298–373). Greek Church Father, bishop of Alexandria, the "Father of Orthodoxy," without interest in philosophy. *(44)*

AUGUSTINE, ST. (354–430). First major philosopher of Christianity. Platonism played a major part in his conversion to Christianity. *(48)*

AUSTIN, JOHN L. (1911–1960). Leading Oxford lingustic analyst. *(17)*

BABBITT, IRVING (1865–1933). Harvard scholar and leader of a new classic humanism; his *Rousseau and Romanticism* (1919) expressed his opposition to the anti-Socratic tendencies in both. *(154)*

BACON, FRANCIS, BARON VERULAM (1561–1626). English philosopher and statesman, pacemaker of the inductive method in science. *(67)*

BACON, ROGER (*c.* 1214–1294). The "admirable doctor," scholastic advocate of mathematics and experimental science; in his encyclopedic *Opus Majus*, an Augustinian in theology and moral philosophy. See the translation by Robert Belle Burke (Philadelphia, 1928) II, 702.

BALZAC, JEAN LOUIS GUEZ, SEIGNEUR DE (1597–1654). French writer, author of *Socrate chrétien* (1652). The title of these discourses on religion means that their model "adds to the 'I don't know anything' of the philosopher of Athens the 'I know Jesus Christ' of the Apostle of the Gentiles."

BARCLAY, ROBERT (1648–1690). Leading apologist and theologian of the early Quakers. (70)

BARTH, KARL (1886——). Swiss founder of the Protestant neo-orthodox Dialectical Theology inaugurated by his commentary (1917) on St. Paul's *Epistle to the Romans*. (278)

BAUR, FERDINAND CHRISTIAN (1792–1860). Founder of the Tübingen school of critical-historical theology; influenced by Hegel. See his *Das Christliche des Platonismus, oder Sokrates und Christus* (Tübingen, 1837), p. 103.

BAYLE, PIERRE (1647–1706). Author of the monumental *Dictionnaire historique et critique,* skeptical of our theoretical knowledge, but strongly believing in moral knowledge. The *Dictionnaire,* however, has no separate entry for Socrates. (177)

BENDA, JULIEN (1867–1956). French novelist and critic, anti-Bergsonian champion of reason, author of an impressive indictment of modern intellectuals for their betrayal of their supernational responsibilities. (211)

BENTHAM, JEREMY (1748–1832). English philosopher-lawyer, central figure of the Utilitarian movement, opposed to "metaphysical verbiage." (83)

BERGSON, HENRI (1859–1941). French philosopher of metaphysical intuitionism, opposed to rationalism, proponent of the *élan vital* and of a dynamic ethics. (208)

BERKELEY, GEORGE (1685–1753). Irish-born philosopher and bishop, known chiefly for his subjective idealism. He wrote *Alciphron* during his stay in New England (1728–31). In *Siris,* he turned to a more Platonic form of idealism. (78)

BLANSHARD, BRAND (1892——). Professor emeritus of philosophy, Yale University; developer of the idealist tradition in American philosophy. (164)

BODIN, JEAN (1530–1596). French humanist and political economist, author of the theory of secular sovereignty of the state. (62)

BOETHIUS, ANICIUS MANLIUS SEVERINUS (c. 480–c. 525). The last ancient Roman after the fall of Rome. A Christian by religion but a pagan in philosophy, he wrote his classic *Consolation of Philosophy* in prison before his execution by King Theodoric's Goths. (38)

BOILEAU, NICOLAS (1636–1711). French poet, satirist, and critic, the "lawgiver of Parnassus." (177)

BONALD, LOUIS VICOMTE DE (1754–1840). French political philosopher of the Restoration period; stressed tradition and authority. (193)

BONAPARTE, NAPOLEON (1769–1821). French emperor. (194)

BONAVENTURA, ST. (JOHN OF FIDANZA, 1221–1274). The "Seraphic doctor," Franciscan scholastic philosopher and mystic. (51)

BOSSUET, JACQUES BÉNIGNE (1627–1704). French bishop, celebrated orator and Christian historian. *(177)*

BOUTROUX, ÉMILE (1845–1921). French philosopher who, in opposing the rule of determinism in science, advocated the autonomy of ethics. See his "Socrate, fondateur de la science morale," in *Études d'histoire de la philosophie* (Paris, 1897), pp. 11, 89, 91, 93.

BRANT, SEBASTIAN (1457–1521). German author of the didactic and satirical *Narrenschiff* (1494). Several references to Socrates in the sections "Of Ready Anger" and "The Wise Man." Translated by E. H. Zeydel as *The Ship of Fools* (New York, 1944).

BREASTED, JAMES HENRY (1865–1935). Eminent American Orientalist and historian of antiquity. See his *The Conquest of Civilization* (New York, 1938), pp. 396 ff.

BRENTANO, FRANZ (1838–1917). German predecessor of phenomenological philosophy who, after his break with the Catholicism of his youth, tried to develop for himself a Christian religion of reason. See his *Geschichte der griechischen Philosophie* (Bern: Francke, 1963), pp. 162-164. *(250)*

BRETT, GEORGE SIDNEY (1879–1944). Canadian psychologist and philosopher. See his *History of Psychology* (New York, 1913), p. 21. *(17)*

BROOKS, PHILLIPS (1835–1893). Distinguished American Episcopalian bishop and lecturer. *(136)*

BRUNSCHVICG, LÉON (1869–1944). French idealistic philosopher, for whom the Socratic conscience was also the beginning of scientific consciousness. *(213)*

BURCKHARDT, JACOB (1818–1897). Swiss historian of art and civilization with prophetic vision, a protagonist of the "free personality" and an enemy of political power. *(212)*

BURLEIGH (BURLAEUS), WALTER (d. 1343). Scholastic philosopher and author of a history of philosophy (*De Vitis et moribus philosophorum*) based on such sources as Cicero and Diogenes Laërtius. *(vii)*

BURNET, JOHN (1863–1928). Scottish historian of ancient philosophy, seeing Socrates' main mission in the "care of the soul," but also crediting him with Plato's doctrine of Ideas. See his "The Socratic Doctrine of the Soul" (1916) in *Essays and Addresses* (1929), p. 158; "Philosophy," in *The Legacy of Greece* (1923), pp. 78-79; *Greek Philosophy*, Pt. I (1928), pp. 131-32. *(16)*

BUTLER, SAMUEL (1835–1902). Victorian novelist and satirist. *(106)*

BYRON, GEORGE GORDON, LORD (1788–1824). English romantic poet and Philhellenist. See Elizabeth Atkins, "Byron and Socrates," *Publications of the Modern Language Association*, XLI (1926), 404-23. *(91)*

CALVIN, JOHN (1509–1564). French Protestant reformer, spiritual leader of the theocratic regime of Geneva. *(66)*

CAMPANELLA, TOMMASO (1568–1639). Italian Renaissance philosopher, strongly interested in Galileo's science and opposed to Aristotelian restrictions on free research. *(280)*

CAMUS, ALBERT (1913–1960). French writer, exponent of a philosophy of cosmic revolt in the name of justice and charity. *(217)*

CARLYLE, THOMAS (1795–1881). Scottish writer, historian in the spirit of "hero worship." *(95)*

garret to escape arrest by the agents of Robespierre. *(192)*

CORNFORD, FRANCIS MACDONALD (1874–1943). British classicist. References to Socrates in his *Before and After Socrates* (Cambridge, 1932), pp. 28, 114, 122, 530.

COUSIN, VICTOR (1792–1867). French eclectic philosopher and statesman. References to Socrates in his *Histoire général de philosophie* (1872). See pp. 28, 114, 122, 530.

CROCE, BENEDETTO (1866–1952) . Outstanding Italian idealist philosopher, critic, historian, and statesman, an uncompromising Liberal throughout the Fascist era. *(283)*

CROSSMAN, RICHARD HOWARD (1907––). Member of Parliament, leader of the moderate left wing of the British Labor Party, originally a professor of classics at Oxford. *(122)*

CUSANUS, NICOLAUS (1401 – 1464) . German Cardinal and philosopher of "wise ignorance" *(docta ignorantia)*, interested in both science and mysticism. *(56)*

DAMPIER, WILLIAM CECIL (1867–1952). English historian of science. See his *History of Science* (Cambridge, 1948), pp. 127-28. *(17)*

DANTE ALIGHIERI (1265–1321). Poet of the medieval world-view, influenced by Albertus Magnus and Thomas Aquinas. *(53)*

DEMONAX (2nd century). Late member of the Greek Cynic school, glorified by Lucian. *(36)*

DESCARTES, RENÉ (1596–1650). French builder of a rationalist metaphysics on the basis of a radical skeptical revision of knowledge; in his ethics close to Stoicism. Other instances of admiration for Socrates in *Correspondence of Descartes and Constantine Huygens, 1635–1647*, ed. Leon Roth (Oxford, 1926), pp. 127, 236. *(176)*

DEWEY, JOHN (1859–1952). America's philosopher of intelligence in action, a proponent of philosophical and social "reconstruction" in a changing environment. *(139)*

DICKINSON, G. LOWES (1862–1932). English author and political thinker. References to Socrates in *The Greek View of Life* (New York, 1932), pp. 155, 163.

DIDEROT, DENIS (1713–1784). Chief editor of the prerevolutionary *Grande Encyclopédie*, and author of most of its philosophical articles. *(189)*

DILTHEY, WILHELM (1833–1911). German philosopher, interested particularly in the theory of the humanistic studies *(Geisteswissenschaften)* and in intellectual history. *(245)*

DIOGENES LAËRTIUS (3rd century). Greek biographer, author of the *Lives of the Philosophers,* one of the most valuable though uncritical sources of information on Greek philosophy. *(vii, 3)*

DIXON, W. MACNEILE (1866–1945). English literary critic, Gifford Lecturer in 1935–1937. *(113)*

DRYDEN, JOHN (1631–1700). English poet, critic, and dramatist; convert to Catholicism. *(69)*

DUNNING, WILLIAM ARCHIBALD (1857–1922). American historian, leading historian of political theory. See *A History of Political Theories* (New York, 1913), p. 21. *(17)*

DUNS SCOTUS, JOHANNES (*c.* 1265–1308). "Doctor subtilis," Franciscan originator of "Scotism," a less rationalistic version of Scholasticism. *(54)*

EDMAN, IRWIN (1896–1954). American philosopher and writer. See his "Socrates on Trial," in *The Atlantic*, 101 (1953), 47-51.

ELIOT, THOMAS STEARNS (1888——). American-born English poet, critic of humanism in his *Idea of a Christian Society* (1940). *(116)*

EMERSON, RALPH WALDO (1803–1882). Leading American Transcendentalist, worshiper of "Representative Men" and admirer of Carlyle, whom he visited twice (1835, 1847). *(129)*

EPICTETUS (*c.* 60–110). Late Stoic philosopher, born a slave, whose teachings were taken down by his disciple Arrian. Cf. Fritz Schweingruber, "Sokrates und Epiktet" in *Hermes*, LXXVIII (1943), 52-79. *(33)*

ERASMUS OF ROTTERDAM, DESIDERIUS (1465–1536). Central figure of Renaissance humanism, advocate of a religious conciliation in the name of a *philosophia Christi*. *(60)*

EUSEBIUS OF CAESAREA (*c.* 260–*c.* 340). Father of Church History, bishop. *(46)*

FÉNELON, FRANÇOIS DE SALIGNAC DE LA MOTHE (1651–1715). French theologian and archbishop, advocate of a mystic "quietism." *(178)*

FICHTE, JOHANN GOTTLIEB (1762–1814). German idealist philosopher. *(230)*

FICINO, MARSILIO (1433–1499). First head of the Platonic Academy of Florence. *(56)*

FISKE, JOHN (1842–1901). American philosopher and historian, leading advocate of evolutionism. See his *Darwinism and Other Essays* (Boston, 1895), p. 116. *(9)*

FITE, WARNER (1867–1955). American philosopher, defender of individualism, critic of Plato and of an uncritical worship of Plato; in a chapter on "Socrates the Martyr" of his book, *The Platonic Legend* (1935), he calls it "absurd to say that Socrates died a martyr to free thought and speech" (p. 112).

FONTENELLE, BERNARD LE BOVIER DE (1657–1757). French writer and popularizer of science. Discusses Socrates' religion in *Histoire des Oracles* (1687), chap. 8; *Oeuvres* (Paris, 1818), II, 115 ff.

FORCHHAMMER, PETER WILHELM (1801–1894). German classical archaeologist, active in liberal politics. For his condemnation of Socrates, see *Die Athener und Sokrates: Die Gesetzlichen und der Revolutionär* (1837), pp. 6, 11, 55, 61, 62 ff., 72, 74. *(16)*

FOUILLÉE, ALFRED (1838–1912). French Platonizing evolutionist, emphasizing the individual conscience as the source of progress, author of a scholarly two-volume work, *La Philosophie de Socrate*. *(201)*

FRANKLIN, BENJAMIN (1706–1790). As a philosopher, a freethinking Deist. *(126)*

FREDERICK THE GREAT (1712–1786). King of Prussia (1740–1786), friend and protector of Voltaire, to whom he as crown prince gave a miniature silver bust of Socrates to be attached to his cane.

FUSTEL DE COULANGES, NUMA DENIS (1830–1889). French historian, student of *La cité antique*, stressing the role of religion in its life. For his views on Socrates, see *The Ancient City*, translated by Willard Small (1874), p. 476.

GALILEI, GALILEO (1564–1642). Italian astronomer and physicist, who in his philosophical ideas followed Plato. His *Dialogue of the Two Chief Systems of the World*, in which he advocated the Copernican theory, led to his trial by the Inquisition. *(280)*

GANDHI, MOHANDAS KARAMCHAND (1869–1948). The "Mahatma," martyr of India's liberation, advocate of nonviolence based on soulforce *(Satya-graha)*. *(285)*

GIDE, ANDRÉ (1869–1951). French novelist, leader of liberal thought, and ethical libertarian. *(212)*

GILSON, ÉTIENNE (1884——). Leading French Catholic philosopher and historian of Christian philosophy. See *The Unity of Philosophical Experience* (New York, 1937), p. 106. *(11)*

GOBINEAU, JOSEPH ARTHUR, COMTE DE (1816–1882). French originator of the theory of the *Inequality of the Human Races* (1915) and of Nordic superiority. See his *Essai sur l'inégalité des races* (1853–1855), Bk. IV, chap. 3. *(14)*

GOETHE, JOHANN WOLFGANG (1749–1832). The German poet and sage for whom the "highest good of the sons of men lies in personality." During his Storm and Stress period *(c. 1774)*, he considered writing a play around Socrates. Two letters to Herder (see pp. 228-29) suggest reasons why this plan was abandoned. *(228)*

GOMPERZ, THEODOR (1832–1912). Austrian historian of philosophy, author of *Greek Thinkers*. In the translation by G. G. Berry (London, 1913), see especially II, 45-46, 109, 111.

GRANT, MADISON (1865–1937). American anthropologist and advocate of the Nordic race theory. *(157)*

GROTE, GEORGE (1794–1871). English historian, a liberal in politics, in ethics a follower of Bentham. See his *History of Greece* (1850), VIII, 400, 465-66, 492-93. *(16)*

GROTIUS, HUGO (1583–1645). Dutch jurist and humanist, whose *De iure belli ac pacis (The Law of War and Peace)*, with its foundation in a natural law independent of divine and human enactments, was a major force in the development of international law. *(63)*

GUARDINI, ROMANO (1885——). German Catholic writer and philosopher, whose account of the Socrates story was widely read in Germany after the end of the Hitler regime. See his *Death of Socrates*, translated by Basil Wrighton (New York, 1948), p. v.

HÄCKER, THEODOR (1879–1945). German Catholic writer, influenced by Kierkegaard. Makes impressive claims for Socrates as the unsurpassed ancestor of existential philosophy in *Der Geist des Menschen und die Wahrheit* (1937); see pp. 143 ff.

HAMANN, JOHANN GEORG (1730–1788). German Protestant writer of antirationalist leanings, the "Magus of the North." See his *Sokratische Denkwürdigkeiten* (1759).

HAMILTON, WILLIAM (1788–1856). Leading Scottish philosopher. References to Socrates in his posthumous *Lectures on Metaphysics and Logic* (1860), I, 57, 75, II, 393-94.

HARTMANN, NICOLAI (1882–1950). German philosopher, known chiefly for his ontology and ethics. Occasional references to Socrates, e.g., in *Ethik* (1926), Pt.

Index of Names

ism, who wanted to base morality on self-love. *(192)*

HÖLDERLIN, FRIEDRICH (1770–1843). German poet and thinker, a romantic worshiper of ancient Greece. *(231)*

HOLMES, OLIVER WENDELL (1841–1935). United States Supreme Court Justice, best known for his minority opinions in defense of civil liberties. *(138)*

HUGO, VICTOR (1802–1885). French poet, dramatist, and leading romanticist. *(199)*

HUME, DAVID (1711–1776). Scottish philosopher, leading modern skeptic, in ethics a proponent of the principle of sympathy. *(82)*

HUSSERL, EDMUND (1859–1938). German originator of the Phenomenological Movement in philosophy. *(262)*

HUXLEY, THOMAS H. (1825–1895). British biologist; though a Darwinian he saw ethics as opposed to the law of "natural selection." *(105)*

ILIN M. (ILIA JAKOVLEVICH MARSCHAK, 1895——). Soviet writer, co-author of a widely used textbook of the history of civilization. See his *Giant at the Crossroads* (New York, 1948), p. 116.

ISIDORE OF SEVILLE, ST. (*c*. 560–636). Spanish churchman and encyclopedist, bishop, author of the *Etymologiae,* a primary source of information about ancient philosophy in the Middle Ages. *(vii)*

JAEGER, WERNER (1888–1961). German-born professor of classics, Harvard University. See his *Paideia,* translated by Gilbert Highet (New York, 1943), II, 13-14, 27-28, 75-76. *(3)*

JAMES, WILLIAM (1842–1910). Central figure in American pragmatism and proponent of "radical empiricism." *(138)*

JASPERS, KARL (1883——). First German philosopher of "existence." In his recent trilogy on the great philosophers, Socrates is the first of the four standard men (*massgebende Menschen*), including Buddha, Confucius, and Jesus, who have determined the existence and essence of human being as no one else has done. *(272)*

JEAN DE MEUN (*c*. 1250–*c*. 1305). French poet who continued the *Roman de la Rose* begun by Guillaume de Lorris. *(52)*

JEFFERSON, THOMAS (1743–1826). American statesman; as a philosopher, an opponent of Plato and a follower of Epicurus. *(126)*

JEROME, ST. (EUSEBIUS HIERONYMUS, *c*. 340–420). Known chiefly for the *Vulgate,* his Latin translation of the Bible; for some time a hermit and an advocate of monasticism. *(46)*

JOHN OF SALISBURY (*c*. 1115–1180). English Scholastic philosopher, later Bishop of Chartres; a Platonist and medieval humanist. See his *Policraticus* I. 29, 154, 179, 256; II. 105, 154, 295, 316. *(6)*

JOHNSON, SAMUEL (1709–1784). Central figure of London literary life in the eighteenth century. *(81)*

JONES, RUFUS (1863–1948). Renewer of American Quakerism, student of mysticism. *(143)*

JULIAN THE APOSTATE (331?–363). Roman emperor, unsuccessful in his attempt to revive paganism; a Neoplatonist in his philosophy. *(37)*

JUNG, CARL GUSTAV (1875–1961). Swiss psychoanalyst. In his *Psy-*

chological Types (translated by H. Godwin Baynes [New York, 1932], p. 181), Jung maintains that Socrates' rationalistic attitude repressed his intuitive functions, so that they had to take effect in hallucinations.

JÜNGER, ERNST (1895——). German writer, originator of the phrase "total mobilization"; later opposed National Socialism. Refers to Socrates' death in *Der Waldgang* (1950), p. 80.

JUSTIN MARTYR (also JUSTIN THE PHILOSOPHER, *c.* 105–*c.* 165). First major apologist of the Christian faith, believed that Christianity was the true philosophy; suffered martyrdom in Rome. *(39)*

KANT, IMMANUEL (1724–1804). German philosopher of Critical Reason as against dogmatism, skepticism, and antirational inspiration. *(219)*

KEATS, JOHN (1795–1821). English romantic poet who wrote "beauty is truth, truth beauty." *(95)*

KELSEN, HANS (1881——). German student of law, now in the United States. In "Platonic Love," *American Imago*, III (1942), 1-11, he argues that the deepest drive in Socrates was the urge for power over other men.

KEYSERLING, HERMANN (1880–1946). German free-lance philosopher, admirer of Eastern wisdom, and founder of a private academy (*Schule der Weisheit*) in Darmstadt. *(268)*

KIERKEGAARD, SØREN AABYE (1813–1855). The "Danish Socrates," fountainhead of existential philosophy and of modern dialectal theology, who finally broke with the official Lutheran church of Denmark. See Jens Himelstrup,

Sören Kierkegaard's Opfatelse of Sokrates (Copenhagen, 1929) and John Wild, "Kierkegaard and Classic Philology," *Philosophical Review*, XLIX (1940), 536-37. *(291)*

KLEIST, HEINRICH VON (1777–1811). German dramatist. He questions the indifference of the greatest heroes of virtue, like Socrates and Jesus, to the reactions of posterity, in a letter of November 12, 1799, to Ulrike von Kleist. See *Werke*, edited by Erich Schmidt, V, 48.

KLOPSTOCK, FRIEDRICH GOTTLIEB (1724–1803). German poet, famed chiefly for his epic *Der Messias*. *(220)*

KROPOTKIN, PRINCE PETER (1842–1921). Russian scientist, naturalist, and monarchist, who tried to base a new evolutionary ethics on the facts of mutual aid in nature. See his *Ethics*, translated by Louis S. Friedland and Joseph R. Piroshnikoff (New York, 1924), p. 90.

KUHN, HELMUT (1899——). Author of chapter on Socrates in Katherine E. Gilbert and H. Kuhn, *History of Esthetics* (New York, 1939); also of *Sokrates, ein Versuch über den Ursprung der Metaphysik* (Berlin, 1934). *(17)*

LACTANTIUS (*c.* 300). Christian apologist and rhetorician, who wrote the first systematic statement of the Christian doctrine. *(44)*

LAMARTINE, ALPHONSE DE (1790–1869). French writer and statesman, leading romanticist, author of a sequence of poems, *La Mort de Socrate,* in which he ascribes to the "sage of the sages" ideas of an admittedly "more advanced" (i.e., more Christian) philosophy: "If a man ever deserved without a doubt to be suspected in advance of sublime inspiration, this man was Socrates" (Avertissement, p. 266). *(195)*

LAMONT, CORLISS (1902——). American scientific humanist. See his *Humanism as a Philosophy* (1949), pp. 14, 16, 41-42.

LANDOR, WALTER SAVAGE (1775–1864). English writer and author of *Imaginary Conversations*. *(88)*

LANGE, FRIEDRICH ALBERT (1828–1875). German protagonist of Neo-Kantian "Critical Philosophy," as such equally opposed to metaphysical dogmatism and antiphilosophical skepticism. *(244)*

LAVATER, JOHANN KASPAR (1741–1801). Swiss preacher, leading physiognomist. *(223)*

LEIBNIZ, GOTTFRIED WILHELM (1646–1716). German philosopher of "pre-established harmony" in the universe; also tried to harmonize Lockean philosophy with the great philosophical traditions. *(218)*

LENIN, VLADIMIR ILYICH (1870–1924). Founder of the Russian Soviet Republic, in his earlier years also a student of philosophy, who criticized positivism in the name of dialectical materialism. *(289)*

LEONARD, WILLIAM ELLERY (1876–1944). American scholar and poet. *(159)*

LEOPARDI, GIACOMO (1798–1837). Italian poet and writer, also a critical scholar; in his philosophy an extreme pessimist. *(281)*

LESSING, GOTTHOLD EPHRAIM (1729–1781). German dramatist and critic, champion of religious tolerance. *(221)*

LIN YUTANG (1895——). Chinese writer and humanist, living in the United States. See his *The Importance of Living* (New York, 1937), pp. 19, 417. *(13)*

LIPPMANN, WALTER (1889——). American author and columnist, a humanist in his philosophy. *(163)*

LOCKE, JOHN (1632–1704). Founder of British empiricism, advocate of religious tolerance and of a moderate Deism. *(70)*

LOTZE, HERMANN (1817–1881). German philosopher, known particularly for his logic and metaphysics. References to Socrates in his *Logik* (1843), p. 313, stressing his opposition to sophistic logic in the field of ethics.

LUCIAN (2nd century). Greek writer of satirical prose, critic of philosophy. In his *Sale of the Philosophers*, he auctioned off Socrates, whom he seems to identify with Plato, at the record price of two talents (about $3,000), whereas most other philosophers either found no bidders at all (Cyrenaics, Democritus, Heraclitus, and the Epicureans) or fetched at most one-sixth (the Peripatetics) or less of that price. In *The Dead Come Alive,* in which Lucian tries to defend this skit, he makes Socrates the leader of a mob of outraged philosophers ready to lynch him, until he obtains a hearing before Philosophy herself. *(36)*

LUTHER, MARTIN (1483–1546). Originator and storm center of the Protestant Reformation, advocate of the sufficiency of Biblical faith for salvation, opposed to philosophy and to Erasmian humanism. *(64)*

MACAULAY, THOMAS BABINGTON (1800–1859). English historian and essayist. *(97)*

MAIER, HEINRICH (1867–1933). German philosopher and Socrates scholar, advocate of the "Socrates gospel." See his *Sokrates, sein Werk und seine geschichtliche Stellung* (1913), pp. 1, 3, 303 ff., 627-28. *(16)*

MANN, THOMAS (1875–1955). German writer. Apparently the only references to Socrates occur in *Betrachtungen eines Unpolitischen* (1915); *Gesammelte Werke* (Berlin, 1925), VIII, 309; *Nietzsche's Philosophy in the Light of Contemporary Events* (Washington, 1947), p. 23.

MANNHEIM, KARL (1893–1947). German sociologist, best known for his sociology of knowledge; on leaving the Continent he taught chiefly at the University of London. See his *Teleology and Utopia,* translated by Louis Wirth and Edward Shils (New York, 1936), p. 9. *(17)*

MARCEL, GABRIEL (1889––). Leading French exponent of a Christian philosophy of existence. *(11)*

MARCUS AURELIUS (121–180). Stoic philosopher who, as Roman emperor (169–180), built up an unusually good record, though he too persecuted the early Christians. See John Stuart Mill, *On Liberty,* chap. 2. *(35)*

MARGUERITE DE NAVARRE (1492–1549). Queen of Navarre, poetess and advocate of religious liberty. *(165)*

MARITAIN, JACQUES (1882––). Leading French Neo-Thomist, former student of Bergson. *(215)*

MARQUIS, DON (1878–1937). American author, columnist, and playwright. *(162)*

MARX, KARL (1818–1883). Founder of dialectical materialism, whose philosophical dissertation on Epicurus was composed during his Hegelian period. *(241)*

MELANCHTHON, PHILIPP (1497–1560). Luther's chief collaborator, professor of classics, "praeceptor Germaniae." *(66)*

MELVILLE, HERMAN (1819–1891). American novelist and poet, whose posthumous fame is spreading widely in Europe. *(135)*

MENDELSSOHN, MOSES (1729–1786). German philosopher of the Enlightenment, also a liberal Jew, who in his dialogue *Phädon* (1776) presented, within the framework of Plato's *Phaedo,* the arguments for human immortality supplied by his own metaphysics. *(222)*

MEREDITH, GEORGE (1828–1909). English Victorian novelist and poet. Stresses Socrates' love for truth in *Letters of George Meredith* (New York, 1912), I, 237.

MERLEAU-PONTY, MAURICE (1908–1961). French phenomenological existentialist who at the Collège de France held the spotlight of French philosophy in the 1950's. For his searching appraisal of Socrates see his *Éloge de la philosophie* (Leçon inaugurale, January 15, 1953, Collège de France), pp. 29-34; translated as *In Praise of Philosophy* by John Wild and James M. Edie (Evanston: Northwestern University Press, 1963), pp. 33-41. *(11)*

MEYER, EDUARD (1855–1930). German authority on ancient history, whose *Geschichte des Altertums* (1884–1902) was the first to include the whole Orient in its scope. See Vol. IV, p. 461. *(11)*

MILL, JOHN STUART (1806–1873). English utilitarian, who added considerations of quality (e.g., dignity) to Bentham's quantitative pleasure calculus; protagonist of liberalism in the interest of individuality, an empiricist in his philosophical method. See also his letter to Thomas Carlyle (October 5, 1833) in *The Letters of J. S. Mill,* edited by Hugh S. R. Eliot (London, 1910), I, 67; also in *Collected Works* (Toronto, 1963) XIII, 181. *(99)*

MILTON, JOHN (1608–1674). Poet, defender of the freedom of printing, a nonconformist in religion, who believed that every man should be his own church. See Irene Samuel, "Milton's References to Plato and Socrates," *Studies in Philology,* XLIV (1944), 50-64. *(69)*

MINUCIUS FELIX (2nd or 3rd century). Latin Christian apologist, author of the famous dialogue *Octavius* between the Christian Octavius and the Roman pagan Caecilius, who is finally converted. For Minucius "either Christians were philosophers or the (non-skeptical) philosophers were already Christians" (chap. 10. See also chap. 13).

MONTAIGNE, MICHEL, SEIGNEUR DE (1533–1592). French Renaissance humanist and skeptical author of the *Essays.* The three editions (1580, 1588, 1595) show increasing interest in and appreciation for Socrates, who, along with Epaminondas, eventually replaces Cato as Montaigne's human ideal. See Frederick Kellermann, "Montaigne's Socrates," *Romanic Review,* XLV (1954), 170-77. *(166)*

MONTESQUIEU, CHARLES LOUIS DE SECONDAT, BARON DE (1689–1755). French jurist and political philosopher, who in his *Esprit des lois* opposes absolute political norms in favor of relative ideals suited to the "spirit" of each nation. *(180)*

MOORE, GEORGE FOOT (1851–1931). American historian of religion. See his *History of Religions* (New York, 1920), I, 477, 492-93, 494, 496. *(18)*

MOORE, THOMAS (1779–1852). Irish poet, friend of Byron. *(91)*

MORE, PAUL ELMER (1864–1937). With Irving Babbitt one of the leaders of the American antiromantic humanists; professor at Princeton University. *(153)*

MUMFORD, LEWIS (1895——). American philosopher of civilization and art. See his *The Conduct of Life* (New York, 1951), pp. 244-45.

MURRAY, GILBERT (1866–1957). British classical scholar. See his *History of Ancient Greek Literature* (1897), pp. 174, 177. *(16)*

MUSSOLINI, BENITO (1883–1945). Italian Fascist leader. Whatever classical education this blacksmith's son from the Romagna had was obviously limited. *(283)*

NATORP, PAUL (1854–1924). Leading member of the Marburg Neo-Kantian school, who interprets Plato's doctrine of Ideas in modern epistemological terms. References to Socrates in *Platos Ideenlehre* (1930), pp. 2, 7, 9 ff.

NEHRU, JAWAHARLAL (1889–1964). Free India's prime minister, for years a political prisoner; liked to compare his master Gandhi with Socrates. See *The Discovery of India* (New York, 1946), p. 363. *(285)*

NEWMAN, JOHN HENRY (1801–1890). Oxford convert to Catholicism, author of *Apologia pro vita sua* (1864). *(98)*

NIETZSCHE, FRIEDRICH (1844–1900). German classicist, later the philosopher of the "superman," who transvalues all existing values on the basis of the will to power. See Heinrich Hasse, *Das Problem des Sokrates bei F. Nietzsche* (Leipzig, 1918); Kurt Hildebrandt, *Nietzsches Wettkampf mit Sokrates und Platon* (Dresden, 1922); Walter A. Kaufmann, "Nietzsche's Admiration for Socrates," *Journal of the History of Ideas*, IX, 472 ff.; Eduard Spranger, "Nietzsche über Sokrates," *40 Jahrfeier Theophil Boreas* (Athens, 1939). *(250)*

NOVALIS (GEORG FRIEDRICH PHILIPP VON HARDENBERG, 1772–1801). German poet and romanticist of Catholic faith. *(237)*

ORIGEN (185–c. 253) Platonizing apologist, philosophical theologian, not always quite orthodox. *(43)*

ORTEGA Y GASSET, JOSÉ (1883–1955). Spanish antirationalist philosopher of life. *(308)*

OVERSTREET, HARRY ALLEN (1875– —). Professor emeritus of philosophy, the City College of New York; writer on philosophical and psychological subjects. *(157)*

PAINE, THOMAS (1737–1809). Pamphleteer of the American revolution and the Freethinkers. *(126)*

PARETO, VILFREDO (1848–1923). Italian sociologist and economist, professor of political economy at Lausanne; teacher of Mussolini, who made him a senator shortly before his death. Pareto has been called the Karl Marx of Fascism. *(282)*

PASCAL, BLAISE (1623–1662). Mathematician, Christian apologist *(Pensées)*, and antirationalist mystic. *(176)*

PATER, WALTER (1839–1894). English essayist and critic, author of *Marius the Epicurean*. *(106)*

PEIRCE, CHARLES SANDERS (1839–1914). American philosopher, known chiefly as the originator of pragmatism. *(137)*

PETRARCH (FRANCESCO PETRARCA, 1304–1374). Italian poet and humanist. *(55)*

PETZOLDT, JOSEF (1862–1929). German positivist. In *Das Weltproblem vom positivistischen Standpunkt aus* (1906) he berates Socrates for his unscientific attitude, while acknowledging the value of his social pedagogy.

PICO DELLA MIRANDOLA, GIOVANNI (1463–1494). Italian Renaissance humanist. *(59)*

PITKIN, WALTER BOUGHTON (1878–1953). American writer-philosopher and professor of journalism at Columbia University, who began his philosophical studies at the University of Michigan. *(159)*

PLATO (428–348 B.C.). One of Socrates' youngest students; the main channel of the Socratic tradition. *(21)*

PLOTINUS (204–c. 270). Major figure in Neoplatonism, interested in Platonic metaphysics rather than in the dialectical irony of Plato's master, Socrates. *(37)*

PLUTARCH OF CHAIRONEA (c. 46–125). Greek moralist and biographer; his *Lives* contain no separate life of Socrates. *(33)*

POPE, ALEXANDER (1688–1744). British philosophical poet; author of "Essay on Man." *(78)*

POPPER, KARL (1902——). British philosopher of Austrian origin. The first volume of *The Open Society and its Enemies*, headed "The Spell of Plato," attacks Plato as the fountainhead of modern totalitarianism. *(119)*

PRANTL, CARL (1820–1888). German writer on the history of logic. See his *Geschichte der Logik im Abendlande* (Leipzig, 1855), I, 27-29. *(17)*

PRIESTLEY, JOSEPH (1733–1804). English-born philosopher-chemist, persecuted as a friend of the French Revolution, emigrated to North America; a Unitarian in his theological views. His last work was *Socrates and Jesus Compared* (1803), with the Latin motto, "Plato is my friend, Socrates is my friend, but even more my friend is the [Christian] truth." Jefferson is known to have read and appreciated this work.

RABELAIS, FRANÇOIS (*c.* 1495–1553). French physician and satirical writer. *(165)*

RADHAKRISHNAN, SARVEPALLI (1888-——). India's chief contemporary idealist philosopher, president of Free India. See "The Spirit in Man," in *Contemporary Indian Philosophy* (New York, 1936), p. 273. *(13)*

RAMUS, PETRUS (PIERRE DE LA RAMÉE, 1515–1572). French Huguenot philosopher, killed in the St. Bartholomew's Day Massacre; his main ambition was a reform of logic based on a rejection of scholastic Aristotelianism. See Charles Waddington, *Pierre de la Ramée* (Paris, 1855), p. 24.

RANKE, LEOPOLD VON (1795–1886). German historian, "beyond comparison the greatest historical writer of modern times" (G. P. Gooch). See his *Weltgeschichte* (1886), I, p. 67. *(16)*

RASHDALL, HASTINGS (1858–1924). British moral philosopher. In his *Theory of Good and Evil* (1907), II, 460, he emphasizes Socrates' limitations as a teacher compared with the saints and heroes.

RENAN, ERNEST (1823–1892). French Orientalist and historian, presenting Jesus, in his *Vie de Jésus*, merely as a superior human being. *(200)*

ROBIN, LÉON (1866–1947). French historian of philosophy. See *La Pensée grecque et les origines de l'esprit scientifique*, translated by M. R. Robie (1929), pp. 148-49, 160. *(16)*

ROBINSON, JAMES HARVEY (1863–1936). American historian. See his *The Mind in the Making* (New York), pp. 100-1.

ROSENBERG, ALFRED (1893–1946). Author of the semi-official classic of Nazism, *The Myth of the Twentieth Century*. He served under Hitler as "Beauftragter für die Überwachung der weltanschaulichen Erziehung" (Commissar for the Supervision of Education in World-View). *(274)*

ROUSSEAU, JEAN JACQUES (1712–1778). French pacemaker of democracy and antirationalist ("le sentiment est plus que la raison"). *(185)*

ROYCE, JOSIAH (1855–1916). American philosopher of absolute idealism in a Christian framework. *(139)*

RUSKIN, JOHN (1819–1900). Influential critic of art and society; in the intervals between his productive spells subject to severe depressions. *(102)*

RUSSELL, BERTRAND (1872——). English philosopher of scientific realism, a relativist in ethics. *(114)*

SANTAYANA, GEORGE (1863–1952). American philosopher of half-Spanish descent, calling himself a decided materialist in natural philosophy, but admitting Platonic essences as one of his "realms of being," though without power over the realm of matter. *(143)*

SARTON, GEORGE (1884–1956). Harvard historian of science. See his *Introduction to the History of Science* (Baltimore, 1927), I, 89-90. *(17)*

SARTRE, JEAN-PAUL (1905——). Leading figure in French "atheistic" existentialism, politically committed to the liberation of the exploited classes. *(217)*

SCHELER, MAX (1874–1928). German philosopher, best known for his new phenomenological ethics, in which he stressed the significance of ethical models. *(265)*

SCHELLING, FRIEDRICH WILHELM (1775–1854). German philosopher of romanticism, for whom nature and spirit coincide. *(238)*

SCHILLER, FERDINAND CANNING SCOTT (1864–1937). British philosopher of pragmatist "humanism." *(112)*

SCHILLER, FRIEDRICH (1759–1805). German poet, historian, critic, and philosopher. *(229)*

SCHLEGEL, FRIEDRICH (1772–1829). Leading early German romanticist, proponent of the theory of romantic irony, which he based on his interpretation of Socratic irony (see his *Lyceum Fragment,*

No. 108, in *Prosaische Jugendschriften*, II, 198); a convert to Catholicism after 1808. *(237)*

SCHLEIERMACHER, FRIEDRICH (1768–1834). German theologian, philosopher, and translator of Plato's works. *(231)*

SCHLICK, MORITZ (1882–1936). Leading German neo-positivist, leader of the "Vienna Circle." *(272)*

SCHOPENHAUER, ARTHUR (1788–1860). German pessimistic philosopher; a brilliant writer who as a teacher failed to attract students. *(239)*

SCHREMPF, CHRISTOPH (1860–1944). German Protestant thinker and translator of Kierkegaard. Refers to Jesus and Socrates as his only authorities in *Sokrates. Seine Personlichkeit und sein Glaube* (Stuttgart, 1927), pp. 4, 181, 184.

SCHWARTZ, EDUARD (1835–1940). Leading German classicist. Impressive statements about Socrates in his *Charakterköpfe aus der antiken Literatur* (1906), chap. 3, "Sokrates und Platon," pp. 52, 54, 59.

SCHWEITZER, ALBERT (1875——). A believer in the power of elemental thinking, a practicing advocate of a mystic ethics of reverence for life. *(265)*

SENECA, LUCIUS ANNAEUS (*c.* 4 B.C.–A.D. 65). First major Roman Stoic, also tutor and counselor to the emperor Nero, who forced him to commit suicide. *(31)*

SHAFTESBURY, ANTHONY ASHLEY COOPER, 3RD EARL OF (1671–1713). English Platonist philosopher of esthetic harmony, and proponent of the theory of a special moral sense. *(73)*

SHAKESPEARE, WILLIAM (1564–1616). Called "a Socrates in genius" (*genio Socrates*) on his monument in Trinity Church, Stratford-on-Avon (before 1623). In his works, the only specific reference to Socrates occurs in *The Taming of the Shrew* (Act I, scene 2, line 71), where "Socrates' Xanthippe" is mentioned. T. W. Baldwin, in *William Shakespeare's Small Latine and Lesse Greeke* (Urbana, 1944), II, 604-07, traces Hamlet's famous monologue via Cicero's *Tusculan Disputations* to Socrates' farewell speech in Plato's *Apology.*

SHAW, GEORGE BERNARD (1856–1950). Playwright-critic of modern society and defender of unpopular causes. *(109)*

SHELLEY, PERCY BYSSHE (1792–1822). English romantic poet of freedom, who tried to "link Athens with Jerusalem." *(93)*

SHESTOV, LEV (1866–1938). Russian literary critic, essayist, and religious philosopher with existentialist leanings. See his *In Job's Balances,* translated by Camilla Coventry and C. A. MacCartney (London, 1932), pp. 230, 338-39, 348, 385. *(13)*

SIDGWICK, HENRY (1838–1900). Prominent Cambridge moral philosopher and historian of ethics. See his *Outlines of the History of Ethics* (1886), p. 31. *(17)*

SOCRATES SCHOLASTICUS (*c.* 380–*c.* 450). Early church historian. *(49)*

SOLOVIEV, VLADIMIR (1869–1900). Prominent Russian religious philosopher, critic, and poet. *(287)*

SOREL, GEORGES (1847–1922). French proponent of syndicalism and of the "myth" of the general strike, advocate of violence; first a nationalist, then, after becoming a Marxist, he gave his final blessing to Lenin (see 4th edn. of the *Reflections on Violence*); Lenin, however, called Sorel "muddle-headed" in *Materialism and Empiriocriticism.* Mussolini, whose nationalist future Sorel seems to have foreseen while Mussolini was still a socialist, and his Fascists canonized him. The book on the trial of Socrates was Sorel's first major publication. *(203)*

SPENCER, HERBERT (1820–1903). English philosopher of evolutionism and of a philosophical synthesis of the sciences, an extreme liberal in political and economic matters. *(103)*

SPENGLER, OSWALD (1880–1936). German philosopher of history; author of *The Decline of the West,* influenced by Nietzsche. *(267)*

SPENSER, EDMUND (*c.* 1552–1599). English poet of the Elizabethan age. *(67)*

SPINOZA, BARUCH (1632–1677). Builder of a geometrically developed system of pantheistic naturalism. *(177)*

STEELE, RICHARD (1672–1729). British essayist and playwright, associated with Joseph Addison. *(75)*

STIRNER, MAX (i.e., KASPAR SCHMIDT, 1806–1856). German advocate of extreme egoism in *Der Einzige und sein Eigentum.* *(241)*

STRINDBERG, AUGUST (1849–1912). Swedish playwright. *(306)*

SWIFT, JONATHAN (1667–1745). English satirical writer and dean of the Church of England; opposed to all freethinking. In his satirical *Predictions for the Year 1708* (*Bickerstaff Papers*) he introduces Socrates as the one "whom I look upon as undoubtedly the wisest of uninspired mortals." *(71)*

TAYLOR, ALFRED EDWARD (1869–1945). Prominent Scottish philosopher and Platonic scholar. See his *Socrates* (New York, 1939), pp. 120-21, 124. *(16)*

TERTULLIAN, QUINTUS SEPTIMIUS FLORENS *(c.* 155–*c.* 222). Christian apologist, founder of Latin theology, advocate of extreme fideism and enemy of all philosophy. *(40)*

THOMAS AQUINAS, ST. *(c.* 1225–1274). The "angelic doctor" of medieval Scholasticism, and effective supporter of Aristotelianism. *(52)*

THOMSON, JAMES (1700–1748). British poet. *(80)*

TILLICH, PAUL (1886——). Protestant theologian and philosopher, transplanted from Germany to the United States; his existential thinking is based on the courage to be, which overcomes the anxiety of nonbeing. *(278)*

TIMON OF PHLIUS *(c.* 320–230 B.C.). Student of Pyrrho, the founder of skepticism; author of *Silloi* ("lampoons"), satirical poems. *(27)*

TOLSTOY, LEO (1828–1910). Russian novelist and critic of Western civilization in the name of a new primitive Christianity. *(287)*

TOYNBEE, ARNOLD (1889——). English proponent of a new theory of history. According to him the breakdown of Graeco-Roman or Hellenic society begins during Socrates' lifetime in the Peloponnesian War. In an Annex to Volume VI of *A Study of History* ("Life and Death of Socrates," pp. 486-95), Toynbee points out eighteen parallels between Socrates and Jesus, suggesting the possibility of an influence, however indirect, of the story of Socrates on that of Jesus. *(117)*

ÜBERWEG, FRIEDRICH (1826–1871). German philosopher and historian of philosophy. In his *System*

der Logik und Geschichte der logischen Lehren (1857) he credits Socrates with the discovery of induction and definition.

VALERIUS MAXIMUS (1st century). Latin author of a very popular book of essays on various topics and personalities, *De factis dictisque memorabilibus libri IX,* main source of many unauthenticated stories about Socrates. *(vii)*

VICO, GIAMBATTISTA (1668–1744). Italian originator of the modern philosophy of history. *(281)*

VOLTAIRE, FRANÇOIS MARIE AROUET (1694–1778). Central figure of French prerevolutionary Enlightenment, the "patriarch of Ferney." *(180)*

WADJA, A. R. (1888——). Indian historian of philosophy (Mysore University). See his chapter on "Socrates, Plato, and Aristotle," in S. Radhakrishnan (ed.), *History of Philosophy, Eastern and Western* (London, 1953), chap. 18, p. 50. *(13)*

WEBER, MAX (1864–1920). Leading German sociologist and liberal politician. *(264)*

WESLEY, JOHN (1703–1791). Founder of Methodism. *(80)*

WHITEHEAD, ALFRED NORTH (1861–1947). Outstanding English mathematician, founder of a new metaphysical philosophy of organism, a Platonist and left-wing liberal, who exerted his major philosophical influence after coming to Harvard. *(111)*

WHITMAN, WALT (1819–1892). American poet and exponent of a democratic philosophy of life and nature. *(134)*

WINDELBAND, WILHELM (1848–1915). German Neo-Kantian philosopher and historian of philosophy. See especially his *Präludien* (1889), pp. 78, 84-85; *History of Ancient Philosophy*, translated by E. Cushman (1899), pp. 134-35; *History of Philosophy*, translated by J. H. Tufts (1896), pp. 94, 95.

WINSPEAR, ALBAN D. (1899––). American professor of classics. Climactic passages in his Marxist indictment of Socrates in *Who Was Socrates?* (New York, 1939), pp. 9, 71, 85.

WOOLF, VIRGINIA (1882-1941). English novelist, critic, and essayist. See her *The Common Reader* (1925), pp. 33-35.

XENOPHON (430-357 B.C.). Athenian historian and general, faithful disciple of Socrates, though not present at his death, having joined the adventurer Cyrus the Younger against the king of Persia; later served in the Spartan army against Athens. (*25*)

YOUNG, EDWARD (1683-1765). English poet of the "Graveyard School." (*78*)

ZELLER, EDUARD (1814-1908). German philosopher and author of the classic *Philosophie der Griechen* (1844-1852). See especially *Socrates and the Socratic Schools*, translated by Oswald J. Reichel (London, 1877), pp. 52-53, 77-78, 97, 234-35. (*16*)

ZENO OF CITIUM (*c.* 336-*c.* 264 B.C.). Founder of the Stoic school. (*4*)

ZENO OF SIDON (150? B.C.). Prominent member of the school of Epicurus. (*28*)

ZOPYRUS (5th century B.C.). Greek physiognomist, known only through references in Cicero and Alexander Aphrodisias, apparently a contemporary of Socrates. (*224*)

ZWINGLI, HULDREICH (1484-1531). Swiss Protestant reformer; in contrast to Luther friendly toward the humanism of Erasmus. (*66*)